PRAISE ...

House o...

"Mr. Dickerson, a former Christian fundamentalist-turned-Catholic-turned-atheist, spent a few years in his late twenties working for the Hallmark card company. His inside view of the greeting-card business is an irreverent portrait of corporate America by a confession-prone geek. . . . And Mr. Dickerson does capture the odd experience of being an almost-thirty-year-old virgin in a culture that assumes sexual proficiency in men at a far younger age. His one attempt at hands-on knowledge . . . reads like a scene from a strange, polyester version of *Belle de Jour.* In any case, there is something refreshing about a memoir that features dutiful card-writers instead of drugs and iambic pentameter instead of incest; and Mr. Dickerson treats the whole notion of personal growth with a light touch . . . a gimlet-eyed view of the 'cube farm.'"   —*The Wall Street Journal*

"At twenty-six, Dickerson, now a noted wordsmith and regular contributor to NPR's *This American Life,* landed a dream job writing greeting cards for Hallmark. Unfortunately, his fundamentalist upbringing and social outcast status hadn't fully prepared him to find humor in topics that often sell cards. His memoir will delight fans of another self-deprecating writer with the same first name—David Sedaris."   —Realsimple.com

"This very funny memoir by NPR regular Dave Dickerson deals with his brief stint at Hallmark as a card writer. A former fundamentalist Christian in a long-distance relationship with his fiancée, yet determined to lose his protracted virginity, twentysomething Dave thinks Hallmark is going to be his dream job. He soon realizes that Hallmark's corporate-cubicle culture is an exquisitely bad fit for his creative personality. His book is laugh-out-loud funny, and Hallmark's loss is our gain."   —*East Aurora Advertiser*

"David Ellis Dickerson is the King of Neurotic Discomfort. *House of Cards* is a profoundly funny book, and it ranks with the best of David Sedaris."
—Mike Reiss,
Emmy Award–winning writer for *The Simpsons*

"*House of Cards* is hilarious and amazing. What a marvelous relief it is to discover, at long last, that there's life on other planets, specifically Planet Dickerson in the galaxy HooBoy! It's amazingly wonderfully weird."
—Bob Shacochis,
National Book Award-winning author of *Easy in the Islands* and *The Immaculate Invasion*

"The only thing Dave Dickerson does better than poignant, funny greeting cards is this poignant and funny first book. A wordsmith, a charmer, and a witty self-effacer, Dickerson proves himself a gifted narrator of hilarious, compassionate prose."
—Sara Barron,
author of *People Are Unappealing*

"The behind-the-scenes material is diverting (you'll never be able to read the word 'special' on a card again without smirking), but it's the broader drama of the profoundly uncorporate Dickerson's doomed efforts to fit into the corporate world that gives the memoir its staying power."
—*Publishers Weekly*

"The stories are often provocative, fun to read, and horribly familiar to those who have worked for large corporations. . . . Dickerson's alternately amusing and painful anecdotes speak clearly to all."
—*Kirkus Reviews*

House of Cards

THE TRUE STORY OF HOW A

26-YEAR-OLD FUNDAMENTALIST VIRGIN

LEARNED ABOUT LIFE, LOVE AND SEX

BY WRITING GREETING CARDS

· A MEMOIR ·

David Ellis Dickerson

RIVERHEAD BOOKS

New York

RIVERHEAD BOOKS
Published by the Penguin Group
Penguin Group (USA) Inc.
375 Hudson Street, New York, New York 10014, USA
Penguin Group (Canada), 90 Eglinton Avenue East, Suite 700, Toronto, Ontario M4P 2Y3, Canada
(a division of Pearson Penguin Canada Inc.)
Penguin Books Ltd., 80 Strand, London WC2R 0RL, England
Penguin Group Ireland, 25 St. Stephen's Green, Dublin 2, Ireland (a division of Penguin Books Ltd.)
Penguin Group (Australia), 250 Camberwell Road, Camberwell, Victoria 3124, Australia
(a division of Pearson Australia Group Pty. Ltd.)
Penguin Books India Pvt. Ltd., 11 Community Centre, Panchsheel Park, New Delhi—110 017, India
Penguin Group (NZ), 67 Apollo Drive, Rosedale, North Shore 0632, New Zealand
(a division of Pearson New Zealand Ltd.)
Penguin Books (South Africa) (Pty.) Ltd., 24 Sturdee Avenue, Rosebank, Johannesburg 2196,
South Africa

Penguin Books Ltd., Registered Offices: 80 Strand, London WC2R 0RL, England

The publisher does not have any control over and does not assume any responsibility for author or third-party websites or their content.

Penguin is committed to publishing works of quality and integrity. In that spirit, we are proud to offer this book to our readers; however, the story, the experiences, and the words are the author's alone.

First Riverhead hardcover edition: October 2009
First Riverhead trade paperback edition: November 2010
Riverhead trade paperback ISBN: 978-1-59448-486-5

The Library of Congress has catalogued the Riverhead hardcover edition as follows:

Dickerson, David Ellis.
House of cards : love, faith, and other social expressions : a memoir / David Dickerson.
p.   cm.
ISBN 978-1-59448-881-8
1. Greeting cards—Authorship.   2. Humorists, American—Biography.   3. Greeting cards industry—United States—Biography.   I. Title.
PN171.G74D53   2009   2009029059
741.6'84—dc22

PRINTED IN THE UNITED STATES OF AMERICA

10   9 8   7   6   5   4   3   2   1

Contents

PART ONE

Welcome! How I Got the Job

PART TWO

Congratulations: My Months in Everyday Editorial

PART THREE

Shared Joke: My Year
in Traditional Humor

PART FOUR

Cope: My Year and Change
in Main Writing

PART FIVE

Get Better Soon: My Months
Back in Humor

Acknowledgments

This book is dedicated to six people who saved my life. Lisa Pollak, Ira Glass, and Adam Chromy saw my work and gave me a crack at a writing career, and I'm forever grateful. But I would have been homeless while writing the book if not for the additional generosity of Jocelyn Beaufort, Tracy Rowland, and especially Sherry Weaver, who together put me up for seven months while I was living on unemployment in New York City. Since I'm an imperfect guest and an indifferent house sitter, I am in awe of their goodness. Let this acknowledgment be your thank-you card.

Prefatory Apology

My dear friends from Hallmark, let me be blunt: there were too many of you. Not only have all your names been changed, but you're likely to find that some perfect zinger you remember saying has migrated to someone else's mouth unfairly. I'm sorry. It's what happens when you try to whittle a copious phone list of vibrant personalities down to the seven or so characters a casual reader can keep track of. Just think of this as the movie version.

I'd particularly like to apologize to Alex, Jen, Christina, Maria, and all the rest of the Friday Foodies group, none of whom rate even a single mention. A good seventy percent of my socializing involved you wonderful people, and yet—in retrospect—none of it was directly relevant to the story arc that it turned out I was living. What can I say? The time we passed together was too happy to be dramatically interesting. It's your own fault for being so goddamned nice.

These caveats aside, the story that follows is true, subject to the hiccups that always attend a reconstruction of this sort. Names have been changed, and there's a composite here and there. I didn't keep a journal, and I can't always remember whether something happened in April or October, and just because someone told me that Mary

Smith once worked as a clown in Latvia, it doesn't mean it's factually proven; it's just what I was told, and have tended to believe, because I enjoy believing interesting things. That said, I made calls and visits and double-checked the best I could, and so the details of this book should ring true to anyone who worked alongside me at the time. While I have compressed time or burnished the odd adjective, I have not invented any of the incidents herein. I'm afraid I didn't have to.

A Note on the Cards

Most of the greeting card sentiments in this book are my own creation, for the simple reason that everything I actually wrote for Hallmark is its copyrighted property now, and it was easier to simulate what a card *might* say than to get permission to reprint what a single specific card *did* say.

That said, I can't promise there won't be overlap. If I mention a sample card that says, "Nothing florid, nothing sappy . . . just a wish for a day that's happy!" I can't guarantee that Hallmark doesn't have something similar on file. In fact, I bet it does. Probably so do American Greetings and Leanin' Tree and any major card company you could name. Any reasonably bright lemur could author such a thing after a single weekend at a card-writing seminar, and probably in the same thirty seconds it took me. In such a case, I'm not infringing; I'm simply trafficking in clichés. You might as well brace yourself now.

On the few occasions where I quote an actual existing card, I have tried to cite its author accurately according to my memory and have tried to limit such quotation to minimal, fair-use snippets.

PART ONE

Welcome!

How I Got the Job

1

Recruitment Day

MATTHEW HAD BEEN GETTING THE PHONES ALL MORN-ing. He and I were the two twenty-six-year-old gofers at the PREVENT program in Tucson, Arizona—a military drug-awareness program with a terribly tortured acronym*—and in early July of 1994 we'd worked together for over two years. So although we were both supposed to answer phones and route calls, Matthew knew that when I was on a creative side project, he had to take up the slack. Today was one of those days.

My side project was this: write a birthday card for our co-worker Dr. Steve's son Elliott, who was turning three. I was sitting at my worktable with a twice-folded sheet of typing paper in front of me, my notepad beside it for composing, and I was tapping my pen on my rhyming dictionary, wondering what approach to take. We didn't have a rhyming dictionary in the PREVENT office, but I always carried one around in my back-

---

* Personal REsponsibility Values Education aNd Training. The navy came up with it.

pack. I also had a real dictionary—*Merriam-Webster's Tenth Collegiate*, in hardback, which had served me from my undergraduate years through my MFA. It lay at my feet now, packed alongside a large movie guide, a TV reference, plus two or three other books I happened to be reading. As a result, I could answer almost any trivia question that ever came up in any conversation, and I could compose crossword puzzles anywhere. My backpack weighed about thirty pounds, but I was a portable genius.

There were basically three options for any card I wrote: funny poem, prose joke, or cartoon. Funny poems were my favorite, but I figured a three-year-old could best appreciate a cartoon. But a cartoon about what? What did three-year-olds like? Trains? Candy? Elephants? Balloons? *Balloons*, I noted on my notepad. Not only were they fun, they were really easy to draw.

Even as I did this, I wondered why I was doing it. No one had asked me to. I was supposed to be answering phones, and I had already spent an hour just staring and tapping and getting up for water, and Matthew was being nice about my lack of working, but my guilt was mounting. This was a huge waste of time for such a silly project. But I also knew that Dr. Steve and his wife would really love the card. My cards were always a huge hit around the office. And my job was so boring, it was a thrill to have any excuse to do something I was actually good at.

Elliott, Elliott. What rhymes with Elliott? I jotted a few lines:

To birthday-baby Elliott:
Although at times you're smelliott,
When you look glad
At mom and dad,
It turns their hearts to jelliott.

FIGURE 1

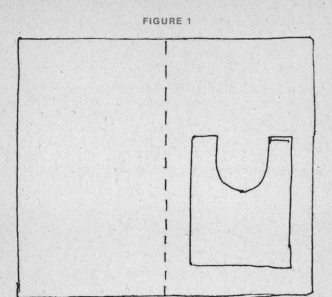

Silly and amusing in a trivial way, but definitely not worth the time I had already committed. (Also, the "glad-dad" rhyme was forced, too easy, and more than a little trite.) Now my pride was engaged. I needed something good.

I flirted briefly with a classic joke that had entertained my fiancée, Jane, back when we had just started dating. It involved cutting a window out of the card as exampled in Figure 1.

So that the final card looked like this (turn now to Figure 2).

I nixed this idea, though. It was amusing for adults, but for a kid it might be actually traumatizing. Handing that to a coworker's child would be not only bad karma, but a potentially disastrous career move.

The problem I kept coming up against was that the kid was three. What good is three? He couldn't really appreciate anything at all. I have only one memory from the time I was three:

FIGURE 2

[Outside]

[Inside]

I was in the supermarket, sitting in the back of my mom's shopping cart, happily reading all the words around me out loud: "Eggs! One dozen! Milk! *TV Guide!* Cheddar cheese!" While my mom was up front paying, the woman behind us, who I remember as young and attractive, said, "Oh, that's so cute!" and to my surprise, she actually kissed me. That's when I knew I was straight. Stuff like that you remember. A greeting card, not so much. Why did people even give cards to three-year-olds?

For the parents' benefit, of course. As soon as that occurred to me, I knew it must be the reason. And that's when I got a great idea: write a card that made fun of the whole concept of giving cards to three-year-olds. I needed a wordy quote to make it work, though.

I had only three non-reference books in my backpack: *Fundamentalism* by James Barr, *Rescuing the Bible from Fundamentalism* by John Shelby Spong, and *On Being a Christian* by Hans Küng. Barr was my favorite, so I found a good tough section and drew the following card (See Figure 3, overleaf; this is the last page flip for a while, I promise):

Inside it said:

I know it makes no sense, but you can't read anyway.
Happy Birthday!

I handed it over to Matthew. I expected him to say what everyone else always said: "These are so good! You could sell these!" And I'd say, "Yeah, I probably could." And then I'd think about printing costs, hiring a real artist, the paperwork for filing for a business loan, for getting a license, for finding a distributor, the receipts, the tax concerns, and I would give a deep shudder and

FIGURE 3

say to hell with that idea. To start your own company, even beyond the risks of debt and utter failure, you would have to actually embrace the idea of paperwork. I honestly don't know how anyone does it. All I ever wound up doing was saving the cards in a folder—the only folder I actually owned and managed to keep track of. For some reason I really liked those cards, and all the names of friends on them. It was the closest I've ever come to having a scrapbook.

Matthew surprised me. He snapped his fingers and said, "I

forgot, I was going to tell you. Hallmark is going to be interviewing on campus tomorrow. You should go."

"Why me?" I said.

He peered at me. "Are you kidding? It's you. It's what you
should be doing."

On the one hand, he was right. I was embarrassingly bad at
my office job—distracted and forgetful, even on basic things like
how to replace the toner—and the only reason I'd held it for so
long, surely, was because my fiancée, Jane, was also the boss's
daughter. I was obviously cut out for something else.

I've been writing poems ever since I first read Dr. Seuss. My
favorite Dr. Seuss book was *On Beyond Zebra!* It posits a series
of made-up letters beyond the usual alphabet: letters like floob,
yuzz, quan, and thnad. And then each letter goes on to illustrate
an imaginary animal ("Floob is for Floobooberbabooberbubs . . ."").
In that book, everything seemed to dance: language, letters, even
the very concept of nature. It's the only Dr. Seuss book I remember keeping with me as I fell asleep, back in kindergarten.
You could say it was the first time I read a dictionary for fun.

Then in college at the University of Arizona, I suddenly,
oddly, developed a habit I'd never evidenced before: I would
come into class twenty minutes early when no one was there
and anonymously write a poem on the board about whatever
we were studying. When my undergraduate English class read
Crime and Punishment, I wrote:

Higglevich-Pigglevich,
Rodya Raskolnikov
Axed an old woman who
Didn't belong.

After long chapters of
Psychoanalysis,
He concludes, finally,
"Murder is wrong."

And when my Reformation class studied a particularly grim chapter in medieval German history, I wrote:

Imperial taxes had jolted,
And Prince Maximilian had bolted.
While trapped on worse land,
Things got out of hand—
And that's why the Peasants Revolted.

I couldn't help it. The words seemed to beg to be played with, and there was no other venue to share my creations in once they were finished. It's not like anyone publishes this stuff anymore. It was fun to stretch my brain and come up with a joke about premodern literature* and then share it as an inside joke with people who would actually get it. For those few years where I had a regular excuse to write it, life had been thrilling.

But when I graduated with an MFA in fiction and looked around, I asked the universe, *Where can I get a job writing silly poems?* And the universe had answered, *Unless you can time-travel back to the thirties and kill Ogden Nash and take his place, you're probably out of luck. Try to enjoy a long, unrewarding life of Plan B.*

---

* Shakespeare,
It's claimed by some, was really Ed de Vere,
While others vote for Bacon. But I say
Whatever answer helps get me an A.

Now I suddenly had a new answer. Hallmark, eh? So that was on the one hand. On the other, I realized that even in this simple act—walk across campus and say hi to some Hallmark rep—I had to face my own worst enemies: my brain and my will, both of whom were skeptical of exerting even this much effort. My life up to this point had taught me two things: (1) All jobs are agonizingly, intolerably boring except the job of writing (either stories or puzzles); and (2) It's impossible to make money writing stories or puzzles. Puzzles in particular were impossible. From the three friends of mine who have done it, I know you have to be a constructing genius and an entrepreneur, and I'm merely competent and loath to hustle.

But even in writing stories for money, the way I was told to go about it was to submit to small nonpaying literary magazines, then get enough published that you could get a story collection with a small press, and then—on the basis of that or of whatever small-press novel came next—get a teaching job at some obscure college no one much cared for. Yet even this simple plan seemed impossible. I could barely manage to submit ten copies of a story and send them off to various magazines (writing a different cover letter every time, making sure you got the editor's name right, including the SASE that was properly weighted, etc.). Just thinking about it made my limbs heavy, and my brain gasped for anything more exciting to occupy it. Mailing off stories involved actual suffering. And for what? For ten rejections to trickle in over the next nine months. And even if I made it (I'd succeeded once in the six mass mailings I'd managed to shoulder through), you got no money and no one noticed you were in this stupid magazine that only other MFA students had ever heard of. You were supposed to do years of this. I could barely handle it for two hours.

With this as my background, the idea of applying for a job with an actually fun company everyone wanted to join seemed utterly absurd. No one gets lucky. That's not how the world works.

But four things pushed me forward that day. The first was the fact that there'd be an actual Hallmark representative present. I've always despaired of ever impressing anyone with my résumé, and my writing so far had gotten almost no attention. But I know that in person I'm charming. It's what I've counted on my whole life to get me out of trouble for being late, or for forgetting assignments, or for all the other difficulties that my absentminded brain gets me into. People are generally receptive to my jokes and my friendly nature, as long as they aren't humorless office manager types.

The second was that I had just come up with this idea for a novel set at a greeting card company (*Strange Greetings*), which was basically an excuse for me to exercise my MFA and write funny poems in a work of alleged literature. I'd worked out the characters and the rough plot, but I didn't know what a card company was actually like. I figured, then, that even if I went to this thing and nobody there liked me, I could still meet an actual greeting card employee and ask some questions by way of research.

The third thing—minor, but there—was that I was starting to hear rumors around the office that our contract with the government might not get renewed. Possibly all of PREVENT could be let go and I'd be forced once more into a work environment that seemed devoid of the security that comes from dating the boss's daughter. I'd actually have to work hard at some mindless job that I knew I'd hate, for as many as eight hours a day. This was so horrifying a possibility that I didn't even dare to take the rumors seriously. But just in case, why not say hi to Hallmark?

Fourth and finally: no matter what happened, it would make a good story for when I called Jane that night. Even when she was in another state, I found her inspiring me to do things I'd never have tried on my own.

SO THE VERY NEXT MORNING I got out the only suit I owned and my striped tie (I had either striped or black, and I thought Hallmark would appreciate color), and left work a little early to saunter over to the University of Arizona's Art Building.

For some reason I imagined that this was going to be something like a job interview, where they bring in volunteers to be interviewed and everyone dresses their best. But the event was in a tiny classroom, and the Hallmark agent/ambassador seemed to bet here to show a movie/PowerPoint presentation about the joys of working at Hallmark and would then field questions.

I found my way in just as the presentation was starting, and as the narrator went on about the excitement of working in a creative environment, the cultural richness of Kansas City, the benefits, the profit sharing, and so forth, I groaned. They were here to recruit for a *summer internship*. For *college seniors*. Real jobs weren't even on the table, and I was way too old to be there. I was surrounded by art students, ranging in age from nineteen to twenty-three, all of whom were dressed in clay-and-paint-spattered T-shirts and jeans, politely slouching through this speech by The Man (she was an Asian woman, but still The Man). And what's worse, it was clear from this presentation that they were recruiting summer *artists*, not summer writers. I felt so out of place that I stood—actually stood—straight up beside the far door, in my thrift-store suit and tie, clutching a slim manila folder to my chest like a mantis with rigor mortis.

Then the presentation ended, the lights went up, and the speaker, Sunny Birnham, fielded questions.

Sunny Birnham! Just thinking about her makes me want to hug something. She was a midsized Asian woman whose age I never quite figured out because she matched a youthful vibrancy with a startling ability to decide quickly about abstruse corporate strategies. She loved colorful scarves and shawls, and this particular day she wore one that was purple with silver-thread highlights: Technicolor with sparkles; the textile equivalent of fireworks. Her earrings were dangly wires in odd shapes. She seemed to laugh constantly, and even the tilt of her head was irreverent. She was the perfect ambassador to artists because everything about her seemed to burst with color and energy. And as it turned out, she wasn't anyone's flunky; she was the woman in charge of creative recruitment for all of Hallmark. And she had come here in person.

After the presentation most of the students filed out, but a few stayed like kids after class, each with a particular one-on-one question for her. I sidled into the line that was forming, feeling very, very silly. And eventually it was my turn.

"Um, I'm not an artist," I said. I didn't even meet her gaze. "But I've written a few cards over the years, and I thought you might want to look at them." And I proffered my thin, beat-up folder.

A look came over her face that I've seen since—the professional politeness that happens any time writers sign autographs and someone hands them a poem or story. You brace yourself for the worst without trying to discourage anyone. She thumbed through the first few blandly—and then her eyes widened in shock. "Oh my god!" she said. "You do humor!" She closed the folder, shoved it back at me with a raised eyebrow, and said, "Here's what you do." A pen appeared in her hand and she wrote on the back of a card. "This is the number of my assistant. I want you to call him and ask for a Humor Writing Portfolio."

"What's that?"

"It's a little booklet that has a lot of sample assignments for you to do, like an application." She looked at my concerned face and laughed. "You'll love it, it's a lot of fun."

"A Humor Writing Portfolio . . ." I said, making a note on the cover of my folder.

"And ask for a regular Writing Portfolio, too. We have both. Why not try one of each?"

I wrote this down and said, "Thanks!" We shook hands.

"This is good," she said, jabbing at the folder, which I had returned to clutch position against my chest. "Good luck!"

I forgot all about asking her research questions for my greeting card novel. I ran all the way home and placed the call immediately. Then I called Jane and told her, and she said, "I'm so proud of you! It's perfect, and you can do it! Hey—can you draw kitty cats? Maybe you should start practicing." Then I called everyone in my family and all of my friends and said, "I met a woman from Hallmark and I think she liked my jokes!" I barely slept for the next week. Partly, of course, I was excited. But some part of me was also nervous about the pressure that comes with being good at something: you have to be just as good later.

2

Performance Anxiety

THE HUMOR WRITING PORTFOLIO APPEARED IN MY MAIL-
box a week later. It was a booklet about sixteen pages long, on
nice speckled paper—the kind that had become a trademark of
Shoebox Cards since Hallmark had launched the line in 1982.
Just touching it was fun. After a standard "So You Want to Work
for Hallmark!" introduction, each page had one or two assignments. "We do a lot of Garfield cards," a page might say. "Here
are two examples. Now write two of your own." "Here's a set
of funny photographs. Choose two and write gags for them."
"Write a twelve-line verse for someone to send to his dentist on
Arbor Day." The more serious, plainly titled Writing and Editing
Portfolio was the same way, only it contained additional assignments like "Here's a poem that doesn't scan. Fix every line that
needs help. Also, there may be misspellings." And there was one
assignment that said, "Hallmark employees have to come up with
new product ideas. So come up with one and pitch it to us."

Then, at the very end of both portfolios, they said, "Now show us what you can do!"

I called Jane and said, "They haven't given me any guidelines at all. What should I send them?"

"Why not send them some of the ones you've written to me? Like the popcorn sonnet. I love that one."

She meant a poem I'd written for her when we were just friends. She'd worked at the student movie theater in concessions and would give me free drinks and popcorn. I paid her back once with a mock-romantic sonnet that began:

> *The popcorn that thou givest unto me*
> *Bringeth emotions I can scarcely utter.*
> *For thou art like this popcorn that I see:*
> *Lively and fresh, though thou contain'st less butter.*
> *And in the carbonated beverage, too,*
> *Which, like the popcorn, thou bestow'st for free,*
> *Though it consist of Brown Dye Number Two,*
> *In it, I see thy hair, and think on thee . . .*

The final couplet was, "My Pepsi tab would founder many banks. / I can't repay you; please accept my thanks."

Once we'd started dating, I wrote her a poem every week or two, starting with one that I attached to the first flower I ever gave her, after our first date: *Casablanca* on the big screen at a local revival house. The poem began:

> *This flower is doomed, and will not last a week,*
> *Cut down in a spasm of masculine pique.*

'Cause that's what, when smitten, we manly-men do.
This flower, my darling, was murdered for you . . .

That's how it went, joking about the love we were in: here's a
flower; don't get too mushy. We called each other "bear" sarcas-
tically, in phrases like, "Are you my little want-to-stop-shopping-
for-groceries bear?" if we were at a market and one of us looked
tired. We got along amazingly well, and couldn't help pointing
out how amazingly we kept getting along. It was pure sentiment
with air quotes, and my poems reflected it. By the time I had
applied to Hallmark, in the five years we'd been dating, I'd written dozens of humorous love cards and hadn't even realized that's
what they were. Jane kept them all in a folder, and that afternoon
we talked it out and I selected four that seemed both good
enough and not too inside-jokey, and she read them to me to
make sure I'd gotten them perfect for my application. "Thanks,
honey," I said. "You know, if I keep sending you these things at
the rate I'm going, you'll have two hundred poems by the time
you're a Ph.D."

"Hah!" she said. "By the time I finish my fucking dissertation,
you'll have written two hundred and fifty."

AS A LAST NON-FUN PART, Hallmark also wanted a résumé.
Mine was pretty thin (three years as a phone-answerer at PRE-
VENT, preceded by four weeks each at a pair of fast-food
restaurants), so I added a note: "If you'd like proof that I'm tem-
peramentally suited for the job, all I can say is, I proposed to my
fiancée in a crossword puzzle magazine, and it made a sidebar in

USA Today." I even added the date—easy to confirm, since the issue was framed on my wall—just in case anyone wanted to check.

Then I waited. Several interminable weeks passed, during which I lived my life as if nothing unusual were going on: I woke up in my apartment with my roommate, walked to work for my eight-to-twelve half-day, then came home and wrote my greeting card novel—which now seemed prophetic—without trying to obsess about Hallmark and my job prospects. I kept wanting to phone and ask what was happening, but was terrified to do it and maybe mess things up. It was maddening.

Since I only worked part-time, I filled the rest of my days with an unusual obsession that comes over me whenever I've got lots of free time and general life pressure: I obsessively wrote cryptic crosswords. At the time, I was probably one of the top five constructors in the country, so it was one of the few things I knew I excelled at. The main problem is that cryptic crosswords are extremely obscure. A normal crossword is simple: if the answer is NIGHT, the clue will be "Evening." In a cryptic crossword, the same clue might be "Dark awful thing" or "Near town after sundown"—and then you might discover that all the clues have extra letters ("Dark lawful thing") that together spell a quote, or that you have to remove RAT every time it appears in a word (so BERATING is entered as BEING in the grid), or the grid is circular and half the clues are entered backward . . . and as the complications pile up, there's simply no end to how demented it can get. No one solves cryptic crosswords except other word obsessives like me. They're even hard to find. Most of my work was appearing in a tiny subscription-only magazine called *Tough Cryptics* that served maybe a couple hundred people worldwide, and which brought in a few hundred bucks every other month, and that was the extent of my notoriety. That's why I could never make a living with my puzzles.

It is, however, how I first noticed Jane. I found myself one night in 1992 at Laffs comedy club in Tucson, sitting at the bar with a virgin daiquiri, waiting for open mike night to start, and I'd brought along a cryptic crossword to solve. Jane came in— this big-boned, broad-shouldered, vaguely butch redhead who I recognized from her hanging around with my fellow comedians. But she didn't do comedy and so I hadn't paid much attention to her. Tonight she sat next to me and saw my crazy crossword with its weird-looking grid. She looked interested, so I sighed, preparing to explain how these puzzles worked, when she pointed at the puzzle and said, "The answer to that one is ALTOONA."

I looked. She was right. "But to solve that, you have to know about Oona O'Neill. How did you know about her?"

She scoffed. "She married Charlie Chaplin. I had to research him for one of my film courses. Once you read about someone named Oona, it's hard to forget. It sticks in your brain like an ice ax."

"Trotsky?" I said.

"Ooh! Ten points," she said, and laughed.* After that, I noticed Jane. I knew I couldn't date her, because she wasn't a Christian like I was. (Evangelical Christians, for all practical purposes, think

---

* Leon Trotsky is the only famous person I can think of who was killed by an ice ax. Jane never needed footnotes.

of themselves as the only "real" Christians doing what the Bible actually demands; Jane was Catholic and obviously liberal, and I'd been avoiding both Catholics and liberalism ever since I'd converted at eight.) But as I watched her over the next several months, I kept thinking, *What a shame. Smart women sure are sexy.* In the conservative Christian churches I'd grown up in, aggressively smart women were discouraged from showing up.

IT WAS IMPOSSIBLE TO CONCENTRATE on anything relevant while I was still waiting to hear back from Hallmark, so I retreated into puzzle making with an unusual fervor, spending two or three days each on crosswords so abstruse and bizarre (there was one based on heraldic symbols, and another about the old seventies kids' show *H. R. Pufnstuf*) that I didn't even send them to my puzzle friends; I simply saved them on my computer and started the next one in a day or two. In a few weeks, I had written seven such puzzles and started to wonder about my sanity. I started to understand, just a little, those crazy guys from the movies who write messages from the aliens all over the walls of their padded cells. It was a compulsion that felt absurdly important, even though I knew logically that no one cared about these damn crosswords. By the time I hit twelve puzzles, the craziness of waiting cracked something in me, and perhaps because I dared to dream I might be moving away from the town I'd lived in since first grade, I decided it might even be time to square things with my dad. That's how I found myself on the far northwest side of Tucson one Sunday a few weeks after my meeting with Sunny, sitting with Dad in the trailer he shared with my twin brother.*

When I say I wanted to "square things," I don't mean there was any actual overt rift anyone could point to. We Dickersons don't seek out difficulties. When they come sharking in, we hunker down like turtles and wait for them to lose interest. So as far as I knew, Dad had merely observed the obvious series of events in my life and drawn his own unhappy conclusions:

1. Dave, who's been a devout and assertive conservative Christian since age eight, goes off to college to get a Religious Studies degree to become a theologian.
2. After a few classes, Dave starts saying liberal things and getting in arguments at family gatherings.
3. In his senior year in college, Dave meets this Catholic (i.e., non-Christian) girl Jane, dates her, and after three years gets engaged.
4. Dave quits going to the family church and converts to Catholicism. (Also, he registers as a Democrat.)

---

* It seems disingenuous to call him simply my brother, yet I can't call him my twin without inviting follow-up questions. But since my brother doesn't feature much in this story, let this footnote suffice: we're fraternal, and we look and act very differently. You can see the divergence in our baby pictures, where I'm smiling recklessly and losing my hair already, and he's got no widow's peak but looks concerned about something off camera. In high school, I was a mere five-eight and a hundred forty pounds, and he was a bony five-ten and one twenty-five. At least one person in our senior class didn't even know we were brothers, much less twins; he just thought we were friends with the same last name. Our voting records haven't overlapped in decades, but we've always been friends; he's an amazing husband, father, and worker; and I would happily take a bullet for him.

It had been four years since Jane and I had started dating, two years since I'd stopped going to my family's church, and just over a year since our engagement and my Easter rebaptism as a Catholic—one of Jane's last acts with me before she went off to Ph.D.-land in Minnesota. I assumed that Dad blamed college and Jane for my apostasy and was praying I'd come back to the fold— perhaps now that Jane had left town? On some level, he must have believed that I was going to hell, since the Bible doesn't offer a lot of wiggle room in this area (doubting hell is *liberal*), and evangelical Christians pride themselves on taking the Bible at its word. But I also knew he loved me. So I assume he was doing what all evangelicals do when their beliefs threaten to lead somewhere unpleasant: crossing his fingers, trusting God, and trying not to think about it too consistently. We'd never actually talked about what had happened.

But even as I saw Dad sitting there across from me, I had to bite my tongue. He had his rough, ink-stained hands wrapped around a glass of water and was wearing his usual habanera shirt and a straw cowboy hat. We each had a beard and mustache, and although his hair was gray now, I thought of how much we'd always resembled each other. *He's fifty-seven years old and he lives in a trailer. He's never had a job he even liked.* I cast my eye over the cheap metal bookshelves I remembered from back when we'd lived in an actual house, each shelf filled with ancient copies of *Don Quixote* and *Lazarillo de Tormes* and Lope de Vega, all from his days studying Spanish literature, none of which he'd read in years. It was depressing to see them all, books with no future.

My dad had been the first from his family to go to college, where he'd gotten a Ph.D., then taught for a time, then had a nervous breakdown, followed by a religious conversion to Bible-believing Christianity. He didn't thump or rail about hell, but he took the morality seriously and taught us to as well. One of those lessons seemed to be to never expect much success from the world. He'd made terrible money as a printer for the twenty-one years we'd lived in Tucson, often barely breaking even, and he'd always raised us to be wary of too much college. "You need it to get by, but never worship education," he'd told us, over and over again. My sister, Laura, got her linguistics degree and promptly got married to a man who supported them both. (She didn't work, since she was planning to have kids. She told me once that God didn't approve of working mothers.) My brother, Daniel, dropped out after only two years of studying French horn and was currently a phone-bank monkey at Intuit Software. I was the only one in the family who'd ignored Dad's advice, who could never get enough of books and learning. I looked at him now, deeply puzzled. This trailer, those books, this inky lifestyle. How could someone I loved so much be characterized by so many things I couldn't stand to be near? And why had it never occurred to me to run farther away?

"Well, David," said Dad, "it's nice to have you here."

"It's nice to be here," I said, which was still kind of true. "Thanks for driving me." I didn't have a car, and since my entire family was way up on the northwest side of a sprawly metropolis, I hadn't seen them much in the last few years. I went to mass at the Newman Center these days instead of to their northwest-side megachurch, and we called or met for lunch only once every two or three weeks. Today, Dad had driven me up in the family car—a big green wood-paneled station wagon I'd called Battlezone when I'd driven it in high school. Like all the cars we'd ever had, it was old and used, and looked it.

Our small talk was over, and after a bit of calculation—there was no easy way to do this, and how many chances did I still have to try?—I simply launched right into my spiel. "You know, Dad, back in college when I had taken all those Bible classes and discovered that"—how to phrase this?—"that the popular way to read the Bible doesn't really stand up to scholarly scrutiny, it was a real blow to me. I mean, I was devastated. The Bible was supposed to be this perfect moral guide, and suddenly I couldn't be sure of any of it. I didn't know how to live. I was terrified that I was going to become some great"—I hated this word, but what the hell—"*sinner* who drank and slept around and all of that.

"And I want you to know that Jane saved me. She was this liberal Catholic feminist, but she was a good person. And she taught me how to be good without"—I wanted to say *worshipping* but I bit my tongue—"without relying so heavily on the Bible. It's because of her that my spiritual life has actually deepened. In Catholicism, I have a spirituality that's connected to history and to literature and to art and to science in a bunch of ways that"—don't say *fundamentalism*—"that worshipping at your church really doesn't do.

"Anyway, if Hallmark calls, and I move away, and we don't see each other so much, I just wanted you to know that. Jane didn't destroy my faith. She helped me save it. I know she swears a lot and seems liberal, but she's more moral than you know."

Dad didn't react much. He rarely does. He leaned back on the cheap sofa and cleared his throat, which was how he always began a measured conversation. "Well, David, I never thought that Jane had . . . corrupted you or anything of that nature." He smiled. "I just assumed you were going through your own thing, and that God would lead you"—he opened his hands helplessly—"someplace good, wherever that was. I know you don't believe in the Bible anymore, and that you think I'm a fool for believing the way I do. But I pray for you and I trust the Lord, and I know it's hard to talk about this stuff . . ." and again he paused, and there was this tense silence where we both wanted desperately to express something honest without being hurtful. "What I can't understand, however, is why these so-called Bible experts can't even read the Bible. You know, they say, 'There's all these contradictions in Scripture!' They actually say that Genesis is two creation stories, and all you have to do is read it and you can see that they're misreading something that's right under their noses. . . ." He let the comment hang there, both a challenge and a plea for understanding.

I knew then that we were stuck. Because even that small bit of conversation raised twenty topics in my head. *Genesis is two creation stories, but the translations smooth them out because that's what sells Bibles. And speaking of Genesis, Jane learned more about evolution from the nuns at her Catholic high school than I did in public school . . . but I'm learning it now and the science is really fascinating. And speaking of science, I became pro-gay because I studied the science and that's where the research led me, not because I wanted to be liberal. And speaking of liberal, I became a feminist because Jane cares about how women are portrayed in the media, and that affects how I look at everything now. And speaking of changed perceptions, here's why I now love the Eucharist . . .* I could barely rein it all in.

On top of this, what I really wanted to say, and couldn't possibly mention at this point, was that Jane and I weren't sleeping together. I was sure that was my dad's greatest fear—evangelical Christians are constantly worried about sex—and I wanted to assure him that while I was more radical in my politics and my theology, I was still very conservative in my actual behavior. I didn't drink. I didn't smoke pot. And after we'd talked about it and prayed about it, Jane and I had agreed to hold off on sex until after we were married. It was my idea, but she respected my beliefs and was willing to go along with them, presumably because she was also a virgin and was as nervous as I was.

As a devout evangelical, I had a lot to be nervous about. Sex education in a conservative church is always the same: they start by saying that sex is a beautiful gift from the Lord, and then warn you not to do it before marriage, not to fool around, to protect your "thought life" from unwholesome TV shows and movies, and in general to ignore the pernicious influence of our culture in general—including any liberal thing you might have learned in sex education at school. Sex comes to feel not like a gift but like one huge warning label on a supposedly tasty bottle of poison. Not only is having even lustful thoughts forbidden (Jesus says in Matthew that having a lustful thought is the same as committing adultery), but sex itself is alleged to be this incredibly tempting slippery slope where if you give in even a little—say, to some under-the-bra groping—the next thing you know you'll be getting pregnant during a three-way where everyone's wearing leather corsets and trying vainly to keep a deep spiritual emptiness and misery at bay. If you hear this warning narrative for long enough, it can become a self-fulfilling prophecy. Lots of young Christians slip away completely because there's no room in the Bible-thumper's morality for a modicum of sex. You either abstain or you're not welcome until you apologize.

Since I was growing skeptical of the Bible's wisdom about sex, Jane and I steered for a middle way that nevertheless stayed close to shore. We certainly fooled around. After some initial experimentation where I fondled her breasts (which she found kind of dull) and tried to finger her (which she found too intense), we'd settled on a middle ground of blow jobs and frottage, and that's where we'd been for a year and a half before she moved away. We had orgasms, but I'd never seen her completely naked. It was an odd situation to be in. Her entire family was sure we were having full-on intercourse, and mine was hoping— and probably praying—that I was doing nothing at all. Our compromise would have made no sense to either side. That, I thought, was what proved we were being wise.

A motor sounded outside, and Dad said, "Oh, your brother's home. I was letting him drive my new car." I turned to the window and saw my twin pulling up in some tiny red sporty thing. "It's an MR2," said Dad. "It runs really well considering it's an 'eighty-five."

"Why did you get a new car?" I asked. New to him, of course. It was old for 1995.

"Daniel needed something for work, and you know, now that your mother's been getting these checks, I can actually afford a few things we've needed for some time."

Mom had supported the family as a nurse for twenty years, and now that she was in a home with Alzheimer's, she was getting a pension from her old work. Even without a memory, she was still bringing in a good chunk of the family money. The car was the most recent new item. With two of the three kids gone and only a trailer to pay for, Dad had also bought a computer, with dreams of doing some design work from home, and he'd bought a fancy full-sized Yamaha keyboard that he was hoping to play at church functions once he trained himself. So far none of these plans had materialized; they'd just cost money. Can you love someone and still hate their life? *If Hallmark hires me, I might make enough to help him,* I thought, *and I bet he'll need it someday.* I felt the first fingers of pressure that haunt the adult breadwinner.

Daniel entered, we muttered our howdies, and that curtailed further talk about Jane or religion, but Dad was okay with that. "Come on out here," he said to me. "There's something I want to show you." And he took me out to Battlezone, went to the passenger's side, and opened the door. "Do you have a pen?"

"Always," I replied.

He opened the glove compartment and fished out a piece of paper, offering it to me. "You should have a car," he said. "So this is the title. You just need to sign it and it's yours."

I could hardly speak. I had mixed feelings for a second. *Can Dad really afford to do this? What if his new car breaks down?* But in the end I decided that, at twenty-six, it was long past time for me to get my first car. If I were going to escape, this would make it easier. I pulled out my handy Uniball Micro and signed the title against Battlezone's hood, which was still warm from the driving earlier, and from the eighty-five-degree August afternoon.

"You'll have to pay for insurance," said Dad, "but with your record I imagine it won't be too much of a hardship. With this car particularly. I can't say precisely what the car's worth but it can't be very much."

"Great," I said. "Do you need to do anything else?"

He shook his head no. "I already signed it. In fact, one thing you could do is, you see that next line below for the next trans-action? If you sign that now ahead of time, if you ever want to get rid of the car in a hurry, all you have to do is go into the glove compartment and hand that to someone and they can fill the rest in themselves."

I blinked. "Dad," I said, "if I do that, then any random thief who finds it can sign it and have legal title to my car!"

Dad shrugged. "I guess that's true. Anyway, here you go." He handed me the keys, and that's as close as I ever got to having ritual maturity conferred upon me. "Drive safely on the way home," he said. "I don't know what all the rules are about my insurance. I mean, I'm sure you're covered, but why take chances?"

Why take chances indeed, I thought on my way back home, driving the actual speed limit. *That's something only rich people with savings can afford to do.* The more I thought about my application to Hallmark and the wild gamble it symbolized, the crazier the whole thing seemed.

ON MONDAY, WHILE I WAS SHOPPING for insurance and taking notes for cryptic crossword number fourteen, Sunny, the creative recruiter for Hallmark, called and said, "We'd like you to do an additional portfolio."

"Oh, no. What does that mean?" I said.

"Well, they liked your poetry, but there are only four or five poems between the two portfolios, so they'd like to see more." Again, she must have heard anxiety in my voice—or maybe it's just a reflex when your job mostly involves offering college seniors their first big gig—so she sounded chipper and soothing and said, "This is a very standard procedure when they're actually interested in someone. The portfolio is very broad, so it doesn't show off everyone's specific skills. That's why they ask for a follow-up."

"May I ask who's reading my portfolios?"

"Everyone," said Sunny. "The writers, the editors, the managers. We try to get broad-based input."

Rats! More waiting. But at least I knew they liked my work. And I now had this advantage: I knew I was being read by people who write poems all day, and I was getting a sense that the company was more creative inside than it looked like from the card counter. That meant I could risk sending them poems that said, "I'm a very talented verse writer, and you can teach me to focus later." So I sent them the most dazzling twelve new poems I could manage to write, regardless of whether I thought they could actually be turned into cards. I remember only one poem in particular, which I chose to demonstrate that I could handle complex rhyme schemes as well as difficult, three-syllable rhymes.

> *Your kindly hospitality's*
> *A thing to put a pal at ease!*
> *You throw off ostentatiousness*
> *And jettison formalities!*

> *With customary graciousness*
> *You share your place's spaciousness!*
> *You give, devoid of vanity—*
> *A model of audaciousness!*

> *With how you cure insanity,*
> *And handle guests' inanity,*
> *Your groovy hospitality's*
> *A model for humanity!*

Sunny was right. It was fun. I read them all to Jane, and she was thrilled and supportive. When I sent the supplement off, I was practically singing.

Yet more waiting. The weeks stretched on, and if I hadn't been weird already, I got up to puzzle number seventeen, a particularly obscure little number based on Wilhelm Reich's nineteenth-century theory of "orgone energy." I kept calling Sunny's assistant and Sunny kept telling me that the people there seemed to like my work, but she wasn't making any promises, and anyway they weren't sure when they were going to have an opening. After my fourth or fifth call, she said, "I wish I had better news, but I really don't know what's next. My advice to you, Dave, is try to put this out of your mind. Get a job where you are. When we call you, we call you. Sometimes it even takes years."

AS IT TURNED OUT, PREVENT didn't get the new contract, and we all got fired after being kept on as long as possible doing ever more tedious jobs, like driving the file boxes an hour away to some storage facility, and then taking careful notes about where everything was. I was so terrified of losing even this crappy work that I actually worked extra hours. I did research and typed up an entire mini-encyclopedia of where to find things in the file boxes, indexed in three ways: by area of the storage space ("C-3 means 3 columns left, third box from bottom"), by date of storage, and by actual object ("Tape, masking—B-7, C-4 [2 reels]; stray clump in D-3"). I spent hours drawing diagrams of ceiling-high walls of boxes, then going back to the site to double-check its accuracy. Everyone said they were very helpful. Then I was disemployed.

Now I had to wager on some kind of future. My unemployment checks would last for six months. Would Hallmark get back to me by then? Would it be yes? Or should I start looking for work here in town like Sunny said, fully knowing that I was possibly going to leave suddenly?

I elected to do nothing and wait Hallmark out. Part of this was because I hated the prospect of job-hunting anyway, and part because my roommate had a whole library of really cool laser discs that I finally had enough time to really get into. But there was another element, too: I had hope. Real hope. A sense that this was the perfect job for me, and that anyone who worked in the biz would surely recognize it. I bought *What Color Is Your Parachute?* and while walking home from the college bookstore, I read the section on Faith and the Job Hunt, where author Richard Bolles says that your vocation, your calling, is "where your great love and the world's great hunger meet." In the middle of the sidewalk, in Tucson's still-hot September breeze, I closed the book to my chest, shut my eyes, and crossed myself with a fervent amen.

I told Jane one night, "When I was an evangelical, I was basically superstitious. Everything that happened to me was a sign from God. I found a parking space, and that's a blessing. I got a bad grade, and that's God chastening me. But even though I don't think God works that way anymore, I feel like this job is my destiny, an actual gift from God. It's not coming from superstition, but from some other place, like deep inside me. Someplace more basic and real."

"That's called self-confidence, honey," said Jane. "Enjoy it. I bet it's very nice."

THEN, IN MID-SEPTEMBER, while working on puzzle number twenty-one (a lighthearted frolic based on the Brontë sisters' masculine pen names), I finally got the call from Sunny. Hallmark had an opening for an editor, and it would pay around $27,000—which, Sunny reminded me, went pretty far in Kansas City. At PREVENT I had been living quite happily on around $10,000, and $27,000 seemed like unimaginable riches. "But of course," she said, "this isn't a job offer yet. We need to interview you. What's your schedule like?"

3

Interviews

THANKS TO *WHAT COLOR IS YOUR PARACHUTE*, I'D studied the standard interview questions ("What's your greatest weakness?" "That I'm not comfortable around clichés"), and I knew the rules: Firm handshakes. Direct eye contact. Talk half the time, listen half the time. Never seem nervous.

I also knew I needed a haircut. At the time I had long shaggy hair and a full beard—the default look of a twentysomething geek too lazy to bother with style. I loved not caring about my hair and I hated getting it cut, but for Hallmark, just this once, I could chop it back for a few days.

"I'm only worried about one thing," I told the stylist as I bent my neck back into the basin. "You see this?" I stroked my hand along my widow's peak. "I've had long hair for years, so I don't know what it looks like short. And I can't tell if this projecting part at the front is attached to the rest of the hair, or if there's a strip of baldness between the main hair and this thing at the front. So could you check before you cut, please: is my widow's peak an island or an isthmus?"

She lifted a flap of hair, peered at my scalp, and said, "I'd say there's some marshy undergrowth."

I laughed. "Cut away, then!" I had pitched an odd phrase; she played along. That's all I've ever wanted out of life: a little repartee to know I'm not alone. This stylist was my kind of woman.

On October 3, 1995, Hallmark actually flew me out for an interview. That date happened to be my twenty-seventh birthday. It was also, by dumb luck, the day of the verdict in the O. J. Simpson trial. What I'm saying is this part of the process was kind of a blur, and I wasn't the only one distracted.

On the flight to Kansas City I read the packet Sunny had sent me, which included a 1992 *New York Times Magazine* article about the company, which filled me in on the basics: that Hallmark was founded in 1910 by Joyce Hall, who had traveled to Kansas City with his cartoonist friend Walt Disney. (Disney did better in California, of course.) Joyce Hall's original greeting cards were all written on three-by-five cards and kept in a shoe box, which is how Shoebox Cards (a tiny little division of Hallmark) got its name. *I draw cartoons. I write poems. I keep them in a little folder.* It felt like I'd looked at an old photograph and seen an ancestor with my same nose.

According to the *New York Times* article, greeting cards are (or were, in 1992) a $2 billion-a-year industry, with an average growth rate of around four percent. It used to be better; from the 1960s to the mid-1980s, greeting cards just kept growing astoundingly. But they sputtered in the mid-1980s with the decline of the shopping mall. One of the most memorable parts of the article was a description of how Hallmark had never once, in its entire history, had any kind of large layoff. In the late

1980s, when it probably should have laid off a couple dozen spare employees the place couldn't use, the workers were instead paid full salary to do community service work until they could get retrained and placed elsewhere in the company.

Thank god. As I'd pictured myself as a writer, I thought about how many times I'd gotten in trouble at work in the past for stupid things: a dog cartoon here, a misinterpreted comment there. But here at Hallmark, when the bosses had every excellent excuse to fire people, they resisted. Who needed to date the boss's daughter? This was just the sort of forgiving employer I needed. And community service work, too. So it was a *moral* company. Hallelujah. As deeply religious as I was, I had been afraid that corporate work would force me to sell a bit of my soul. Maybe here I wouldn't have to.

Once I landed, I got shuttled in a paid-for cab from the Kansas City airport, feeling like a sultan. No one in my family had ever been flown anywhere without holding a fund-raiser first.

HALLMARK IS A SET OF four tall buildings in the heart of downtown Kansas City, Missouri. My first impression from the cab ride was of a long series of midsized skyscrapers composed primarily of cinder block. We passed row after row after row of similar-looking high-rises, all in the same color scheme of sandstone and cement. Hallmark—and the shiny mall across the street from it, called Crown Center—is a much-needed break in the drudgery. The city's residential areas, I soon discovered, are flat-out gorgeous, especially down on Ward Parkway, where stately forty-room mansions are poised near one another like happy monks, each in its own serene prayer bubble. But if you're being flown in for an interview, your first thought is apt to be, *Somewhere in this city is a factory that makes factories.* It's depressingly redundant.

The ride from the airport wound up taking an hour, but I was getting reimbursed for that, too. *My god*, I thought as I left the cab, *I'm saving a receipt*. My testicles grew two sizes that day.

I walked into the lobby and felt immediately overwhelmed by the unassuming power of the place. "We're successful and we know it, so we don't show it off," the place seemed to say. I went through a revolving door and realized, weirdly, that I'd only ever seen them in the movies or when traveling. Now it was possible I would live in a revolving-door city. Things were surreal for me before I'd even crossed the threshold.

I signed in, got a visitor's pass—my first sign-in; my first visitor's pass—and waited for Sunny. While I waited, I was free to look around in the lobby, where they were showcasing the work of a few artists who seemed to work in gently shaped stone: a disk of obsidian, three gray sandstone obelisks about four feet tall, etc. It was the sort of art you expect to see in a bank: inoffensive but solid, matching fluid artistic gestures with the security of incredibly heavy weight. But what immediately struck me, above all else, was the smell of paper.

I'm sensitive to the smell of paper because I spent so much time in my dad's print shop that eventually I could lift a ream of twenty-pound bond and know if it was fifteen sheets short. So although a lot of businesses across America smell like paper, I still maintain that Hallmark smells more like paper in motion than any non-magazine business I can imagine. And I think this is because part of Hallmark's corporate culture is to supply everyone with little stacks of three-by-five cards, the same size (apparently) as the ones that Joyce Hall used when he was writing the cards with which he would found the company back in the day. So the card stock is a little thicker than the paper most offices use, and because it's produced by cutting (done somewhere on the premises, I imagine), it carries just a little dust with it. And that dust goes everywhere, it gets in everything, until every suit you own carries with it a spritzing of transient industry.

Speaking of which, I was wearing the same suit I'd worn when I met Sunny the first time, as I still had only one. And since it was my birthday and I had a job interview, I was wearing a new tie, even more colorful than my other navy one. This one was yellow with blue stripes, and it was actually silk, and I was terrified of spilling something on it. I was about to meet some HR person, and I suspected they liked things just so.

With only a little time left, I crossed myself, kissed my thumb, and prayed, *Bless me, Saint Vitus. I'm going in.**

An elevator dinged and Sunny appeared, smiling. "Still dressed up, I see," she said.

I shook her hand firmly and made eye contact. "Yes indeed."

"That won't last long. Follow me." We went up in the elevator to her office, and she handed me my itinerary. "Here's what's happening. You're going to talk to fourteen different people today for about a half-hour each."

"Fourteen? I thought you had like some HR person who was a gatekeeper type who—"

---

* Saint Vitus is the patron saint of comedians. There are other patrons of comedy, like Genesius and Lawrence of Rome, but Saint Vitus also has a disease named after him—St. Vitus's dance, which we now call Huntington's chorea—and the perversity of this made me like him the best when I was shopping for a patron.

"That's not how we do things. You have to work with a lot of different coworkers, and they all have different concerns. It's easy. You'll see. Just be yourself, be honest, and then you'll fly home and we'll talk about you behind your back." She laughed, but then she saw I was smiling nervously. "No, really, Dave. Relax. I'm sorry. That was just a joke. Now let's look at that itinerary while we travel."

"No problem," I said, and I actually did relax a bit. It was nice that she'd mis-joked. It made this process feel more human.

I would meet an editor, then the editorial manager, then a main-staff writer, then a writing manager, then I would go to the Idea Exchange, meet the manager there, and be escorted by a few of their writers to lunch in the Crown Room. Next stop: the Humor Department, then over into the Reed Center, off to Shoebox, and . . . She paused and added, "I hope those are comfortable walking shoes."

"So do I," I said.

I was ready. *Eye contact. Handshake. Talk half the time. Never seem nervous.* As far as that last goes, I was sweating horribly, and since I'd rarely worn formal shirts, I didn't know I was supposed to wear an undershirt. I just kept the jacket on and checked myself in every passing reflection to make sure my suit's armpits weren't darkening, because for all I knew it could happen. Could I get a new suit in a hurry?

My first visit was with Tammy, an editor in Season, whatever that was. She was a thin, smart-looking brunette who was wearing an orange sweater on which she sported an artsy brooch of a cat that moved its tail and paws, bobble-head style. "That's a fun brooch," I said as I approached.

"Thanks," she said. "It was a gift."

I offered her a firm handshake and direct eye contact. "Let me just say that I'm really glad to have the opportunity to interview here."

She laughed with surprise and said, "Please relax. You're making me nervous."

I unclenched just a little. Was this a trick? She glanced at an open folder on her desk, where I recognized a copy of my résumé. "So!" she said. "Did you really propose to your fiancée in a crossword puzzle magazine?"

"A puzzle magazine," I said. "It wasn't exactly a crossword." It was a grid-type thing where all the clues were based on *Casablanca*. Names, places, trivia. When you solved the puzzle, the shaded center area spelled a quote from the film: NOBODY EVER LOVED ME THAT MUCH. The instructions said, "Another part of the grid contains a message intended for only one member of the solving community." The top and bottom rows read JANE BELLEVUE / PLEASE MARRY ME. But that was a lot to go into, and I was still trying to talk only half the time.

My interviewer almost gushed at me. "Did she solve it?"

"Not technically. She read the instructions, knew it was for her, and couldn't wait, so she just skipped to the answers."

"And she said yes."

I sighed. "Actually, she said, '*Placet*,' which is Latin for 'It pleases me,' which is what Harriet Vane said to Lord Peter Wimsey when he proposed to her in the book *Gaudy Night*. My fiancée is really into classic mysteries."

"Wow," said Tammy, politely.

Which is why I sighed. I was sure I'd overshared, and that she would have preferred me to say just, "Yeah, she said yes." But that wasn't technically true, and I couldn't just lie. Tammy looked down at her sheet again. "And you're from Tucson?"

I nodded, then remembered and said, "Yes. Yes, I am." That was about half, wasn't it?

"Well, you'll find it pretty cold here."

That was it. The tough questions never came. It was just a fifteen-minute chat, and then she walked me to my next interview, which went exactly the same way. The next was like the first two. An hour and an half into the day, I'd had six interviews, and not one person had asked me anything about the job, and literally every person had said, "Relax," in the face of my firm, direct handshake. Everyone said "Happy Birthday," too. (No cards, though.) I had to tell the proposal story several more times, because apparently people loved it so much that they called ahead to my next interviewer, who often had further questions. ("*USA Today* ran it in a sidebar under wacky news just above a story about an avant-garde fashion show that included bras made out of plungers." "No, no date yet. She has to get her Ph.D. first." "*Casablanca* was the movie we saw on our first date, and we saw it again on Valentine's Day the first night we slept together in the same bed. We just cuddled, but still. Whenever it's on TV, I'll call her and we'll try to watch it together.") Three people smiled and told me, "You'll never wear that suit again."

It gradually dawned on me that my hiring must be a foregone conclusion, and that this interview process was a way of either justifying their decision after the fact, or possibly weeding out any overt lunatics whose craziness didn't come across on paper. I began to relax for real now, and to focus less on my posture and correct responses and more on simply finding my way around. I tried to picture myself doing the job. Where would I sit? Who would be my neighbors? What would my cubicle feel like?

And so I began to get a sense of the geography. The area around Hallmark is quite hilly, and so there are four buildings, all the same height, but with different numbers of floors because the terrain keeps rising. The main entrance is the 2480 building, nine stories high, where most of the business end of the company works and lives. When I was there, the ninth floor was the home of the main writing staff, and the seventh and eighth floors were for the editors. Then there's the 2460 building, which is seven stories tall. At the bottom of 2460 was where Humor lived. Then, a little farther out was the 2440 building, five stories, one room of which housed Mahogany/Tree of Life, which is the home for the African-American and Jewish cards, respectively. Then, in the last building in line, was 2420, also five stories, where you could find Shoebox. When I was there, it was, in fact, the only thing there was to find: above Shoebox was mostly vacant space, chair and cubicle storage, held in abeyance against future expansion.

That much I grasped. Mostly, though, it was all such a blur that there are only four strong memories I carry with me.

Memory #1: I met Magda, the Everyday Editing manager—a sober-looking woman with stylishly cropped blond-and-silver hair, a textbook example of what happens when a young head-turning beauty runs hard against twenty years in a sedentary job. She was the model Hallmark manager: bright, judicious, cautious in all things. And she was the only person I met all day who seemed dubious about me. "You seem . . . very educated," she said, with real concern. "Our average consumer isn't a college graduate. Do you think you'll be able to stay interested in the job? Do you think you can write for people at a . . . less academic level?"

"Well, sure!" I said, and told her about my dad's background and humility, and how I'd been raised knowing that getting a Ph.D. doesn't make you better than the other folks in the trailer park. "In fact, every so often someone for some reason will tell me, 'You're really smart,' and I always reply, 'My mechanic thinks I'm an idiot.' That's how I think of it. I'm not pretentious, and I'll happily write for anyone." That seemed to satisfy her. It was the only interrogative hurdle I actually noticed all day, and I was confident I'd cleared it. But I also thought, *Yeesh. I hope I don't have to work with a person who seems to hate me already.*

Memory #2: I visited a place called the Idea Exchange at the bottom of 2440 and was utterly blown away. Most of Hallmark consists of the same cubicles you see everywhere: battleship-gray 1980s-era squares festooned with the personalities of their occupants: photos of puppies and kids; the occasional movie poster or robot toy. The artists' areas were often much wilder and more interesting, but the editors' and writers' spaces I had seen up till now were basically sedate: more decoration, more cartoons, but still essentially cubicley.

Not in the Idea Exchange. The Idea Exchange was a staff for creative forward thinking: the writer-artists of unusual proven skill who were tasked with handling plans for the future, as well as with troubleshooting any needs that might demand a quick solution. And the Idea Exchange had no cubicles. It was more like a fantasia of doors and windows: antique doors, Dutch doors, barn doors, peppered with small bursts of stained or decorated glass. Each of them was hanging from the ceiling on various wires, so that a workspace might have a gently rocking door serving as a wall, and a dangling colored pane at an angle to alter the light slightly. It was a perfect example of what Hallmark does best: the transformation of everyday objects into warm, expressive art—art that, in the process, gives those same workaday objects the gift of gentle motion. There was also a timeless quality to the design: people worked at rolltop desks and leaned back, staring at the ceiling, in old-school business chairs like they don't make anymore: stiff leatherette, knobby metal wheels. It was surely not expensive, but it looked like a helluva lot of fun.

"I want to work here!" I said in my interview with the area's manager and chief instigator—a short bulldog of a woman named Addie Apian with the quirky voice of a born comedienne.

"Everyone does," she said. "We've got a line this long of people wanting to get in here. So I get the best. I'm really proud of my staff. Work long enough and do good things, and maybe I'll see you here someday."

"It's a deal," I said. And for the rest of that morning, I kept remembering the Idea Exchange. It became my default dream job.

Memory #3: I had lunch with a guy named Josh Broward, who seemed polite and smart, but we didn't talk much. Mostly he was interested in getting out of the Crown Room—that's Hallmark's somewhat swanky cafeteria—and off to the Humor Department, where they had a television and where they would soon be announcing the results of the O.J. trial. So my actual strongest memory of my interview is me, standing next to Josh Broward in the back of a crowded room, in a building I was lost in, crammed full of people my age whom I didn't know, and watching in disbelief as O.J. was declared innocent. I had a lot of theories about the trial, but I was trapped—stuck in practically the only place in the world I could have been at the time where, interviewing as I was, I wasn't free to express myself, and I couldn't read the people around me. Happy Birthday.

Memory #4: A miracle happened.

After lunch I met Max Stentor—a tall, shaggy-headed man of forty-eight with a wide smile and a voice so powerful you could sometimes feel it in your chest like the drums in a parade. It wouldn't be quite accurate to call his voice deep, though that was part of it, and you couldn't quite call it piercing, though there's truth there as well. Mostly, his voice was just really, really loud. Later on I discovered that even when he was back in his cubicle, talking on the phone about the company's woes or secrets, you could still hear him as clearly as if he'd walked up to you and started murmuring. If it helps, try to picture a jowly, boisterous Elliott Gould. That was Max Stentor.

So Max strode up to me, clapped my hand in one of his huge ones, and said, "David. I know I shouldn't say this because it'll take this interview off topic right away and we've only got a little bit of time. But I'm a big fan of your crosswords."

I think my brain exploded. It turns out he was one of the few hundred subscribers to *Tough Cryptics*. Because of my work there, within the puzzle world I had, and have, a following. And when all us puzzle writers and editors get together at conventions and gatherings, people say nice things about me. But when Max said, "I like your crosswords," it was the first time I've ever heard a sentence like that coming from a civilian. It's now been over twelve years, and I've lived in two other states since then (three if you count New Jersey), and I've still never heard anything like it.

"Did you see the thing I did in the latest issue?" I asked, and he said, "That was a really creative use of the grid!" And we were off, talking about favorite clues, well-loved themes, and the constructors I'd met and knew. Every fear I had about this job melted away. Clearly, this was the place of my people. Max was the manager for me. If I was ever going to be understood in the working world, this was my best, clearest shot. For the next ten minutes we chatted about puzzles and words and the joys of solving, and I knew this was where I wanted to work. We parted smiling, and that smile lasted all through the day, and the whole plane ride home. I somehow managed to drive Battlezone back from the airport and collapsed into my bed, exhausted but happy.

Sunny called me the next day. "You did good," she said. "Congratulations. You're hired. They're offering you thirty-two thousand to start."

"Thirty-two?" I said. "You said it was twenty-seven."

"Like I said," she replied. "You did good."

To this day, I am convinced that in person, I am $5,000 more charming than I am on paper.

PART TWO

Congratulations

My Months in Everyday Editorial

4

Orientation

THEY FLEW ME OUT AGAIN TO FIND A PLACE, AND THEN, in a miracle I've never experienced since, they paid for honest-to-god movers, real professionals who even did all the boxing up and wrapping in Tucson while I sat on my roommate's couch watching his laser discs. Jane took time off from school to come and help me move, so with just two suitcases, two sleeping bags, and a pair of pillows to carry along with us, she piloted Battle-zone all the way up from Tucson to Kansas City, Missouri. (It was a natural division of labor. I hated driving, and she hated how I drove.)

When we got in at eleven P.M., the apartment was completely unfurnished—just three decent-sized rooms with hardwood floors and a steadily hissing furnace in the corner. We had gotten here way faster than the movers. We crashed into slumber, cuddling each other on top of our bedrolls. We didn't fool around, even a little, even after six months apart. We were that exhausted.

She stayed the whole weekend, though, and it dawned on me that this was the first time in our three years of dating that we had ever actually had privacy. We had both lived at home, or with roommates, and now here we were, completely on our own, with no one to report to. We could do anything. It was terrifying, really, because what if we slipped up? With sex so tempting and so easy, how could we stay true to our values?

We managed. We christened the floor of the apartment with a traditional session of blow job and frottage, and by Sunday she was on a plane back to St. Paul. The movers arrived a few days later, the week before my job officially started, on Tuesday, November 1. ("Why don't I start on Monday?" I asked Sunny, and she said, "Hallmark pays by the month. Just take Monday off and have a Happy Halloween.")

ON HALLOWEEN NIGHT, 1995, I wandered the neighborhood, partly to soak it all in, partly to avoid any kids who might knock and ask for candy. I was right across the street from the Plaza, which is one of the only really pretty parts of Kansas City. Based on the Plaza in Seville, Spain (there's even a fancy clock tower), the Missouri version dates back to the early 1900s and it's simply gorgeous: curved Spanish roofs, colored tiles on the walls, classical fountains everywhere you step. I found myself walking through it with the heady sensation of being a foreign tourist, looking at all the high-end boutiques, and thinking, *I could buy stuff there now. Or there. When Jane moves here I'll buy her nice things.* The stores were so classy that they didn't even have paper pumpkins in the windows. But it still felt like Halloween as I'd always pictured it. There were actual trees here, whose leaves had actually turned color for the fall, just like in *Peanuts*, and they were starting to look stark in the moonlight. There was an actual nip in the air, like I'd always heard about but never really felt in the desert. In the distance, a guy with a saxophone wailed into the night, just like in music videos. *Oh, right. Jazz and blues are big here. I can go see concerts now, too.* October itself seemed to electrify me. Finally, I was in a city that felt big enough to hold my ambition. And you know what else? It wasn't all that cold. I laughed out loud. I jumped. I danced a few silly steps. I could get used to this.

THAT NIGHT, THOUGH, the night before my first day at work, I had a nightmare. In my dream, the Antichrist had taken over the world. There wasn't even a plot, really; I just woke up and read the newspaper and knew it had happened. The earth was now under a one-world government with a completely demonic world leader, and everything was about to end. I went to the window and saw clouds gathering like an inverted A-bomb, and the sky darkened with locusts that began screaming above me. A huge black-clad horseman floated out of the sky in action-movie slow motion, wielding a sword and silently bent on some unspeakably dark purpose. Even the grass had browned and withered. The sun was red and dying. Everyone I loved was gone—raptured up to heaven like all the good Christians—and I'd been left behind to suffer the strange wrath of God.

The thing is, I didn't believe any of this. I hadn't for years. In my dream I kept trying to scream, "This whole scenario doesn't even make sense! Why would anyone vote for a one-world leader when everyone knows about the Antichrist already? Once he demanded to be worshipped, wouldn't people think he was kind of nuts? And why would a God of love and forgiveness suddenly act like a morbid teenager who's into Goth metal? It's a wholly idiotic reading of Scripture that only worked its way into Christian thought in fundamentalist America in the eighteen hundreds . . ." I never heard my own voice. It turns out you can't argue with dreams; their engine is somewhere besides thought. My next urge was to laugh, but that didn't work, either. To make a joke, you need to have some initially rational foundation, and there was no logic here—only dread. I stood, horrified and helpless, as the air turned cold and I smelled distant charnel burning and the terror washed over everything in all its operatic finality, and I woke up in a flinching position, feeling as exhausted and achy as if I'd been running. I was still on a sleeping bag on the carpet in the living room.

"Goddammit," I said aloud. I'd had Antichrist dreams in the first anxious months after leaving the evangelical church, but they hadn't troubled me in years. Why now, out of nowhere? It was like I'd been duped in my sleep. I was furious. I actually rummaged through my boxes of books to find my Bible so I could fling it against the wall. But when I found it, it was a Catholic Bible and I didn't have the heart. The Catholics have never taught this idiocy. I couldn't take it out on them.

I still had two hours before work. I grazed among my boxes, collecting soap and a towel and a razor . . . and then I realized I still had no shower curtain. I took a long bath, and I washed the dream from my head with a full-immersion baptism.

AFTER A BASIC RUN-THROUGH with Sunny—where I got my picture taken, got my employee badge, and was handed a huge folder full of tedious-looking fliers—my first meeting of the day was with young, vibrant Regina, who was the head manager of all the writing staffs. Her office was up on Main Writing, ninth floor. Hallmark then had four staffs: Main Writing (the serious cards), Traditional Humor (Garfield and pop-ups), Alternative Humor (Shoebox), and the Idea Exchange (experimental R&D). I wasn't joining any of them today. It was almost cruel, like walking me through a candy store on the first day of Lent.

I didn't mind for long. Regina welcomed me warmly into her office—she had an actual office, unlike other managers—and I remembered her from the blurry day of interviews; where most of the people I'd met had been polite and almost lackadaisically calm, Regina was a young creative optimist who was radioactive with encouragement. She was like if Katie Couric was in Mensa and seemed to be flirting with me.

"Let me tell you why I like you," she said, smiling the whole time like a kid revealing a great secret. "What I saw in your portfolio was a kind of energy and creativity that we don't see very often. For the longest time, we were in a rut, doing all the same things, you know? All our cards sounded the same. *Da-duh-da-duh-da-duh da*; *Da-duh-da-duh-da-duh*. It was like that for eons. I know we can do better. The consumer is changing. She's more open to new things. My dream is to do cards that are actual poetry, and we're starting to get some of it out there. Our writing staff—you know, we try new things, but it's hard. A lot of them are used to doing things in a particular way, so I'm trying to shake things up. You"—and here she pointed in a gesture that seemed to bestow some of her magic on me—"are the kind of writer we need for the future of the company. It's going to be really exciting."

"Uh, wow," I said, feeling giddy. "I'm really honored." I'd just thought I was a good enough writer to squeak through and get a job, like a dog grateful for table scraps. I'd had no idea I was going to be part of a revolution.

She paused and looked at me with sympathy so obvious she could have projected it from a stage set. "I'm so sorry we don't have a writing opening right now. But we wanted you right away, and editing was the first opportunity we had."

"That's fine," I said, and as I said it, I started to feel the way she apparently saw me. Was that hope I was feeling?

"You'll be reporting to Magda—she manages Everyday— and you'll be working with Edith McNicely, who's just a wonderful person. They're going to help you get on your feet here so when you do start writing, you'll be ready. And believe me—I want you to be writing. We all do. But this is the best we can do for now."

"I understand," I said. And I did. Her belief in me had acted on me like Percocet, and I suddenly felt that I could do anything, and I felt it so confidently that there wasn't even any need to rush. "Really, I'm just happy to be here. My whole life I've been writing poems and silly jokes and I never thought there were other people like me, you know, with those same obsessions, and a company where we could all work together. Being here now—I don't know. It's like the world suddenly makes sense."

Regina grabbed her chin thoughtfully, as if struck by something, and she frowned at my face a moment. "I can tell," she said, "that you are an old soul."

When I woke up this morning, I was a terrified eight-year-old. "I think you're a good influence," I replied. We beamed at each other, the meeting ended, and I strode downstairs to my first assignment, feeling a little like Jesus must have on his first day of shop class. *I've gotten a special message. I'm meant for more than this.*

MAGDA WAS THE ONLY WOMAN who had doubted me during the interview process. Today she seemed happier to see me—at least on the surface—and showed me to an empty, distant gray cubicle. It was really more of a desk-booth, with no sides to speak of. She said, "You'll be working with Edith McNicely. She's waiting for you in the wings. You'll be spending a lot more time there than you will at this cube." Thank goodness.

We threaded through adult-sized cubicles to a room off to the side with a door marked WEDDINGS AND BIRTHS in flowery script, and there I saw Edith, who had apparently heard us coming, because she wasn't working when we came in. She was just standing there expectantly, composed and upright. When I extended my hand, she actually pumped it and said, "Hiya! Welcome aboard." She was in her late forties to mid-fifties, with gray hair that she kept in a fun pixie cut. She had dressed up for work, with a cameo brooch and a jacket with an interesting, vaguely floral fabric pattern. As she showed me around, she always seemed on the verge of tittering, and I could maybe see why they'd put us together. She was the quintessential cool young grandma. After five minutes in her presence I guessed two things about her: (1) that her refrigerator probably bore a copy of the poem "When I Am an Old Lady, I Shall Wear Purple"; and (2) that she must love the hell out of babies.

"These are the wings," she said, and spread her hands to in-

clude both sides of the room. All along the walls, and in a portion of the center, was a series of frames on hinges, like the kind
you see in stores where they sell posters. Each was about the
size of a large business suit. She flipped through them with a
series of clunks and showed me that each frame held twelve
cards—three across in four rows—and each also was stapled to a
computer printout of some sort. (And I thought, *It's 1995 and
we're still using dot-matrix printers with spindle-reel paper? Embrace the
inkjet already.*)

"This is every card in our line," said McNicely. "This is Wedding, and over there is Births, along with a few minor things, and
of course we've got them all divided by subcaption. You know—
wedding announcements, bridal showers, cards to put on the
wedding gifts, and all of that stuff." When she called it *stuff*, it
didn't come off as flippant or ironic; she was talking about good
friends she could be casual around. "Plus of course there's To
Daughter and From Both of Us and all the usual subs we have
with every card. There's even Wedding Humor, which I guess
you would like.

"They're ranked in order by sales, most popular to least for
each caption. A guy from marketing comes in every two weeks
and updates the wings. You'll see him—a nice young black man
named Sherod, so don't freak out if you come in and he's poking around. He belongs here. What you need to know is, we
don't touch the wings. We just read them and use them in our
planning, okay?"

"My god. There must be hundreds of these."

She laughed appreciatively and I realized I'd just compli-
mented her garden. "Most of them aren't in every store. That's

why we rank them. Some of our stores, they only have room for
two of our six Wedding-Religious-from-Both cards, so we send
the two top-ranked ones."

I'd always imagined that cards were just dreamed up wholesale
by writers, but that's a small percentage of the job. Mostly they're
created by an editor who looks over the lines, gets a sense of
what's in it, sees what's selling and what's not, and then, periodically over the course of a year, fills out a series of requisitions
for new cards that sure would be nice to have in order to keep
the line fresh. The requisitions are handed to writing managers,
who give them to writers they think can do the job.

Although most of the wings were taken up with cards, there
was a station at the front with two chairs and two computers,
and one of them was clearly where Edith had been working.

"Is that other one my desk?"

"Oh, no. That's for the line designer. You'll meet her later,
maybe." She led me to her desk and showed me a sample requisition, which was printed on a half-piece of paper and looked
something like this:

WEDDING CONGRATS—3.95   8 TO 12 LINES,
VERSE OR PROSE

POSSIBLE THEMES: WJOY, WHAP, HMYM
We need a card suitable for friends who are very fond of each
other but who haven't hung out in a while: warm about the
connection, vague about specific details of their lives these days.
Other successful cards in this category refer to "your special day"
and "you bring joy with you," so while we'd like to see this same

idea, we need it from a slightly different angle, maybe referencing a shared past with universal specifics.

Due date: November 16

"What are those things under 'Themes'?" I asked.

"Theme codes. That's the first thing you need to know. Here." She fished in a folder and pulled out a paper. "Go to your desk and memorize these. They're really, really important, okay? Then come back here and read through the wings and see how they match up with the cards. I'll be right here when you get back. Take as long as you need."

IT TURNS OUT theme codes are used as shorthand for the general emotional gist of a card. There were only about sixteen of them, and each was four letters long, so I'm still not sure why she wanted me to go back to my desk. My desk was empty of everything except for two things: the new-hires folder I'd just placed on it, and a little plastic standard-issue holder full of those omnipresent three-by-fives. Was I supposed to make flash cards?

I stared at the list and kept telling myself, *This represents seventy years of Hallmark's experience and wisdom. It can't possibly be as silly as it looks.* The list went like so:

THOY (or TOY) = Thinking of You
HMYM = How Much You Mean
TYDS = Things You Do and Say
FRND = Friendship
QLIF or QLIFE = Quote About Life

. . . and so on. I hadn't even gotten a third of the way down the page when I realized, with kind of a vague unpleasantness, that this wasn't just a code. It was an alien concern to me. In every card or poem I'd ever written, the question to myself was always, "How can I amuse someone on their birthday, or say good-bye in a funny/sweet way?" I had never bought a serious card in my life, and it had never occurred to me, at any time, that I might want to tell a friend of mine, "You know, you're a really great friend," or to share a quote about life. I stared at this list and wondered, *Who are these people who send all these cards?* Then I remembered my reading: women. Ninety percent of the card market. The sheer girliness of it all started to weigh on me like a deadly mountain-sized scented pillow.

Men showed up, too, here and there. The most popular male theme was Seldom Say (SELD). These, I learned, applied to cards whose thrust was "I know I don't say it very often, but for what it's worth, I love you and here's a card." Again, even among my own gender, I felt alienated. Who are these inarticulate dicks, and why do their women put up with them? Jane and I said, "I love you," constantly. We didn't need Seldom Say. If anything, we needed Seldom Shut Up About It.

A significant subset of these themes included various wishes: for happiness (WHAP), joy (WJOY), fun (WFUN), success (WSUC), luck (LUCK). Most popular of all was General Wish (GENW). These, I learned, are cards that present positive regard with no specific aim. A card that says, "Birthdays are fun! Birthdays are great! So blow out your candles and clean up your plate!" might get categorized under General Wish, since it's saying almost nothing at all. Again, I was buffaloed. Happiness, joy, and fun all felt exactly the same to me; I'd always simply wished

my friends whichever one seemed the handiest to rhyme with.
Greeting card buyers must care a lot for companies to subdivide.
Similarly, they had two different codes for cope (COPE) and
encouragement (ENCG), and I crossed my eyes trying to imagine expressing only one of those two in a card. With a sinking
feeling, I realized that if Hallmark was right about this sheet,
then I'd been kidding myself for years, and Wish for Success
maybe wasn't the same thing as Wish for Luck.

I actually made flash cards to kill time. I soon felt silly staring
at them, though, and anyway an hour or so had gone by, so I
went back to the wings.

Edith wasn't there. A beautiful woman my age was sitting in
the other chair. She had long, straight black hair, mysteriously
pale skin, and what looked like a hand-sewn jacket festooned
with purple and red spangles and beads. Very artsy. Very fun.

"Hi!" I said. "You must be the other person."

"Oh, you're Dave!" she said. "I'm Deedee. I've heard a lot
about you." She had a slightly husky voice, too. She was a Hallmark version of the whole Morticia Addams package. I quivered
inside.

"Wait—you've heard of me? I've got a reputation?"

"They say you're quite a character. I've been looking forward
to meeting you." Never mind that *quite a character* wasn't necessarily a glowing review. I already had a rep, and she wrinkled her
nose when she smiled. After some hours of feeling lost and ill at
ease, one gorgeous greeting and I was messianic again.

She was a line designer, which meant that she was the artistic
equivalent of the editor. "We have researchers who tell us all the
new color palettes that are becoming hip for our customers, and

we have to update our designs accordingly. So I make requests and pass them on to the artists. It works for patterns, too. Like when argyle came back a few years ago, we threw a few little argyles into the line."

"Argyle came back? I guess I wasn't looking."

She smiled. "I guess you're not a woman."

"Thanks for noticing," I said, touching my beard. "Actually, even if it came back, I don't think argyle is me. They ought to have a book like that for patterns, you know? Matching your personality, like *Color Me Paisley*."

She laughed. *Score!*

"Gosh," she said, shaking my hand again—and was there a flush in her cheeks? "I've got to get back to work, but it was really good to meet you."

"Likewise—Deedee, was it?"

IN THE COURSE OF my relationship with Jane, I had never really been seriously tempted to cheat. The only other women I fantasized about were the *Playboy* models from the odd magazine I bought now and then, whose pictures were so unreal that they never confused me. On the occasions where an actually attractive real-life woman had come along and seemed unduly friendly and I felt my body respond, I had a safety procedure. Meeting Deedee seemed like a good time to do it again. After a show of good faith ("Well, Edith isn't here. I guess I'll walk around and look for her"), I went to the nearest bathroom and stared myself down in the mirror. "Come on, Dave. Let's do a serious comparison here. Is this other woman as brilliant as Jane? Did Deedee get a perfect 800 on the Verbal part of the GRE? Okay then. Would this other girl get your jokes and throw them back at you? Would she share your joy in *Star Trek* and *The X-Files* and *Mystery Science Theater 3000*? Didn't think so. And even if all this were true, would she be on your same moral wavelength? Especially, would she put up with *not having sex until marriage*, like Jane's doing?"

No temptation survived to the end of this litany. Most didn't even make it halfway. An attractive woman usually served only to remind me how incredibly lucky I was to be engaged to Jane. It happened this day as well, since Deedee had probably not gone to grad school at all, much less taken the GRE. (Not that she seemed dumb, but she was young, and seemed like she'd been here for years already. Where would grad school even fit?) But even as I reached the end of my routine, a little sliver of my brain raised its hand to point out that I was in a completely new city, with no one from my past to watch me, and with an actually sexy-sounding and interesting job now. Would the old college-era methods of dissuasion still work?

Of course they will, I told my brain. *I've always been interesting. It's other women who, nice as they are, never measure up to Jane.* Then I smiled, victory complete, and went back to the wings, where McNicely was waiting this time. After a recap, I spent the rest of the day with the theme codes in one hand, flipping through the wings with the other, and concentrating very hard on Weddings and Births.

AT THE END OF my first day at work, I took the bus home, feeling relieved and happy. Then I walked into my apartment and was struck by the utter emptiness of everything. Not just the apartment, but my life. It was six o'clock now. Bedtime was ten or eleven. What the hell was I going to do for the next four hours? I didn't even have a television, just my computer, with boring old dial-up. This was long before they had clean streaming video or TV shows online.

I called Jane—that was a no-brainer—checked my e-mail, and then walked around the block some more, trying to enjoy the cool of the evening and the ambience of this new city that was my home now. This time, though, instead of feeling excited as I passed nearby apartments with shadows moving behind various lit-up curtains, I felt nervous and off balance. I was really and truly alone. Walking around like this in the evening had gotten me in trouble before. Was I in control these days, or would I go crazy again? It was a problem I hadn't even thought about in years.

Back in early 1992, after I'd noticed that Jane existed, but many months before we started dating, I found myself in the grip of a dark, shameful compulsion. It started when, in one of my classes, a girl bent over in front of me to pick up her backpack . . . and in a brief flash, I looked down her exposed shirtfront, and I saw both her breasts, as plain as day. I literally gasped, and a warmth rushed through me like a drug. After almost a decade of avoiding pornography, of resisting masturbation, of closing my eyes in R-rated movies, these were my first real-life breasts ever— and I had been *completely innocent of naughtiness*. I'd just been in the right place at the right time, and what celestial jury could convict me?

This guilt-free sexual experience affected me profoundly, and almost against my will I found myself walking around the University of Arizona campus obsessively, staring at women and hoping one of them with a low neckline or a loose shirt would bend over near me so I could maybe see another actual breast. It affected the routes I took to class and started taking up more and more of my thoughts. And the whole time, this made no sense to me. I was a Christian! I was morally pure! Why in the world would I be acting this way? But it happened, and I was surprisingly helpless. Within a week I found I literally couldn't study or even sit still in my room: I was sure that out there, somewhere, some woman was revealing her bra—or possibly an actual braless breast—and I couldn't pass up even one opportunity to maybe get a glimpse. I wandered for hours—and, by the way, saw almost nothing worth reporting. I'd have been better off simply staying at home with my eyes glued to the fuzzed-out porn channel on my cable system, waiting for a second of areola. But of course, that would have been immoral.

So I wandered, justifying it somehow, and I stayed out later and later, and felt more and more creepy, and powerless to fix my life's sudden dangerous slide. I had become something like a stalker—a stalker terrified of stalking, perhaps, and with incredibly low standards, but I still knew the grip of the obsession, and I knew I occupied a stalker's place in the sexual food chain, however harmless I might be.

Finally, on one particular evening walk, I noticed that I had stopped and had actually stood outside a house for almost fifteen minutes, staring. There was a woman inside—you could see her shadow on the curtain from the bedside light—and she was walking around and might have been getting ready for bed. Was she naked? It was impossible to tell. It was fascinating and I was so curious. . . . And then I did a terrible thing: I walked onto her lawn, and right up to the window. I actually craned my neck slightly to peer through the curtains. I saw a glimpse of her head—she almost saw me—and I jerked my face back and ran home, terrified at what I'd done. I'd gone from being an extremely lame, PG-13-seeking stalker to an actual Peeping Tom. I could have been arrested. And I would have deserved it.

With what felt like my entire life in danger of total collapse, I turned myself in to my pastor, and I found myself referred twice: once to Sex Addicts Anonymous (where I was the only virgin in the room, and no one took me seriously, so I stopped going after my second meeting), and once to a Christian counselor, who had my whole problem pegged in less than ten minutes.

"Do you have a girlfriend?" he asked.

"No," I said.

"You've never dated anyone? And you're how old?"

"Twenty-two. Twenty-three next month."

"Do you masturbate?"

"Of course not," I said. "That's lustful."

He gave me a look that was some mixture of kindness and impatience. "So you don't have lustful thoughts, you don't masturbate . . ."

"Well, I try not to." I had lied. I did masturbate, but I always felt horrible about it, and apologized in my diary every week or two. "The apostle Paul says we have to take every thought captive in the name of—"

He waved at me to shut up. He knew what Paul said. "So you don't have any outlet at all for . . . Hmm." He stopped taking notes, leaned forward, and said, "Here's your assignment. I want you to go home tonight and buy a *Playboy* or something, and masturbate. Give yourself permission. God's grace will cover you,

right? So do that—it's an order; let's say just one time this week—
and come back here next week and tell me what happened."

Barely believing the weirdness of it all, I went to my local
convenience store, bought two *Playboys* (I just couldn't decide),
took them home . . . and five minutes later, I was completely
cured. The guilt was gone, the pressure was off, and I could get
back to concentrating on my real life. It felt like a medical miracle. I was deeply grateful for the porn industry that day, and
even now I find I still get slightly defensive when anyone says
mean things about Anna Nicole Smith or the Swedish Bikini
Team. They were there for me when it mattered.

I went back to that counselor the following week, almost
speechless with gratitude, and he said, "Your next mission should
be to find a girlfriend. Is there anyone in your life that might be
a prospect?"

"There's a girl among my comedy friends," I said, "named
Jane. She's smart and funny and I know she likes me. But she's
not a Christian."

"Relax," he'd said. "Just ask her out and see what happens."

It took weeks of training to give me the courage, but what
happened next was straight out of a storybook. I had the first
date of my life on October 10, a week after my twenty-third
birthday. Jane and I saw *Casablanca* at a local revival house. It
turned out we were both terribly romantic, and I finally had an
outlet for all my pent-up poems. I wrote her the "this flower was
murdered" poem the very next day, and gave it to her with a
wilted supermarket daisy because I hadn't known the flower
mattered, too.

You survived in Tucson without Jane for over a year, I told myself now. *You can survive just fine in Kansas City. Nothing's changed. You're not going to turn into a stalker, you moron. With your new money, you can even afford Cinemax.* Still, just to be safe, I went back inside and called Jane again. "I know it's late now," I told her, "but I just wanted to say thanks again for helping me move. And I love you."

"I know how you feel, sweetie," she said. "It really fucking sucks to be alone."

BY THE END OF THE WEEK, I had started to get a grasp of how things worked in Everyday. Editorial at Hallmark—and really at any decent-sized card company—is divided into two sections: Everyday and Season. The Everyday cards are things that people might have occasion to buy on any day of the year: Birthday, Wedding, Thank You, Congratulations, and the like. Season cards are, as you'd expect, the ones that go with actual events on the calendar, and which are therefore easier to schedule: Christmas, Mother's Day, Valentine's Day. Season also includes the minor holidays like Earth Day and Secretary's Day, as well as the "season" of Graduation. Weddings and Births, where I was, was an Everyday caption.

I should point out here, as was pointed out to me three times in my first week, that Hallmark has never invented a holiday. This makes sense when you think about it. When was the last time anyone bought something merely because Hallmark wanted them to? It's not like they're sending out sternly worded memos. What mostly guides Hallmark's choices in which holidays to carry is, "Will people use the day to buy cards?" This is the only reason they even bother to have cards for Sweetest Day or Arbor Day—people actually complained when they weren't available at the card shop. When a new holiday comes along, it's not always a sure thing. Secretaries Day caught on pretty quickly, but it was decades before Hallmark developed a line for Kwanzaa, the most famous invented holiday of modern times.

THE SECOND HALF OF the editor's job, after writing requisitions, is reviewing the sentiments that come in. These are voted on at what's called a sentiment meeting. Usually it's just a meeting of the writing manager and the line's editor, as they read each piece aloud and give it a thumbs-up or -down. Occasionally writers sit in, too, though, because it's a really good way to figure out what a certain editor likes.

By the end of the week, McNicely had me sit in on a sentiment meeting—my first ever. This one was for Births rather than Weddings. Specifically, McNicely had been requisitioning new Baby Congrats.

McNicely was meeting with Constance Blandish, a happy Carol Burnett type who was one of the writing managers for Main Writing. (With thirty writers on their staff, Main Writing was so large that they actually had two managers.) It was a small room, large enough for just one table, and it was so out of the way it felt just a bit like we were conspiring in Stalag 17. The meeting proceeded as I expected it would: Constance read a verse, McNicely listened and nodded, and then they discussed its merits or debits. ("That's punchy and cute; let's try it" or "We already have twenty of those.") I sat and tried to learn, but it was hard. Even by the standards of Weddings and Births, these seemed awfully gooey. This was, however, where I first heard the phrase "have sim." That's short for "we already have something similar on file." Since Hallmark has seventy years' worth of cards on file, "have sim" is not an uncommon reaction. ("That sounds have sim to me.") The sentiment is usually marked "have sim" and sent back, as a way of telling the writer, "We can't use another one of these, but congratulations on your aim."

Finally, with only one paper left, Constance's eyes lit up and she said, "I waited until the end to read this. I really think you'll like it."

It was a long poem that I won't bore you with, but here's the upshot. "You have a baby girl now, and she'll change your whole life. You'll buy new little suits, and there will be toys all over the floor. She'll be fussy, she'll challenge you, and she'll bring you all kinds of joy." (It's quite possible that "joys" rhymed with "toys.") The final stanza, however, still sticks with me. As you'd expect, the child will also grow up and make you proud:

But even when she's fully grown,
You'll never forget the day
That little girl came into your life,
And stole your heart away.

This sounded just like all the others to me, but as I was puzzling this out, I heard a sniff. McNicely actually reached for her purse and dabbed her eyes with a Kleenex. *She was crying over a greeting card.* The manager was a little moist-eyed, too. I suppose the smart-ass cynic reaction would have been to roll my eyes and think, *I'm surrounded by idiots.* But that's not what I felt. What I felt was bafflement. A huge emotional moment had just happened, and I hadn't even been able to tell what was different. Two thoughts came simultaneously: First, *McNicely must be the best greeting card editor in the world, if she's moved by her product the same way the consumer is.* And second, *If this is what the job requires, I am totally fucked.* I'm a sensitive guy, but I didn't even cry at *Where the Red Fern Grows.* At this point in my life, I didn't really get the baby thing. And if you don't get it naturally, how in the world can you force yourself to? Was it an unfixable trait, like color blindness or a tin ear? Or could my heart of cool granite be transplanted with a heart of sweet sponge? And could it happen quickly, before my first performance review?

5

Deedee

FOR THE NEXT FEW WEEKS I WAS RELEGATED TO WHAT Hallmark called the Competition Room—an ill-used backwater area where you had to go through a dark windowless passage that felt like a dungeon (when you can see the pipes on the ceiling, you know they don't bring visitors this way), then swipe your card to get past the windowless metal doors, and then sign a register to explain why you were there. (There were no guards or anything; I assume someone just came in and collected the register every few days.) This area contained copies of all our opponents' cards, right down to their display cases and signage, along with a Post-it on each that listed the date a card was added and how long it had been in the line.

"We just want you to take notes," said McNicely. "See what seems to be working and what isn't. A successful card has been around longer. What themes show up in each caption? What designs look compelling? We want you to come up with a theory or theories about what our competition is doing, and what we should do differently."

Since I doubted they gave a damn about my corporate strategy, this sounded like busywork. Either they didn't have anything
else for me to do, or else it was just as I feared: they could tell
that I didn't understand what made a serious card good. And
instead of training me on this with a mentor, they were simply
throwing me in the water and hoping I'd learn to swim. Was I
in trouble already?

"You actually have everybody's cards," I said, impressed.
"American Greetings, Carlton, Dayspring. Do you have secret
agents working throughout the industry?"

"Actually, we do!" said McNicely, with a gay laugh. "That's
what they say. The whole industry is the same way." She leaned
in conspiratorially. "You know our daily newspaper, *The Noon
News*? As soon as it hits the stands, it's already been faxed over
to our competitors within fifteen minutes." *The Noon News* was
a corporate propaganda rag that blandly praised everything Hallmark was doing. I can't imagine it was worth the cost of the fax
paper, unless they were really interested in articles with titles like
"Up-to-date Wrapping Paper Helps Package the Season."

"How do we know that?" I paused for thought. "Wait a minute.
We have moles at our competitors' companies? We pay people to
betray their employers?"

"That's what I've heard, anyway," said McNicely. "I bet it's not
hard. Most other card companies are cheap." She smiled at my
shocked look. "This a serious business."

"I guess so."

"In fact, Dave, I've also heard that if you quit Hallmark and
move to"—she named a big competitor—"they'll automatically
give you a thirty-thousand-dollar bonus in addition to matching
your Hallmark salary." She smiled. "Don't do it, though."

"I wasn't planning on it."

"You just got here, after all. We like having you around!" And with another gay laugh, she left me alone to do research.

AT THE END OF SEVERAL HOURS, I returned with my notes. "Edith, I've got one word for you: bunnies," I said proudly. "It looks like they're absolutely killing with images of bunny rabbits."

"In our competition?" said McNicely. She was in the wings, at her computer, and looked distracted. "Maybe they're trying. But that's not what does well."

I froze in mid heel-click. She hadn't even looked at my charts. "What do you mean? Bunnies don't do well?"

"Unless you're doing Easter, no. You must be looking at the wrong things." She wheeled in her chair to face me and counted off on her fingers. "Bears and chipmunks are always number one. Then mice, then bunnies, and then squirrels. Then pandas. Every so often our artists give us skunks, just to be different, I guess. I wish I could just tell them, 'Guys, skunks aren't cute!' They just aren't. Even pandas are a risk, I think because they're black and white."

I tried a bad joke. "Why? Are our customers against miscegenation?"

She shrugged off my comment gently, the way you would ignore a friend who'd just farted. "Pandas are two colors, and the most popular animals are one. And with pandas, the colors are in odd places, like black around the eyes. They're more confusing to look at."

"But bunnies and squirrels are one color. They should be popular."

"Bunnies have long ears, and squirrels have long tails. Depending on the artist, it can throw off the proportions. That's why chipmunks work. They're like squirrels with no tail."

But chipmunks have stripes, I wanted to say, but I knew she'd have another answer, and I knew it would be something I'd never thought about and probably didn't understand. Christ. I felt completely overwhelmed again. So I made another joke. "What about snakes?"

She smiled politely. "We don't do snakes," she said. "That would be terrible."

Neither did they do humor. Not in Editorial. That, I was starting to see, was my whole problem. Not only was I in the wrong job, but I still didn't have any friends.

IT WAS PRETTY CLEAR THAT Hallmark in general, and Editorial in particular, didn't know what to do with me. It was now only two weeks until Thanksgiving, and the coworkers who hadn't vanished already weren't really in a working mood. This state of affairs would presumably continue until after Christmas and New Year's. So after my initial grounding in Theme Codes, I was told to keep visiting the Competition Room to take more notes. It was the equivalent of the lazy camp counselor tossing the kids a bunch of balls, yelling, "Just do whatever!" and waiting for the lunch bell.

I had one opportunity for actual creative work. For some reason, Everyday Cards was moving from the eighth floor to the seventh, and since the seventh floor didn't have windows, there were concerns about morale. So on November 13, Magda announced that they would be having a little weeklong contest to come up with the top ten best things about moving from Eight to Seven, with the winner to be announced just before everyone left for Thanksgiving.

As it happened, my very first paid publication had been a top ten list. Back in 1990, I'd submitted a series of top ten lists to a Christian satire magazine called *The Door*. (Top Ten Televangelist Pet Peeves, that sort of thing.) They were so popular I was asked to submit a few more, and then a Christian publisher called, and one thing led to another, and in 1992 I became the creator of a religious "non-book" called *The Potluck Hall of Fame and Other Bizarre Christian Lists*. (That's when I learned that you don't always get to choose your title.) The whole book was nothing but top ten lists like "Top Ten Least Popular Precious Moments Figurines" and "Top Ten Christian Bestsellers" ("#7: *Controlling Your Thought Life by Reducing Its Volume*"). Here in late 1995 the book was still in print, and I'd just gotten an end-of-year royalty check for $135. Over the last five years, top ten lists had netted me almost $3,000 total. How could I not submit to this contest?

More important, though, I thought, *This is how I'm going to find my friends*. They'll post my list somewhere, and people who pass by and get my humor will see that I'm funny and will actually seek me out. It was like posting a singles ad for a smart, creative play pal. I just had to make sure that the list I submitted was really top-notch. I wasted more than an hour on the project, and it reminded me of the time I wrote that card for the three-year-old. Had nothing changed?

I came up with a beauty: ten meticulously crafted good things about moving to Seven from Eight. "*Seven* was a popular movie starring Brad Pitt, while dumb old *Eight*'s still in turnaround";

"Going up one less floor on Monday helps us get to work that much faster so we can stumble to our desks and sleep"; and my favorite of all: "We are now that much *less* likely to be killed if a meteor comes through the ceiling, but we're still safe from floods." I read it a dozen times over, and it felt irresistible. After almost two months at this allegedly creative job, this was my first chance to actually express myself.

For the next few days, I looked forward to that top ten list contest more than anything else in my life—which makes sense because there wasn't a lot else out there except the Competition Room and my quiet apartment. Magda was going to post the final results on the big filing cabinet near her cubicle after lunch on the twentieth. So after lunch on the big day I raced over . . . and saw not my list but a compilation of ten different people's ideas. Apparently I'd gotten the wrong impression, and this was a team-building exercise. Still, I must be in there somewhere, so I read down:

7. We are closer to the lunchroom! (Barb Hazelwood)
6. Fewer stairs to climb when the elevator is out. (Edith McNicely)
5. We are safe from floods, fires, and tornadoes. (David Dickerson)

I felt like I'd been stabbed with an icicle. How had this horrible thing happened? Who would read this and know that I was funny? Where would my new friends come from?

I ran to Magda. She was at her desk, staring at papers, and the second she glanced up at me—sideways, sharply, not a good day—I knew I couldn't exactly complain. "Um, I was just wondering why you'd, sort of, changed the wording of my entry."

She smiled and made a dismissive wave. "It doesn't matter. It was a funny idea. I just thought, you're new here so you don't realize we're concerned about tornadoes a lot more than—what was it? Asteroids?"

"Meteors." I stood helpless for a few beats, then walked away fuming. *No,* you *don't get it, Magda. My joke was funny. It was about height. It was absurdly logical. How does moving down one floor make you safe from tornadoes? And wouldn't it put you closer to a fire? You don't make any goddamned sense, and my offering deserved better treatment.*

I was so incensed that when no one was looking I actually took the list down, photocopied it, and replaced it, just so I had a copy of my own that I could carry around and complain about. Of course, I didn't have any friends to speak of yet. Would acting like an aggrieved clown be such a great introduction? *Take a deep breath, Dave. Compromise.* So I brought it to McNicely, my interpreter of Editing culture, and said, "I wrote a great joke I was really happy with, and now everyone thinks I wrote this boring thing instead."

"Oh, don't worry about it, Dave," she said. "The point of the contest was basically to be upbeat and happy. Your version sounds a little violent, and I think that's why she fixed it."

It's not funny, though, I wanted to insist, but read futility in her mild expression. I became obsessed: this was my chance to find friends! When would another contest arise? So much for deep breaths and compromise; I lost it. I knew it was crazy, but I actually wandered through Everyday Editorial, looking for a friendly

face, someone I could buttonhole for some sympathy, someone who would understand why this was so important to me. I
passed cube after cube of nice quiet non-edgy people and finally
found myself in the hallway outside our area, list in hand, standing alone. I sighed, put the list in my pocket, and resigned myself
to another day in the Competition Room.

I was only halfway there—not even to the elevator—when I
looked down and everything started coming apart. On my Competition Room notepad I had hand-drawn a grid of rows and
columns: I was cataloging cards by price point and caption, and
was marking off "verse or prose," "line length," "rhyme scheme,"
"illustration notes," and so on, all across the page. And with a
gasp like when a snowball hits you in the chest, I recognized this
same grid from my job at PREVENT. I was just making goddamned catalogs again to kill time. Only instead of indexing the
three-hole punch in box C-5, I was marking the place where
4-line verse A entered mouse cartoon B.

Where had my dream gone? Had I really traveled halfway
across the country to face exactly the same frustrations? Maybe
all jobs are really just the same. On the other hand, what was I
really thinking? Was I expecting a magical framed display case
for contest entries instead of a top ten list taped to a filing cabinet? Did I really think writing cards for money—or, okay, editing them—would somehow achieve escape velocity from the
drudgery of business? Did I really think I'd have more friends
here than I'd had at home? I felt a hot stinging at my eyes and
rushed toward the cool solitude of the Competition Room.
God, help me, I prayed. *I miss Jane.*

I swiped, signed in, and then, once the metal door clanged

behind me, I realized in mid-sigh that I wasn't alone. Someone else was moving among the Dayspring and the Carlton.

"Hello?" I called.

"Is that . . . Dave?" It was Deedee, our line designer. Today she was wearing a white blouse topped with a red, lace-trimmed toreador-style vest, and a short-plaid skirt with black hose, and something inside me lurched like a drunken ox.

This was the second raw physical lurch I'd felt in a month. The last time was when I'd been ambushed by a TV ad for *The Craft*, coming out in six months. It looked to be a horror movie about four Catholic schoolgirls who get involved in the dark arts. From the very first shot of Fairuza Balk in her schoolgirl outfit looking terribly, terribly naughty, I couldn't look away. I was jolted into another state of consciousness, where I just kept trying to stare harder and make time freeze. *So this is how fetishes happen*, I'd thought. *And mine is naughty Catholic schoolgirls. Who knew?* It was overwhelming, like a conversion. My primitive reptile brain cried, *I want those women to do dark, unspeakable things that I am helpless to prevent*, and my forebrain said, *I am watching that movie even if it's every bit as awful as it looks.* Perhaps this is what I'd been terrified of in my years of tamping down my sex drive. But there was a real joy to giving in that I'd never felt before: the anticipation of the roller coaster's next dip.

"Deedee," I said, trying to keep my eyes focused on her face and not the plaid skirt or the too-tight vest. Jane did not wear sexy clothes. "I thought I was the only person who ever came in here. Did you do something wrong?"

She smiled and said, "No, I just—wait. Are you okay, Dave? You look upset."

I thought a moment, then figured I'd try again. "I know it's silly. But . . . dammit, I wrote a really funny joke for this competition . . ." and I proceeded to explain what happened. I even showed her the list.

"Oh god, that's terrible!" she said. She read it a moment in silence, shaking her head, then pushed it back to me. "You know, I wanted to warn you that first day that I didn't think the Everyday folks were going to get you."

I could have hugged her. I suddenly felt neither hopeless nor insane.

"You're in Everyday," I said.

"But I'm an artist. Well, a designer. That's different. The editors . . ." She struggled for words, then waved them away. "Just—chin up, okay?" And she actually chucked me under the chin with her fist. I may have blushed. "You'll find your people. We're all over the place."

"We," she'd said. I heard community. Then I noticed that she was actually packing to go. "You're leaving?"

"Late lunch," she said. "The Crown Room is still open until two. Have you eaten?"

"No," I lied. "Let's go."

AS AN INSTINCT, all the way down on the elevator I started looking for reasons to find Deedee wanting. Not that I felt necessarily tempted. I hadn't even had intercourse with my own fiancée; I could resist anyone. But I knew it might look bad, the two of us eating together, and I needed to find something wrong with Deedee as proof that we were just friends. Also, so I could characterize her to Jane later.

Strike one was when we got to the fourth floor and a guy on the elevator held the door for her. "Thanks," she said.

"That's so absurd," I said, as we disembarked and went for the trays. This late, there wasn't a line. "Why would that guy hold an elevator door? Does he think you're that weak?"

"He was just being nice," she said. "It's part of the culture here."

"But the message," I replied. "Don't you think there's a connection between a culture of men holding elevator doors for women and the fact that there isn't a single woman on the North American Management Team? In a company where ninety percent of our consumers are women?"

"You know," said Deedee, "back in college I used to get upset about all of that. But I just wound up being angry all the time, and what's the point? Life's too short." She pointed to the corner. "I'm just getting a salad. Meet you at the napkins."

She didn't care about politics or gender. Strike two.

THE CROWN ROOM is Hallmark's commissary, with a fifth-floor mezzanine where you could buy prewrapped snacks (like sandwiches and fruit cups) in the off hours. On any tour you take, they'll tell you that the Crown Room is an award-winning lunchroom, and it's easy to believe. Not that the food is particularly great, but it's so not bad. There are a host of regular choices—chicken, burgers, salad bar, fresh fruit, steamed vegetables, chocolatey–Jell-O-ey desserts—plus the special of the day, which was always something one step up the ladder like rice pilaf, fried salmon, or beef Stroganoff. It was also consistent: if you wanted, you could eat breakfast, lunch, and dinner there all week and have bacon and cheese with every single meal. Which is almost what I did. I had never learned to cook.

We met at the napkins and, because it was late, actually found seats by the window. The Crown Room has impressively tall ceilings and two-story-high windows along one breathtaking wall. "I wish it was snowing today," Deedee said. "I love watching it when it snows." I had never seen it snow here, so I stayed quiet. I was just thrilled to be staring out at a bunch of tall buildings. I was in a real city now. It felt powerful.

"Today's napkins are Scooby-Doo," I announced. The Crown Room napkins were the main way you could tell you were at Hallmark—that and the giant crowns around the hanging lights. Hallmark recycled all its napkins, so you could tell at a glance what wasn't selling. "Such a shame about Scooby. You think it was the design?"

"I think they made a huge mistake not going with Scooby-Dum," said Deedee.

"Or Scrappy Doo. And who was the Southern female Scooby? Scooby Dee?"

"God, I hated that character." And we were off, bantering about pop culture. It was a huge relief to not have to explain why this was funny. Deedee was one of my people, like she'd said, even if she had two strikes against her. Three, if you counted her probably nonexistent GRE scores. As an additional safety wedge, I said, "God, I miss Jane." That led to the whole story: how we met, the *Casablanca* romance, the puzzle proposal.

"It must be so great," said Deedee. "To finally find the person you were meant for, after all those years of kissing frogs."

"Actually, I never dated anyone before her."

"Really?" She paused her fork. "Wait. Then how do you know she's the one?"

"A million reasons," I said. "For starters, we agree on everything. We've never even had a major quarrel."

"You really never dated anyone else?"

"I never saw the point. With most women, I can tell already that something is going to be a problem. She's not religious enough, or she can't keep up with me, or maybe she doesn't like puzzles, which are really important to me. So why even try to date someone if you know it's not going to last?"

"Are you kidding? And do you know how arrogant that sounds? How can you know what's not going to work if you never . . ." Deedee trailed off, looked at me baffled, the way my counselor had when I said I didn't masturbate, and I saw the first frown I'd ever seen on her face. It was aimed at me. I wondered if I'd just gotten strike one. Maybe two strikes: arrogant *and* naive.

She tried again. "Why? For the *experience*, you silly man. I've had a lot of bad relationships, but I've learned from every single one. I wouldn't trade them for . . ." She thought a bit, cocking her head and staring at the space above my head. She pursed her lips when she thought; it made her look like Betty Boop. "Well, one of them I'd trade, I guess. No, two. But mostly, you know, it's been great. And very useful."

I had no response. This entire concept was new to me. There are people who willingly rush into certain failure?

"Still, if you have the fairy tale," said Deedee. "I mean, that's the whole dream, isn't it? I guess if I met the perfect person the first time, I wouldn't be antsy either." She stopped staring above my head and met my gaze, smiling again as if we'd negotiated a deal. "It must be great for you. You're Prince Charming and she's Princess Whatever."

"Except she saved me. But yeah. It's really wonderful. *" I told this Deedee person all about you,* I decided to tell Jane later. *She's a big fan.*

HALLMARK EMPLOYEES get paid only once, at the end of every month. I'd started on November 1 and got my first paycheck just before Thanksgiving. On such short notice, and with an incomplete check, I couldn't afford to go home for the holiday, nor could I fly to see Jane in Minnesota. Instead, I celebrated the way most lonely twenty-seven-year-old bachelors do: I bought a big TV.

"It's a Sony Trinitron, thirty-two inches," I told Jane. "You're going to love it. It took two hulking workmen to move it in here."

"Did you get picture-in-picture?"

"Of course." I'd gotten it for her. She liked channel surfing, while I liked to stay put. This was a compromise we'd long discussed. "And it'll look great at the foot of our new . . . king-sized bed."

"King-sized? Really? I love you!" Jane tended to roll and twitch in her sleep, and found touching another human disconcerting at night. A king had always been her other dream. I got to deliver two that day. At least over the phone.

"Well, that's not in yet," I said. "Next month, next paycheck. But your dad's furniture arrived, and our bed comes next month, and then our apartment is all ready. I'll just be keeping it warm for you for the next . . . when you graduate."

"Two years."

"Man, this sucks."

"I miss you, too, sweetie." After we said good night, I stayed up late, sitting on Jane's dad's furniture—which was a series of weird, low, rounded chairs with early-eighties cushion patterns, but Jane liked it and I didn't care—and watching my new TV. I watched a lot of TV that winter, anything to keep the sadness and longing at bay. Mostly Turner Classic Movies, with occasional guilty dips into Cinemax. I still felt uncomfortable with anything harder than very mild soft-core porn since I was trying to save as much mystery as possible for marriage. So I couldn't even bring myself to enter an adult video store for fear of seeing too much. But I set up my VCR and would record the occasional glimpses of breast you could see on Cinemax's late-night erotic dramas. It became a sort of side project, filling a six-hour cassette a dozen seconds at a time. I labeled it "Lonely Tape."

My other major purchase, with the last few hundred dollars I could afford, was a corporate look. As I shambled around among my fellow Hallmarkers, it had become clear that I needed to stop dressing like a college student, put away my years-old hand-me-downs, and actually wear responsible grown-up clothes. I had money now, and what else could I possibly require? Why, surely getting a new look was as simple as buying the nearest one you liked.

So after work on my first real payday, I marched across the street from Hallmark to the Crown Center mall and walked into the first store I saw that I'd always dreamed someday of having enough money to shop in: The Gap. In my entire life I'd never paid more than $20 for a shirt or a pair of pants, so to be suddenly surrounded by shirts and pants that ranged from $35 to

$50 was a heady extravagance. And there, in the store, I decided to live a dream I'd thought of for years: to wear exactly the same outfit every day so that I, with my color blindness and distractedness, never had to waste time fretting about clothes again. I could do it now. I had enough to buy several things at once.

What I pictured was a kind of corporate casual: white shirt, khaki pants, a simple belt. Then, to spice things up, I could start a collection of wacky ties that I could switch among—though that would have to wait for another payday. None of the shirts were the oxfords that I'd pictured, and they seemed a little baggy, but I remembered reading a year or two back that baggy was in, so I thought what the hell and bought six of them in white. The khaki pants were also imperfect—I was a thirty-five-inch waist and the closest they had was a thirty-six, and I have twenty-nine-inch legs and all they had was thirty. But I bought six of those, too, along with a single black belt. When I told Jane what I'd done, she said, "That sounds wonderful. I wish I could see you."

"I wish you could, too," I said. "I'm not always good at buying clothing alone, but I think I did okay. Anyway, it feels good to have a kind of uniform now. With all the stress I'm feeling right now, it's one less thing to worry about." What I didn't bother to say was that I was also hoping that this new look might be another way to attract my kind of people: here was a look, I imagined, that said, "Guy only halfway willing to sell out," with nice pants and nice shirt, but no jacket and (eventually) a wacky tie or two. Throw in my long hippie hair and wild beard, and I figured my people would recognize a kindred spirit now. I hoped so. I needed it to work.

6

Ruby Jubilee

I DIDN'T EAT WITH DEEDEE FOR A WHILE AFTER OUR first intense lunch, precisely because she immediately became the only person I *wanted* to hang out with, and that neediness worried me. Also, I figured she had her own friends and didn't need me clinging to her all the time. So for all of Thanksgiving week I simply ate alone, which was even more depressing than it had been before, now that I knew what conversation was like. Then came Thanksgiving and Deedee was gone, and I stared down the barrel of my first long weekend by myself, without even coworkers to talk to.

On Thanksgiving, everyone was talking about going to the Plaza Lights ceremony like it was the biggest thing ever, and since I lived across the street from the Plaza, that seemed convenient. It was a way to initiate myself into the ways of this big Midwestern city, with its storied past and actual historic skyscrapers. I was willing to be impressed. In Tucson, few of our multistory buildings were even older than me.

The lighting ceremony was enormous. The Country Club

Plaza fills about fourteen smallish blocks, and even before seven on Thanksgiving night the streets were crammed with 250,000 people, some of whom had parked miles away. That's about half the population Tucson had when I left. I put on my U of A sweatshirt and ventured over. Instead of jazz like I'd expected, the music was carolers and bagpipes. At seven-thirty, some locally chosen child flipped a switch and the hundreds of thousands of Christmas lights burst into life; everyone applauded and cheered. The lights really are something to see—they outline every contour of every major building, including all the way up the clock tower, and then there are even more in the bushes and trees. With this bright, celebratory mix of old stone and new little bulbs, there's no way to avoid the word *charming*. What's more, the Spanish architecture reminded me of Tucson, and for a moment I felt like I had my own part in this; my heart was light and joyous and I joined in the applause and singing.

Then I crashed, emotionally dislocated the moment I stopped singing, and everyone around me kept at it. The second I chose not to join in, the second I differed from the crowd, I not only felt lonesome, but I also felt demonstrably and provably alien-ated. I should have realized that if your main problem is loneli-ness, the last thing you need to be doing is hanging out with an enormous mass of happy people who don't even know you're alive. I edged away, admiring the lights from farther and farther off, and then I simply turned my back and trudged back to my place. I told myself it was in order to avoid the huge crowds that would be leaving shortly. I even told myself I didn't care.

When I turned on the TV, though, *Casablanca* was on, and I called Jane in Minnesota. She didn't answer—no doubt she was out with her friends from grad school—and I left her a message:

"Check Turner Classic Movies! Call back the second you get this!" *Casablanca*, the sort of theme movie of our relationship, and I felt completely abandoned because Jane wasn't watching it with me. I almost never cry, but I cried then, with the lights off and the sound low, wondering if this pain would ever stop. It was strange. I had never been like this before.

Jane called back less than halfway through the film, so we were still able to watch many of the best lines together, including my proposal quote, "Nobody ever loved me that much." So that was nice. But for the forty minutes or so when the floor collapsed beneath me, I had been in a shocking amount of pain. It was time to do something new.

WORK OBVIOUSLY WASN'T giving me a social net, so that weekend, while eating Thanksgiving ham across the street at K.C. Masterpiece steakhouse, I decided maybe a church home would help. The good news was there was a Catholic chapel just a few blocks from me called Visitation Parish. The bad news—which I found on that very Sunday, after days of waiting impatiently for the service—was that everyone there was forty years older than me and grumpy. I'd just converted to a Catholicism housed in a university setting, with all the vibrancy and hipness we expect from our nation's youth. This Missouri church was one of the oldest such buildings in the city, and it looked like the parish elders had stopped recruiting altogether in the sixties for fear of a sudden guitar mass. In many ways it was familiar—the kneeling, the singing, the passing of the peace. But no one was smiling. No one seemed happy to see their friends.

I stood in a pew almost entirely to myself, in an impressive

stained-glass dreadnought of a chapel that was only one-third
full, and during the passing of the peace an old lady turned
around, gave one smile at me, and nodded. It would have been
too long a distance to walk over and actually shake my hand. I
don't blame her. Possibly she had a touch of the rheumatiz. But
in my old Newman Center during the passing of the peace,
people had actually hugged. Here, the line for communion was
an entire line of white-haired people who hunched forward and
shuffled slowly. When the priest set down the chalice a little
hard against the altar with a clang, I heard a distinct echo in the
hollow distance.

On the way out, I asked the one youngish couple I could
find, "Um, where are all the younger people?" "Downstairs at
the next service," said the man. It was where people brought
their children. "Kids aren't popular up here," said the woman,
looking a trifle pained.

Since I had nothing else to do, I pulled a double mass and
tried it, and it was clear that the kids' service brought with it a
serious drop in status. It wasn't in the chapel, but in the basement,
which was weakly tricked out with a mike stand and some metal
folding chairs. If you took away the priest's robes, the whole
thing would have looked like any local fundamentalist start-up,
like you can find in your nearest strip mall.

The kids infected everything. Even as the priest started in
with "Dearly beloved," you could hear the squirming and the
bangs of little feet on clunky metal. Parents shushed and tiny
voices grumbled. Every part of the mass was held aloft on a river
of unruliness, on whispers of "I want—" and "Not now" and
"Shhhhh . . ." on cries of pain ("Don't hit!"), plus of course the
occasional baby's actual, full-throated wail. I felt irritated, since

it looked like the priest was fighting the chaos and was destined to lose.

The noise and running around didn't abate all through the homily, and finally the priest raised the chalice and said, "And on the night he was betrayed, he took this cup . . ." and a girl of maybe five ran down the aisle, came to a puzzled stop at the feet of the priest, looked up, and waved at him: "Hi!" The priest smiled, nodded, and continued.

I actually laughed, as did all the people around me, and that's when I got it. This was the perfect service for me. Even as a Catholic in good standing, I'd always been aware of the rather abrupt artificiality of switching from the secular world of things to do and money to make to this rarefied atmosphere of the holy place in the sanctuary, where suddenly things were supposed to be tranquil and meditative and meaningful. I've never experienced life that way. For me, the happy meaningful moments of life always seem to come in the middle of the rush. I'll see a little girl with an unusually cute backpack, or I'll spy a lizard darting across the road, or someone will say something fun to overhear, and I'll smile and try to remember that moment of joy. (In college once, I passed a girl who was telling her friends, "I'm just so happy about yams." I've remembered that sentence for twenty years.) Now, it seemed, I'd found a church that did the same thing: instead of pretending that you could separate the rambunctiousness of kids from the holiness of the mature adult spiritual world, this priest had essentially camped on the shore near to where childishness was surging all around, and with his vestments and his wafers he was going through the ritual, describing all the right lines in the air and saying all the right words, and vainly trying to get everyone's attention.

So it wasn't about winning after all. All the priest was doing was raining a sort of sanctification on the lives that were already happening all over the room, and as a result, it felt more like spirituality as I knew it than anything I'd ever experienced in a church. This was a service where God met you in mid-verb, and that's the way I've always felt. I can be awed by the night sky or by standing on a seashore, just like anyone. But the stories of grace I remember most and love best are the ones where joy comes as a complete surprise, the bird that flutters accidentally onto the bus. I looked around at this awkward, well-intended, completely human happiness and thought, *If they can keep this up every week, I'm definitely coming back.* I didn't actually meet anyone there that time, but the place was so promising I didn't even mind.

THINGS AT WORK changed on Monday when McNicely called me into the wings. "We think you're ready for your first project. We need you to write a requisition for a Ruby Jubilee card."

"What's a Ruby Jubilee?" I asked.

"It's a priest's fortieth anniversary of being a priest."

"Really? Because I'm Catholic, and I've never even heard of . . ."

McNicely nodded, abashed. "It's a very small category."

Cards are ordered up in a three-stage process: Research the past. Think about what new different thing you want. Express it in a requisition. In theory it was exactly what I'd been doing for the past week in the Competition Room. There was just one problem: in Ruby Jubilee, there was nothing to research.

The first step was to go to the computer database and look up everything else that had been written for the caption. If you could find something decent that hadn't been used yet, or hadn't been used in a while, you could simply claim it (entering your name on a "to be designed" entry line), and that was that. But the database was also highly useful for newbies like me who just wanted to get a sense of what had and hadn't been done.

The database, back in 1995, wasn't even on actual computers: it was on old-fashioned CRT terminals that could only write highly pixellated text in white on a brown or black background. This was retro even for me; the visual equivalent of a card catalog. You'd search in the "Caption" line for BIRTHDAY BROTHER and you'd get a series of screens that looked something like this:

0112349 SKU: <u>BD057-0112349</u> Caption: <u>BROTHER BIRTHDAY HUMOR</u> Verse or Prose: <u>Prose</u> Ratings: 1.6 1.4 1.1 1.3 .8 .5 Writer: <u>L. Newton</u>
Hey Brother—
What's the difference between these two pictures?
(image: identical babe photos)

. . . I couldn't find any either! But I thought you'd enjoy looking! Happy Birthday!

Then under this there would be a list of baffling details about the six lives this sentiment had been through: who had planned each version, what year and line it had run in, and how it had performed. There were also notes on the actual art each time, so that you might learn that a verse that had a 1.4 rating when illustrated with VASE OF FLOWERS had dropped to .8 with SLEEPY KITTEN. The chief flaw in the system, however, should be obvious: it was all text, so you couldn't see the product. It was impossible to judge whether a certain card had failed because the verse was growing trite or because the line designer had made it a hideous shade of avocado.

By the way, before you ask, "What do the ratings mean?" I honestly don't know. I worked with them for four years, and the ratings were discussed in every writing kickoff I ever attended. I once even got singled out for praise because a card I had written scored an apparently unbelievable 2.8. A score of 1.0 was average, and technically a 2.0 rating meant a card had sold twice as much as average (well, twice as much "as counter," they always said, which was apparently different from something else). But this number was also factored against the individual caption and the line as a whole in Byzantine ways beyond my ken; I was forever saying something like "This card only did a .6" and hearing someone else say, "Actually, that's really good for Christmas Niece." (And I'd hear the exact same thing in reverse if Christmas Niece did a 1.4: "Well, that's a small caption.") You could never get a straight answer from anyone on a question like, "Well, how many copies of this one card sold?" All I knew was that anything from .8 on was respectable, and anything above 1.2 was very good indeed . . . and probably already taken by another editor.

The problem on my particular day was this: "Ruby Jubilee" didn't show up in my search. I got nothing back but a blinky cursor. With Hallmark's reputation for quality suddenly in my maladroit hands, how the hell was I supposed to figure out what worked in this caption? I went to McNicely, fretful, and told her my problem. And she said, "Well, that might have been over-looked when we first made the database. Hmm. I'd just go into the wings and see what's there already." So I did that, and I saw the one Ruby Jubilee card we were already selling. It was a fairly nondescript eight-line verse that said, in essence, "Good job. Congratulations on forty years of serving God." It rated a .7. And that was my only data point.

Deedee happened to be working in the wings at the time, and I asked her if she had any opinions about what made Ruby Jubilee work. She looked puzzled and said, "What's Ruby Jubilee?" I explained, and she looked just as baffled as ever. "I have no idea. I've only been here about four years. I've never even heard of that caption before."

Then it dawned on me: *Nobody cares.* I had been given, quite literally, the least important job an editor in Weddings, Births, and Occasional Jubilee Cards could have been given. Even Silver Jubilee (twenty-five years) would have been a step up, because at least more people got them.

As I prepared to create my first requisition, I found myself torn between two impulses. On the one hand, now that I knew the caption was invisible, I had all sorts of horrible ideas for cards, all of them variations on the same obvious theme:

On the fortieth anniversary of your ordination, I just want to
   say . . .
   . . . seeing a sixtysomething virgin really puts my own dry
   spell in perspective.

Or

> In forty years, you've woken up every morning with at least
>   1,460 erections you've never used.
> . . . I bet your penis is furious at God.

I didn't know it at the time, but this was classic "bottom drawer" writing, and card writers do it with some frequency: brainstorming their way through offensive or unsuitable ideas as a way of getting past them. And since some of them are funny, you wind up sticking them in a bottom drawer somewhere so they're still around to amuse you if need be.

My other impulse was to think about any priests I knew personally, to think about what I might say to them. This is another thing card writers do: use their own lives as springboards for emotion. If you can actually picture the person sitting right beside you, it makes the sentiment more focused and easier to write. The priest I thought of was Father Grady, from the Newman Center at the University of Arizona, where I had eventually converted to Catholicism a year before.

Father Grady was not only the spiritual head of the Newman Center at the U of A; he was also a professor in my Religious Studies classes. A beatific, pale, ruddy-cheeked Irishman with white hair, he bore a surprising resemblance to Clarence Oddbody, the angel in *It's a Wonderful Life.* When I was still an evangelical Protestant, determined to be the next C. S. Lewis, I had made no secret of my aspirations to answer big theological questions. I argued in every class, and everyone was pretty clear about my (evangelical, literalist) stance on things then. So when I actually visited my first Catholic mass at the Newman Center (dragged there by a study pal, but I was curious anyway), I was informed enough to know that I, as a Protestant, was not technically allowed to take the Catholic communion wafer. On the other hand, I had enough of a young man's idealistic asininity to try to take it anyway on principle. But when I got there, I realized the jig was up: Father Grady was officiating. He knew who I was, so I wouldn't be able to pull a fast one. Still, I figured it'd be nice to say hi, so when it came time for the Sacrament, I went up for the blessing they give you instead. When I got to the front of the line, Father Grady, to my shock, offered me the wafer. I shook my head, he gave a shrug and crossed me, and I sat down. Afterward, I went to his office hours and I said, "Father Grady! You know I'm a Protestant! Why did you offer me the Host?" And he smiled and said, "I figured Jesus would have."

That stayed with me. My own evangelical church had been far more likely to stick to principle rather than be dangerously lax in the rules. Father Grady was the first priest I ever knew, and he was nicer than any religious person I'd ever met.

IN FATHER GRADY'S NAME, THEN, I wrote up a requisition—one where I decided the direction to go this time was less congratulations-to-you-and-God and more thanks-for-all-you-do-for-the-community—and brought it to McNicely. "Now what?"

"Normally you send a bunch of them to the writing manager, who assigns it. But this is just one, so why don't you contact a writer personally? To see if they've got time."

"Who do I call?"

She mentioned a woman I'll call Dolorosa. "Try her," said McNicely. "She used to be a nun. She's good with religious."

So I called Dolorosa and said, "I have a requisition for a Ruby Jubilee card."

"What's that?"

I explained.

"I've worked here for almost ten years and I've never heard of it," said Dolorosa.

"It's sort of a small caption," I said. "I'll bring it up."

I had just had a brilliant idea. She was only one floor away. She was an ex-nun and still apparently Catholic. So she was probably religious, probably not conservative anymore, and a writer like I wanted to be. We already had a lot in common. Maybe she was one of my people; another person who could be my friend.

DOLOROSA WAS A HEAVYSET WOMAN in her forties or fifties, with straight salt-and-pepper hair cut short, like a tenured lesbian poet. She looked like she was always expecting bad news, but had already decided that whatever it was, she was screwed anyway. As eager as I was to make friends, a little voice told me not to mention health issues. She looked like she might be vocal about her symptoms.

I said, "I understand you used to be a nun," and she asked if I was Catholic, and of course we both were. So when I asked the obvious question, she said, "I just got disillusioned with the whole system. You know, the image is that the sisters are focused on goodness and decency and helping others. But in reality it's just another job. You see the same things in the convent that you see here at work. Some people were really petty. They took credit they didn't deserve. There were the popular people and the outsiders. It was all so incredibly political."

I tried to picture it, but couldn't. As I've said, I only knew non-asshole Catholic clergy. But rather than ask her to relive a painful part of her life, and to lighten the mood, I said, "So really, it's just like high school! Everything is like high school. We can't get away! Ha ha." In chess, this offering of valuable material is called a gambit.

She didn't smile, but nodded soberly. "That's really true."

Humor gambit declined. I regrouped. Maybe she just wanted a different kind of joke.

"So did you sisters ever play pranks on each other? Like put your, I don't know, cassocks in the freezer or whatnot?"

She smiled mildly. "No. We were all pretty serious." I could see how. Gambit declined again. And with that, I realized that Dolorosa was not going to be the sparring partner I realized I'd been fishing for. Again I'd had my hopes up, and again I'd been disappointed. We chatted a bit longer, and then I left her with the req.

One interesting thing happened, though. When I returned, I checked the clock and realized we'd talked for over an hour. But no one had even noticed I was gone or seemed to have thought it weird that I'd been walking up to the ninth floor. *My god*, I thought, *maybe I'm allowed to walk around. Maybe I'm not limited to making friends in Everyday.* Relief flooded me. I could feel a fresh breeze from somewhere in the dungeon.

Dolorosa's verse came back the next day, and no matter how hard I stared at it, it looked . . . generic. It rhymed "today" with "all the souls you've touched along the way," and the last rhymed

couplet ended with "you!" which, even with my limited experience, I suspected was something of a greeting card cliché. Of
course, if you have only one card to send to every single priest
who has this milestone, maybe dull is the point. Just to be safe,
I checked with McNicely and she said, "Looks fine to me. Congratulations!" I entered it in the system, Dolorosa got a credit,
and that was my first card.

But it hadn't looked fine to me. It had looked insipid and
toothless. I was sure I could have written something better in a
fraction of the time the whole process had taken. But I still
hadn't been able to show anyone what I could do. I was starting
to feel desperate, which is the only way I can explain what happened at the Christmas party.

TECHNICALLY, IT WAS the holiday potluck, which was held after
work at Magda's actual house. (We got off work early for it,
which made it the only actual paid vacation I was getting that
year.) Magda's house was intimidatingly lovely. I remember waist-
high vases containing tree-sized plants, and a fancy rug and a
fireplace—and, of course, an enormous Christmas tree, bedecked
with such an eye for color scheme and balance that it was obvious no kids had been involved. Her home wasn't huge, I suppose,
but there was a mansionlike opulence to the place, compared to
the trailer-ready starkness I'd been raised with. Here, every knick-
knack was clearly chosen for a very specific effect. Every wall
hanging seemed to carry a subliminal message about the impor-
tance of not renting. Even if I'd had the money, I could never
get a place to look like this. I'd still have the one couch, the one

table, and not buy plants or paintings at all. I could see how decor added to a place, and it had never occurred to me before. I felt stylistically impoverished.

The high point of the evening was supposed to be a standard "white elephant" gift exchange, where you're supposed to trade lousy, silly, or other poor-taste gifts among one another. I'd attended countless such exchanges in the past, because they're a very good choice for broke college students: you have to buy only one gift, and it literally can't be any good. In my past experience, the most successful gifts were ones that played on past pop culture: a Fonzie beach blanket, a "nanu nanu" T-shirt, a pope-on-a-rope, etc. My own traditional cheap-ass gift was to take a bar of soap and carve it into a paisley shape, complete with hand-scratched filigree. It usually got a laugh, and was sometimes even vied for. But I had little hope that such a thing would go over well in this crowd. So I had done something a little extreme: I put together a tiny sixteen-page collection of my light verse poems. They included such hits as:

The Kennedys
Are used to having all of the amenities.
Their wealth's so great it even beggars
Schwarzenegger's.

And:

There once was a fellow named Wood
Whose limericks weren't very good.
He said, "Though I rhyme

Most all of the time,
Every so often my scansion breaks down completely and I forget
what the hell I'm doing."

I was very careful to make sure I hit every possible target audience. One-third of it was literary jokes for the English majors. One-third was pop culture references, like the Schwarzenegger one. And one-third was just pure silliness that anyone could get. That way, I figured, no one would risk feeling completely alienated.

I typed it up, printed it out, made a nice cover of cardboard (at Hallmark, art supplies are always handy), and stapled it together into a little five-by-seven book. It wasn't a very good white elephant gift, since it was deliberately trying to be entertaining. But surely someone would be entertained by it. Diverting people wasn't just my strong suit; in situations like this, where no one actually knew me very well, it was the only suit I had. My dream here was the same as I'd had with my top ten list: you couldn't choose my gift without reading it aloud, and since it was funny, people would laugh and applaud and see a side of me that hadn't found expression yet. Even if it was only a moderate success, still at least one person at this party would surely find it amusing and talk to me later. That person or persons would be someone I could be friends with.

I knew it was a risk. Everyone would be expecting objects and I'd be offering text. Everyone would be offering one kind of joke and here was something else. I would definitely stand out. But I also thought, at the kind of gift exchanges I'd always loved, my poem book would still be a hit, because people cared more about laughter than rules. I had a sense that maybe things were different here, but I told myself that maybe things were different here only because they didn't have a young brash whippersnapper like me around to remind them what white elephant parties could be like. If I converted even one person, it would be worth it.

So there we all were, the entire Everyday Editorial staff in civilian clothes, opening gifts and displaying them. Mine kept not getting picked and not getting picked for the very excellent reason that it was tiny. Instead, people opened up a series of really dull "bad" presents. A mug shaped like a cow. A wall hanging made of yarn. Then McNicely, god bless her, chose my present. "Oh, look! A collection of light verse by Dave Dickerson!" She opened to page one and read aloud my "Higglevich Pigglevich, Rodya Raskolnikov" poem. There was silence. "Huh!" she said, sounding plausibly interested. Then she read the Schwarzenegger one. Another pause.

"Very creative," someone offered. A few others nodded politely.

"I'll read this later," McNicely said. "Thanks for doing this; it was really unique."

Oh, Jesus, I thought, as I looked around at everyone moving on quickly. *I just sent out a cry for help, and everyone heard it, and no one is coming to save me.* I felt dizzy and a little sick, like I'd been lightly chloroformed. Finally, while I cringed into my overstuffed chair, out came the pièce de résistance—a package from McNicely that was biggest of all, and that she'd actually been saving for the end. Magda opened it—and everyone roared with laughter. It was the clear winner of the evening. It was some sort of blown-glass horse, possibly in several colors.

"Oh my god! That's horrible!" said someone.

"Wow! It's amazing!" said another.

"I know!" said McNicely. "I saw this two months ago at a flea market and I said, 'That's going to be my white elephant this year!' "

I was terrified. I actually couldn't see what was wrong with the horse. It was nothing I wanted to own, but it didn't seem categorically worse—or, for that matter, any more interesting—than anything else we'd unveiled this evening. But to everyone in the room, it was like Jim Carrey had just told a joke. (Or, considering the age of the crowd, maybe Mort Sahl.) I suppose the problem might have been that I'm color-blind, but I suspected something far worse: I had no taste. I had already just embarrassed myself with my poetry gift; I didn't want to further bring down the room and add more awkward silence by asking someone to explain the horse. So I just sat quietly in my corner, and when it came time for food, I cautiously tried to make post-game conversation. The discussion, however, centered entirely around room decorations (I don't decorate), recipes for the various foods we had brought (I brought deviled eggs, which was the only thing I knew how to cook), and the hilariously bad taste of the various gifts we'd just seen. Mine was not mentioned.

I left the party early, felt my face flushed all the way home, and spent the next two hours on the phone with Jane, alternately cursing and sniffling, pacing in a random circle that made a volvulus of my phone cord. Jane said all the right things—"It's just a party, nobody hates you, you've only been there two months, you've got a great job and it could be so much worse, like for instance you could be in grad school"—but none of it sank in. I realized then that there was a core part of me that couldn't listen to reason. Although I had been trying to put a nice face on it, I was doing boring busywork, I couldn't seem to make friends with anyone, I was hugely disappointed in the whole job, and this was all building up into actual rage. This was unthinkable. Two Christmases before this, I'd survived three days waiting for standby flights at O'Hare with Jane, waiting for the next flight, and not getting on, and waiting for the next and failing there, too, and even though we got depressed, in the whole three days I'd never even raised my voice to anyone. And I was feeling rage *now*? What did this mean?

Fortunately, I had some time to decompress because of the holidays. But when Christmas and New Year's were past, I knew something had better change, or I was going to explode. And since I'd never exploded before, I didn't even know what might happen after that. As I went to sleep that night, with my heart and face still boiling with embarrassment and anger, I thought, with an acid chill in my chest, *Oh my god. I wonder if this is what Dad felt like before his nervous breakdown.* I wanted to call someone for help, but who? Jane didn't understand my anger; hell, she'd never even seen me angry. Dad would simply tell me to pray. If this was a disaster in the making, I was going to have to face it all alone.

I wanted to believe I was up to the challenge, but I knew, as a former voyeur, that I'd failed myself before. I didn't even bother to pray for strength. I just drifted into troubled sleep, keeping a wary eye on my unruly heart, afraid of where it might bolt to.

7

My People

FOR THE ENTIRE WEEK OF CHRISTMAS, THE ONLY PEO-
ple in the office—nine huge stories, remember, plus whoever
was in the other three buildings—were late-in-the-year new
hires like me who didn't have any time off to use. Only half the
lights were on—the ones above the cubicles. The hallways were
darkened, lit only from the distant work lights and the sun outside. You could sit—as I did all that week—and just marvel at
the profound silence. Not a creature was stirring.

In fact, it was so eerily silent that I didn't want to just let the
silence win. So I found myself making deliberate noise whenever I walked anywhere: I pretended I was in a musical. I skipped,
I hummed, I tapped my feet, and I did little drum riffs with my
fingers on passing file cabinets. One time, right before getting
on the stairway, I put one hand on the rail and kicked my feet
together while leaping onto the first stair. A man coming up the
steps saw me and raised his eyebrows. "You shouldn't do that,"
he said. "They've got cameras everywhere."

Cameras? Really? And what would I get in trouble for? Rambunctiousness? Intemperate mirth? I couldn't figure out what this guy was concerned about, and by the time I thought to ask him, he was gone. But he was older than me, and in an actual decent-looking suit, and he seemed to know the score. So I spent the next few days in a lot of silence and being very very very very bored. But at least there were no meetings and no irritating conversations. I felt normal again for a time, like I didn't have to swing my fists at all.

CHRISTMAS WAS SPENT calling my family uncomfortably ("God bless you, Dave") and calling Jane frustratingly ("I wish you were here, too"), and watching movie after movie on my big new TV until they all started falling structurally together, and I had no one to comment to. *Where do people get friends from?* I wondered, and realized I should have thought about this before the holidays, since everyone was gone now.

I went to midnight mass at the same nearby church I'd been going to, and a strange feeling of outsiderness overcame me. It wasn't just that this was the boring-grumpy-sexagenarian adult service. I looked at the candlelight licking across the old stained-glass windows, heard the breathing all around me, saw the priest in his robes raise the Eucharist to the heavens, and thought, *Sociologically speaking, this is an odd thing for people to do.* I had studied the sociology of religion in a class with Andrew Greeley and I remembered what he'd said: "Even if Catholicism weren't true, it would make great theater." In the past, I'd always laughed at the comment and focused on the truth. Tonight, for whatever reason, I focused on the theater. Tonight, as much as I wanted to feel it, there didn't seem to be anyone behind the curtain.

As we filed out, I actually clutched my arms together, as if I was afraid of being touched, and as I stomped down the stairs and homeward, my feet felt benumbed and distant from the other jacketed people murmuring homeward as well, and from the dim forms in the cars whose lights flicked on, whose motors purred to life as they rolled to one home or another, far away. *I must be depressed. This is the dark night of the soul that Saint John of the Cross talks about. It's the feeling Saint Thomas Aquinas had when he said, "Everything I've written is mere straw." Martin Luther got depressed all the time. I'm in good religious company.* But as I walked home, I had to admit I didn't feel very religious. I felt like a regular guy who happened to be walking home alone. The night had turned colder; I made a note to buy a better jacket.

Once inside I felt sad, and wondered why, and then the absurdity of my situation struck me. I had just had physical communion with no real emotional communion; a ritual with no warmth. Did I really think one would satisfy without the other? *Religion is pointless without friendship*, I decided. *Either I need to make friends here, or find a friendlier church, or I need to stop going altogether.* For the present, I made a mental note to go to the bookstore on the Plaza tomorrow and buy Saint John of the Cross. Maybe a version with some kind of scholarly commentary. My brain was feeling understimulated, too.

WHEN WE ALL CAME BACK after Christmas, Magda called me into her office. She smiled kindly at me—it turns out she had a gorgeous smile when she chose to use it—and she said, "You're new here, and so we won't actually be giving you a performance review this time around. But I wanted you to know that you're talking too much."

Before I had a chance to reply she tossed her head—the equivalent of an embarrassed eye-roll, to get us past this brief unpleasantness—and then said, "Edith has a new assignment for you. Congratulations, by the way. You're going to be pulling replacements now."

I walked away confused. Talking too much? Had I just gotten chewed out? I tried to understand what had happened. It had seemed, structurally, like a warning. But it had two flaws. First, it didn't feel in any way threatening. Second, it didn't make any kind of sense. Talking too much? I barely talked to anyone in Everyday. If I wanted to talk, I went up a floor to Main Writing, or over one area to Design, where I chatted up any artist who didn't seem too busy, not exactly making friends, but just asking about the job. No one had ever complained or told me to go away. My garrulousness to other people must have seemed to Magda like overwhelming talkiness just because she was so quiet herself. But how did she even know? Were people gossiping? Had someone complained to her and not to me? That would be silly. Obviously she was overreacting. Which was more proof that I belonged somewhere else.

Edith's assignment was simple, in theory. She plunked me down in front of her computer in the wings and said, "I've got a list here of ten cards that I'd like replaced. You need to look online in the EDS system to find replacement copy from the files. If you can't find anything, you can write a requisition for new copy, but you shouldn't need to. It's a lot easier to just find something."

The only problem, it turned out, is that other editors were poaching the same sentiments. A sentiment that said "On This Special Day . . . Just wanted to tell you you're loved" would work in damn near every caption, and so I was actually in a race against the clock and against other editors to grab the best stuff first. "When I find a really good piece of copy that's already been claimed," said Edith, "I'll actually check on it every month to see if it's free yet. You'll find out. Editors wind up with lists as long as their arms."

I'm not an editor. I'm a writer. I don't belong here. "So how do I know if something's been taken?"

She made me look up a sentiment. "You see on that line, where it says SEASHORE MOTIF but there's no rating? If you look at the date on the far right, you'll see it hasn't been planned yet. That's just been claimed by another editor. That's how you do it. You look at the date. And of course you look at the ratings, too. There's no point in pulling copy that didn't do well the first time around, unless maybe you see something in it where it got misapplied. In my experience, that's not something you want to count on."

"What's that one line, BUTTERFLY W/FLITTER? Do the butterflies move?"

"Oh, no!" Edith said, cupping her hand over her mouth in mirth. "No, that means they used Flitter on it. You see this?" She pointed to a brightly spangled card on her desk, a rainbow of specks. "Flitter is a special kind of glitter. It's really tiny, and when you touch it, it comes off on your fingers. It gets on everything. Our consumer loves it."

"Why?"

Edith shrugged. "People just like shiny things, I guess."

"I see." I scanned the EDS screen and its ratings and senti-ments. It looked simple. In fact, it looked moronic. But maybe Magda had just put me in a bad mood. I looked at the top card—Wedding to Couple—and started typing.

"Oh, I'm sorry, Dave," said Edith. "I'm using this computer. You'll have to find something else."

"But . . . I don't have a computer at my desk."

"There are lots of them around. Just find any one."

"Any one?" A timber that had fallen over my heart shifted slightly. "So . . . anywhere in the company? As long as it's online?"

"Sure," she said. "Don't get lost, though! Ha ha."

Find a computer somewhere else? You bet your ass I will, I thought. *Somewhere where no one's going to think that a little friendly conversa-tion is "talking too much."* I was relieved. I actually had an excuse to get the hell out. I would wander all day if I had to. Ten cards. How long could that possibly take?

AS I STARTED UPSTAIRS to Main Writing, a thought struck me: the power of anywhere. This meant—I could scarcely bring myself to form the thought—that I could actually wander sev-eral blocks over to Traditional Humor, where Max Stentor was, the only manager who liked my puzzles. The job I actually wanted. I could hang out there and do my work, and I'd just gotten permission to do it.

That's how I found myself in another building altogether for the first time: the 2440 building, first floor, where Traditional Humor lay. The moment I walked in, I found myself standing before a monstrosity: someone had taken a medium-sized piece of ugly green carpet and draped it like a towel over a disused freestanding coatrack in the middle of the aisle. A Burger King crown hung lazily on top, and there were a few things safety-pinned to the carpet: a drawing of Homer Simpson, a twisted pipe cleaner, an old brown button, a name tag that said "Hi, I'm _____."

Max emerged from around the corner and, *mirabile dictu*, smiled to see me. "Dave! What brings you out here?"

I explained that I needed a computer. "What the hell is this?" I asked.

"That's our Christmas tree," said Max. "Sorry—our *holiday* tree. The guys just put it together and we've been adding to it. We're not a really celebratory crowd here."

I laughed. I was similarly inept at decorating. So inept, in fact, that this eyesore actually felt a bit like home. Certainly more at home than Magda's holiday party.

I found my ten sentiments—it only took maybe two hours—and on the way out, I thought about taping something of my own to the ugly carpet-tree. Maybe one of my old doodles from back at PREVENT? But I held off. It really wasn't my place.

WHEN I RETURNED TO EDITORIAL, I handed Edith the list of sentiments, and she said, "I'm too busy to look at them now."

"What should I do in the meantime?"

"Well—you know the EDS system now. Just go online and read through the sentiments. It's good grounding to know what's out there."

More busywork. I grumbled, found a computer one department over, and read silently for hours. It was almost as boring as mailing off short stories. When I came back, it was late, and Edith caught me. "Eight of those sentiments you chose don't work. One of them just isn't very good—I don't know what it's doing in there, to be honest—and the others have already been claimed." She then went over the procedure again, and I stared at the goddamned screen and tried to make sense of it, but she might as well have been saying, "Flense the beerbibber past rixatrix and always check the zanjero for bradykinin." She was so confident in me, I would have felt stupid saying, "Could you just point at the number I'm supposed to be looking at and tell me what level is bad?" So I nodded, convinced myself I understood, and vowed to try again tomorrow. Or possibly the next day. Whatever assignment McNicely was giving me, it didn't seem especially urgent to anyone.

I DIDN'T WANT TO DEPEND too much on visiting Humor for my mental health for the same reason that I didn't want to always have lunch with Deedee, so I mixed it up and occasionally went up to the Main Writing Staff on Nine. While I was working there one day, Dolorosa came into the cubicle area, wanted to use the computer, but saw me and said, "Oh, sorry!" and turned away.

"Wait a minute," I said. I had seen a flash of cartoon. "What's that under your arm?"

"It's a collection of poetry from our last retreat," she said, holding it up. *Renewed Celebrations*, it said. It had a deliriously happy Snoopy-like dog on the cover.

"Retreat? You have retreats?"

It turned out that every few months, in what they called "creative renewal," the writers would go off and do some sort of one- or two-day workshop, with titles like "Using Imagery" or "Classic Verse Forms." Just hearing this made me salivate. What's more, the work from these workshops was often published in-house, and one such collection was what Dolorosa was carrying around. There were others, she said.

So one day for lunch—another lunch alone, but at this point who was counting?—I found a stash of retreat-workshop book-lets on the ninth floor and grabbed the most entertaining-looking one. It was called simply "Rhyming Workshop." The assignments they'd been asked to do were exactly the kinds of things I'd chal-lenged myself with when I was applying: *Write a poem where the rhyme is always the same throughout. Now do a double dactyl. Now do a poem that uses at least four three-syllable rhymes.* Just being near it all was like a contact high.

Under each assignment, the seminar leader/booklet producer had given examples along with the names. Most of them I could attach to a face, but that was all. And truth be told, for the most part I had a hard time telling anyone's work apart. With one exception: a man named Josh Broward. He always seemed to start obliquely: where most people opened with "It's your birth-day! Hooray!" Josh had a tendency to go with, "Time is the author that writes us." But he could also bounce with the best of them: I recall a poem about a Birthdaysaurus that stuck out precisely because it wasn't the twee thing you'd expect ("Look! I'm combining a dinosaur and a birthday, and that's the only idea I have!"), but it really entered into the kinds of things kids like about dinosaurs, the things I'd always loved: the Birthdaysaurus tromped through town, knocking over buildings, eating huge amounts of food, and scaring adults. Josh was consistently good on every page: always discernibly different, always raising the

level of the assignment. I could have slapped myself. We'd actually had lunch together on my interview day! How had I met
the guy and not noticed his whimsical genius? (I could blame
O.J., but still.) I decided at that moment that I wanted him to
like me, and I wanted to show that I could participate in the
same sort of workshop with the same sort of flair.

To hell with replacement cards, I decided. I spent the next
hour writing the following rhymed letter:

My dear Mr. Broward—for weeks now you've towered, in
legend and rumor, at mythical heights. Folks say that your
writing is fun and exciting—so good that they ask you to turn
down your brights. I'd heard this and nodded, but just now I
spotted some pieces of yours in a workshop on rhyme, and I
just have to say that they blew me away, and I found them
(you'll see this word coming) sublime. Your scansion has rigor!
Your word choice has vigor! You only drop puns from
positions of strength! There's no use in hiding: the waves that
we're riding would seem to be of a commensurate length.

If I'd only known sooner, our sadly sublunar noon meal,
when I interviewed, could have been stellar! Like T.S. and
Pound, we'd have kicked verse around, and I'm sure I'd have
found you one heck of a feller! We should totally meet, both
to chat and to eat—I have Q's you could helpfully A over
lunch. So the next time you're free, send an email to me, and
we'll see what we see. (Fingers crossed . . .)

Thanks a bunch!

Doing this made me surprisingly sad. It was without a doubt
the most fun I'd managed to have at Hallmark since I'd been

hired two months previously. And it had nothing to do with my job. After lunch I sighed and, realizing I'd probably already wasted too much time, dropped it in the nearest mail tray and returned to my usual work, which involved borrowing someone else's computer so I could look up ratings and sentiments. When I got back to my desk a few hours later, Josh had already replied via phone message and wanted to meet. We had lunch the next day in the Crown Room.

TECHNICALLY, EMPLOYEES HAD forty-five minutes for lunch. This was a tradition more honored in the breach than the observance, and in fact the only time I ever invoked the forty-five-minute rule was in future months when I'd made a misfire and was eating lunch with someone boring I needed to get away from. That first day with Broward, we went about seventy-five minutes.

I'd seen him the day I'd interviewed, of course, and had stood next to him during the announcement of the O.J. verdict. But I hadn't been paying much attention. He was about forty, graying at the temples, and wore thin wire-framed glasses. He was trim and handsome, and when I found out that his older brother was an actor in Hollywood, it made sense. Broward wasn't head-turningly handsome, but his entire face—from his close-cropped hair to his laugh lines to his oddly interesting nose and chin—seemed composed of solid, symmetrical character.

"It's nice to meet someone who really likes verse," he said. "I brought something to show you." He gave me a page-long poem, maybe thirty-two lines.

"It's for a poem parody competition I read about in *Poets & Writers*. I'm doing Dylan Thomas."

My eyes bugged as I scanned the page, thinking furiously. *Dylan Thomas, Dylan Thomas* . . . I knew he'd written "Do Not Go Gentle into That Good Night," "A Child's Christmas in Wales," and "Under Milkwood." The last two were prose and I'd never read them. So the only thing I had to go on was "Do Not Go Gentle," and nothing on this page was anything like that. It was called "Bending My Sponsor's Ear, I Feed the Ducks," and read in part as follows:

> *Raise high our Kool-Aid toast to the higher*
> *Power that trussed us, lashed us lush*
> *As whiskey's sour*
> *Mash to the black-baked coffee tower,*
> *The three-month chip, the milk moustache.*
>
> *I tread twelve steps that tumble down*
> *The sky-roofed hill no heaven marks;*
> *What does that mean?*
> *My caffeine blood can scarce explain,*
> *Through sober craft, my sullen art.*

If I'd been writing a Dylan Thomas parody—and I'd never even have considered him as a target—I'd have taken his most famous poem and turned it into a joke with a punch line, maybe played with that line from *Poltergeist*: "Don't go gentle into the light!" What Broward was doing was infinitely more subtle: there was no overt joke in the piece; no Hiawatha trying to take photographs or prunes in the icebox. This was a riff on Thomas's writing style, and even though I didn't get any individual joke—although it was clearly alluding to Thomas's own alcoholism—this was different from the alienation I'd felt at the Christmas party. Back there, faced with the glass horse, I'd felt simply style-blind and helpless to improve. Here, I felt that this poem was something I could actually master with enough diligence. It was the kind of challenge I could have fun with and hadn't seen in a long while. At the moment, of course, I just needed to say something smart about this parody that I could barely understand to impress a person I had only just met.

Fortunately, I'd had years of practice with this in grad school. Rule number one is: steer the conversation to the one thing you *can* understand. "I'd have to read more Dylan Thomas to really get all the references," I said. "But it's gorgeously written, the language is absurdly baroque, and it's very impressive how you've enjambed every line in that Kool-Aid stanza to within an inch of its life."

Broward laughed, and even his laugh was natural and yet energetic, like a mountain brook flowing with seltzer. "That was really fun. It's a direct parody of 'This Bread I Break,' and I wanted to capture his windy oratory. That gets overlooked in a lot of the criticism." *Windy oratory. He talks like I do.* Josh took the poem back and seemed to readjust his focus. "So how are you finding Kansas City?"

I told him it was a weird adjustment, and he gave me a few tips on things to do around town (barbecue, live jazz), but the whole time I was thinking, *This is a guy who apparently reads poetry criticism in his spare time. He's read more than I have, which is something I never face in Editorial. He subscribes to* Poets & Writers, *which I only ever did when I was taking writing classes. This is an MFA student all grown up.* We talked about what we wanted to do—I was writing my greeting card novel, plus some cartoons and verses, and he was writing a screenplay, plus this poem, and a few ideas for Hallmark product he was thinking about. We had both read a lot and liked thinking. In theory, he should have come across just as restless as I did. Why didn't he?

While we ate, he did something I'd never seen anyone do before: he stopped eating his sandwich two-thirds of the way through, just because he wasn't hungry anymore. It was just one more expression of his quiet composure. Years later, in the *Tao te Ching*, I read that the true sage does everything without seeming to move at all, and I thought of Josh in that moment: all that creative energy whirling around all that stillness. At the time, all I knew was that I'd run into the first person I'd met in Kansas City who I actually wanted to be like. It was scary to like someone that much that fast, and to feel my own inadequacies so keenly.

Lest I give the wrong impression, remember that this conversation was mostly light and fun. Among the other anecdotes that day, Josh told me that early in his career at a brainstorm meeting, surrounded by a bunch of fellow writers, he'd scrawled a terrible joke on a card, which was later read out loud: "Enjoy your birthday now . . . because after you die you'll spend all of eternity giving blow jobs to Satan." The next day he had come to work and there had been one of Hallmark's omnipresent index cards on Josh's chair. It had a cartoon on it from a coworker of his named Stanley that read "Josh's Hell Equipment." It showed kneepads, a crash helmet, and a bib. Josh doesn't draw, but he hand-wrote Stanley a quip about extra-strength mouthwash, and before they knew it a tradition was born. "Every few days for almost a year, we were trading cartoons and jokes about giving blow jobs to the devil," he told me. "Jokes about what Satan's penis would be like, how awful the semen would be . . . it got really disgusting. I bet I still have them around somewhere."

Jesus, I thought. *I have* got *to work in the Idea Exchange as soon as possible. That's a place where people actually return your jokes.*

THE CLOSEST I HAD COME TO working in the Idea Exchange was to continue to hover near Trad Humor, where Max liked my puzzles and there wasn't a years-long waiting list of people dying to get in. No one started their career in the Idea Exchange, but it was just possible to get hired into Trad Humor if they ever had an opening. When I visited the IdEx, I felt like a silly, childish wannabe. When I visited Trad Humor, I felt like I was among equals.

My second stab at Wedding replacements worked just fine, for reasons I couldn't fathom, and McNicely tasked me with a dozen more, due date several days from now. With all this time to kill, I kept going back to Traditional Humor to familiarize myself with the line—not of Weddings, but of actual joke cards, like the ones I wanted to write. It was far more interesting. I could read them for hours.

One day I deliberately timed my trip so that it would run into lunch. I'd noticed that several of the guys would wander off to the Crown Room together, then return with trays of food. They'd go into the conference room, close the door, and you could hear some sitcom playing on the TV and occasional bursts of laughter. On this day, as a pair of them left, I said, "Hey . . . could I join you?"

"Sure! Come along," said the first guy, who looked about my age—skinny, dark hair, glasses.

"We're watching *Seinfeld*," said another—shorter and stouter, with a dense but trim brown mustache. His voice was high and declarative, like he was used to giving instructions. "Edgar here is taping them when they rerun at night. We're just starting the third season."*

"Oh, thank goodness," I said. "The second season was the worst. After all the everyday observation of the first season— the parking garage, the movie theater—suddenly in the second you have this awful wackiness with the clown assassin and—"

"I'm with you!" said the first guy, who was apparently Edgar. "They found a sort of balance in season three, but you can see the pains in two."

His friend added, "But if you haven't seen season one in a while, it might surprise you. Especially the first few episodes don't quite hold up. They don't have their pace down; the characters aren't sharp. Even the lighting is bad."

The first guy's full name—a terrible one for a greeting card writer—was Edgar Allan. The second guy I'll call The Professor, but his nickname around the office was The Old Atheist. They'd been friends since college. The Professor had a Ph.D. in philology—that's Latin and Greek classics—and Edgar Allan had majored in English and done a good bit of cartooning in Chicago before joining his friend at Hallmark.

When we returned from the Crown Room, we were joined by a third guy—an older meat-and-potatoes type with a gray-

---

* Back in the mid-nineties, before TiVo, people "taped" TV shows using cassettes with magnetic strips inside them on a plastic reel-to-reel. Ask your parents!

speckled mop and an easy laugh. Blues Man, I'll call him, since he was an actual blues musician and you could feel it in his languorous, unhurried speech. We watched the show, and when it was over twenty minutes later, we all sat around shooting the breeze, debating the merits of this or that season of *Seinfeld*. It was an honest-to-god conversation about what made humor work—the kind of talk I hadn't had since I'd hung out with comedians back in Tucson. I was so happy, so hopeful around them, that I pulled out what had now become my litmus test: I told the story of my top ten list in Editorial and how it had been butchered.

The Professor groaned. "I hate when that happens. It just never gets any easier."

Edgar Allan laughed. "You should see. I've got a stack about this high of cards where the editor or the artist just destroyed a perfectly good joke."

"He really does," said The Professor.

"Get used to it," said Blues Man. "It's part of the gig."

"So I'm not crazy," I said.

"Well, we don't know *that* yet," said Blues Man. "But welcome to the club." He offered me his hand. I shook, we all laughed, and I half expected credits to roll.

WHEN I CAME BACK TO my desk in Everyday, Edith had left me a voice message. "Dave, four of those pieces you picked were already claimed when you picked them. Remember that you have to look at the frammidge line on the banjax screen and check that the mumpsimus isn't embrangled. Okay? Great!" Click.

To go from a land where everything made sense to one where

I couldn't even understand a simple set of instructions set off some kind of depth charge in my soul. I flipped out as much as a repressed person can. Against all my training, against every inclination instilled by my father and my own timorous nature, I actually actively rebelled. That afternoon and on past the usual closing time of five, I wrote Regina, the Writing Overlord, a poem. Since it had worked so well in meeting Josh, I even borrowed the same rhyme scheme. I also dared to subtly allude to the fact that she'd called me an "old soul." Then, when it was late and I knew she'd gone home, I slid it under her door.

Dear Regina—
Each day here's a fun day
I smile when it's Monday
And my soul knows that one day
I'll totally get it.

Just being here's thrilling
And I'm thoroughly willing
To shill what needs shilling
And helpfully edit.

But to polish our brand
Isn't quite what I planned.
It's a post I can stand
But it's not that exciting.

And though normally I'd
Keep these feelings inside,

I just feel really fried
And I'd rather be writing.

Now, I hope you're not worried
Or feel overhurried.
No judge and no jury'd
Accuse me of shrieking.

The point of this spiel
'S just to say how I feel.
You've got grease, I'm the wheel
And this verse is me squeaking.

Regina called me the next morning and said, "I got your note. It was wonderful, and I just want you to know we really are working on this. Trust me!"

I honestly can't prove the poem did anything, but days later, Magda called me into her office and, with another of those smiles that seemed mildly put-upon, told me that I was being transferred to Traditional Humor. I walked out on a cloud and called Jane the second I got off work. "Honey!" I said. "They gave me my promotion!" It wasn't a promotion at all; it was a sideways move from being an Editor I to a Writer I. But I didn't care. The clouds had parted. The curtain had ripped. The spirit had descended like a dove. And from now on, I imagined, I could actually look forward to Monday. For I was Regina's beloved son, with whom she would soon be well pleased.

PART THREE

Shared Joke

My Year in Traditional Humor

8

The Ways of My People

AS MAGDA WAS GIVING ME WHATEVER PAPERWORK I needed to hand to my new boss, Max, she said, "I'm surprised you didn't like it here. When we get extroverts, we usually place them in Editing, because writers are so quiet." I nodded, but then thought, *Wait a minute. Is she suggesting that even though I applied as a writer, they were actually planning to make me an editor all along?* Then I remembered what Regina had said about my writing being the future of the company, and I relaxed. My whole posting in Editing must have been some crazy fluke. And most important, it was over.

In Humor, I handed Max Stentor the folder and he sat me down in his double-wide cubicle, which was mostly business with a few dollops of cartoons. He leaned back in his chair, consciously avuncular. "As the manager, I see my job as protecting you guys from paperwork and baloney. I absorb all that so that you can just keep writing. So this is an easy staff to work on if you just keep your focus. There's just one thing you should remember, and I tell this to all my people. This is a big company, with a lot of history. Let me just save you a lot of time right now: change won't happen. This company is a huge machine and it will assimilate you. You will not change it. It will barely notice you're alive. Learn to be a happy cog and everything will work fine." He said it the way he said most things: with a smile that expressed both irony and pain, and with an edge of sarcasm that served to separate himself from the tedious truths his job obliged him to tell. I wondered how a guy who'd started as a joke writer wound up the way he was now, but I could scarcely calculate all the pressures involved.

I pretended to listen, but the whole speech made no sense to me. Did I seem like a diva? What problems could he possibly be seeing ahead of me? I liked Hallmark, and the way it did things presumably made sense, because it was a really successful company. So why in the world was Max warning me away from hope before I'd even done anything? *And Regina thinks I'm the new voice of Hallmark, and she's Max's boss. So Max doesn't even know what he's saying. I've had higher-level confabs.*

"Got it," I said, because it seemed the easiest way to get started on my job already.

But then Max asked, "Do you have any questions?"

I couldn't resist. One big question had been eating at me. "Why aren't there any women on this staff?"

He sighed. "I don't know!" he said, and there was that frustrated helplessness again, covered with a smile. "We recruit like crazy. I try every chance I get. I would love to have more women here. That's our consumer! But they never want to stay. Every time we get one, they only last a few months. They move to Main Writing or the Idea Exchange or they go off and become editors. I honestly don't understand it."

I nodded. I didn't get it either. The guys were truly nice, and you couldn't imagine any of them sexually harassing anyone. Some days you could hardly imagine them having the guts to speak to a woman without written permission. And although foolish people will occasionally assert that women aren't funny, this is idiotic.*

What's more, Shoebox—also called "Alternative Humor"— had a much more even, fifty-fifty mix on its staff. So why weren't women staying at Traditional Humor? This is something I still don't have a strong answer to (although our office was much uglier than Shoebox). I do, however, have a theory.

Years later I had a terrific writing professor who also had a reputation for being down on women. There was absolutely nothing to it. Many of his favorite writers were women (he introduced me to Alice Munro and Margaret Atwood), he always seemed equally helpful to everyone, and he corrected writers

---

* A brief list of women I find hilarious: Ellen DeGeneres, Lucille Ball, Amy Sedaris, Wanda Sykes, Rita Rudner, Roseanne Barr, Maria Bamford, Judy Tenuta, Whoopi Goldberg, Paula Poundstone, Sarah Silverman, Cheri Oteri, Jaime Pressly, Tina Fey, Joy Behar, and Chelsea Handler, to say nothing of the dozens of women I've seen perform on stages without their own sitcoms (including Ophira Eisenberg, Cyndi Freeman, and Sara Barron), and the dozens more I've known personally—friends who aren't professionally funny but who have always made me laugh when I needed it. Lizz Winstead invented The Daily Show. The Onion has at least one woman—Carol Kolb—in its list of past editors. My favorite writers are all witty: Sarah Vowell, Mary Roach, Molly Ivins, Judith Martin, Anne Lamott, Jennifer Traig, Sloane Crosley, reaching back to Jane Austen and going forward forever. Our culture would have been far poorer without the work of Elaine May, or Gracie Allen, or the comic performances of Judy Holliday, Katharine Hepburn, Myrna Loy, Jean Arthur, Thelma Ritter, Claudette Colbert, Barbara Stanwyck, and Rosalind Russell. To wish it otherwise is clearly demented. This is clearly a sore point with me, and you don't want to get me started. If you think women aren't funny, you're wrong, you're a braying jackass, and you should shut the hell up, no matter how much Esquire wants to pay you.

when they'd made their female characters into flat sexist types instead of real people. But he was a guy-type guy, with occasionally rough manners (applied equally to everyone) and a certain good-old-boy redneck bonhomie. And it's just possible that women—particularly the sort of women who go into writing programs, we bookish types who observe every detail with an eye to its larger meaning—simply didn't feel comfortable hanging around him. If you came in thinking masculinity was inherently hostile to women, you were very likely to pick up hostility from this professor—not because it was there, but because the guylike behaviors of liking sports, barhopping, watching action movies, talking about cars, and such were all deeply ingrained in him in a way that would have been unspectacular at a NASCAR rally, but were rather jarring at a big liberal-arts university. As a nudist friend of mine once told me, when everyone at the same retreat is naked, you start to really notice people's socks.

In the same way, I suspect that Max Stentor was unusually guylike by Hallmark's highly feminized standards: he was unremittingly sarcastic, uncomfortable with emotion, socially blunt, obsessed with odd things (he was tireless on the subject of the Lindbergh trial) . . . and (as I've already said) he was more than a little loud. In the land of the polite, the noisy guy might seem sexist by comparison. I was disappointed not to be working with funny women, but I told myself there was an upside, too: less temptation. That was answer enough for now. This was going to be a fine place to work.

BEFORE I CAME TO HALLMARK, when I was writing my greeting card novel, I had a rather simplistic picture of what greeting

card writers would be like. Because I wanted to sell the film and
TV rights, I pictured the humor staff as being sort of like the
sitcom *Friends*, with three main characters: one brainy guy like
Ross, one wiseacre like Chandler, and one womanizer like Joey.
In supporting roles, I pictured three other guys: one wise, slightly
older married man who could offer wry moral counsel, one old
guy who wasn't funny but had been around forever, and one
angry, bitter guy who hated everyone and somehow turned out
really nice cards anyway. To generate my plot, I decided the staff
would be all men, and the story would begin when a woman
joined the team. Presumably hilarity would ensue. That was my
made-up, Hollywood idea of a greeting card staff.

So on this day, once I joined Hallmark's Humor staff myself
in real life, I was surprised to discover that my simplistic TV-
ready picture was actually true. There were a few differences—
like, for instance, there were no women on staff at all—but in
general everyone lined up astonishingly well according to type.

You've already met the lunch crowd: Edgar Allan, The Professor, and Blues Man. As I got to know them, it became clear that
Edgar Allan was the Chandleresque quippy guy, and The Professor was the brainy Ross type, with an actual Ph.D. The Professor
was married; Edgar was single. They'd both been at Hallmark
for less than five years.

The Joey character was another writer, whom I'll call Romeo
because that's what we sometimes called him. He was actually a
supporting player, not a main guy, because he was single and so
handsome that he was usually off seeing some woman for lunch
and didn't hang out with the rest of us. Instead, the other main
character was Blues Man, who was slightly older and married,
and really did offer wry advice to nervous tyros like me.

The Non-Funny Guy Who'd Been Around Forever was a Mormon geek of Max's age with Coke-bottle glasses and a nervous chuckle and whose jokes were so corny that he always seemed this close to saying, "Working hard or hardly working?" Plus he was so religious and so conservative that he really didn't mesh well with the rest of us—particularly me, since he represented the very past I had worked so hard to escape. Max clearly hated the Mormon geek and his non-funny ways, but Max didn't fire him because—and this is why I'm mentioning him at all— the Mormon geek was absolutely brilliant at writing not-funny humor cards, which it turns out there's a good deal of demand for. One time he got an acceptance for what must have been the dullest card ever. Outside, it showed Mickey Mouse in a space suit saying, "Here's Hoping Your Birthday . . ." Inside: ". . . is the best in the UNIVERSE!" That's it. We real writers were all scratching our heads, so I asked the editor why she'd accepted it, and she said, "Because we didn't have it! I couldn't believe it. We had 'hope your birthday's out of this world,' 'hope it's star-studded,' and 'have a cosmic birthday.' But no 'best in the universe.' It was simply unbelievable how we'd missed it all these years." When I told the Mormon geek about what she'd said, he laughed. "I know. I checked before I wrote it."

The other person worth mentioning was the Bitter Guy Who Hates Everyone But Writes Surprisingly Sweet Things. I'm calling him Black Peter. He was a dark-haired man a bit older than me with a perpetual scowl, and the first time I said, "Good morning," he pushed right past me without even looking in my direction. He came in every day, and—through some arrangement with Max—simply claimed the conference room as his own. When we needed to have a meeting, or when the guys came back to watch movies at lunch, you'd have to knock and wait for him to unlock the door and let you in, but he never joined us—he just scuttled immediately to his cube and never said a word. The first time he ignored my friendly hello, he wore such a look of unwarranted hatred that I was terrified to go near him afterward. There's a lesson here: if you're surrounded by nice, passive people, being even a little bit of a jerk gives you tremendous power.

You may note, by the way, that in my novel, as in my life, there was no room for me. I figured I'd write myself in somehow along the way. As the youngest guy on staff by about six years, I imagined I'd be the precocious wunderkind. It was my story, after all. Why shouldn't I be the star? If Regina was right, the next obvious step was just to uncork my genius and stand back.

ALTHOUGH THEIR PERSONALITIES had turned out to be surprisingly archetypal, the actual working day of the Humor staff was not the way I'd pictured it in my novel. There, it had been a kind of nine-to-five Algonquin Round Table, with everyone cracking wise and playing pranks. But Magda had actually been right: they were mostly introverts—friendly and funny, but introverts—and the cube farm, with its two rows of four low cubicles each, wasn't what you'd call uproarious. The place was small enough and quiet enough that you could just remain seated and talk—"Does anyone know what the soup is in the Crown Room today?" "Minestrone"—and there'd be no great break in the silence and no cause for undue exertion like actually standing up. Every so often you'd hear someone get a great idea and chuckle quietly. But that was it. If someone ever makes a film about greeting card writers, the director is going to have to decide at some point whether to be factually inaccurate or visually tedious.

I had also pictured occasionally having the characters write from home, e-mailing ideas in on their computers. This was also false. For as long as I was there, Hallmark didn't allow anyone to write cards for them remotely. You want the job, you move to Kansas City and you show up to your cubicle five days a week. At a time when the Internet was exploding, Hallmark's higher-ups were late adopters. I guess it was a way of making sure their employees were really committed.

Even my image of myself, furiously typing away for eight hours, turned out to be wrong. I hadn't thought about it before, but writing involves a lot of staring into space very quietly. So if you were to wander into the Trad Humor Department, you might not even see anyone jotting down actual words. We'd be reading magazines (you never know when reading something will trigger an idea), or listening to music, or doodling in hopes that a visual joke would take shape. And of course there were all the things you can do to avoid writing: checking e-mail, looking up card ratings, making lunch plans, going to get soda.

Soda was my favorite delaying tactic. Trad Humor shared the bottom floor of 2440 with Office Planning, and if you went past their cubicles into a back room filled with carpet swatches and used blueprint paper, there was a magical soda machine: one of those 1970s-era types with the sliding screen door at the receiving end. They had them all throughout Hallmark, technically: put in a quarter, and a plastic cup would tumble behind the screen, ice would fall, then generic carbonated water, then (most dispiritingly) a squirt of whatever soda concentrate you'd ordered. I favored Diet Coke, and in this form it didn't mix well, so when the drink was delivered you'd often see brown tendrils of Coke syrup in the cup, trying desperately to osmose. There wasn't even much soda in the things. Frankly, it wasn't worth a quarter.

But what made our soda machine magical was that it was free. All day, all night, we could have all the soda we wanted. For a caffeine hound like me, it was worth the occasionally gloopy aftertaste. No other writing staff had this particular perk, and I indulged it tirelessly. So one day I went into the back room for a drink and saw that The Professor was ahead of me at the machine. He acknowledged me and punched a button. "So how are you liking things so far?"

"It's quieter than I expected. When they told me I'd be joining a Humor staff, I expected more like *The Dick Van Dyke Show.*"

He smiled. "We don't have many Morey Amsterdams here."

"No Rose Maries either, I notice."

We stared for a minute as his cup began filling desultorily with syrup. "Mostly," I said, "it hadn't occurred to me how much of the job would involve just quietly staring into space."

The Professor's eyes brightened. "There's a story there. What I was told is that a few years before I arrived, some suit from Business walked through here, saw that everyone looked like they were goofing off, and became irate. At some high-level meeting, he suggested that writers should keep track of how much time they spent creating actual product, to cut down on all this idleness. But Max was at the meeting, and he went off. 'You must be joking,' he said. 'Do you even know how writing works? You know, I had an idea for a card in my car on the way home yesterday. Do you want me to bill you for that? I get a lot of ideas when I'm in the shower in the morning. Sometimes I get up late at night and jot things down by my bedside. I've been doing that for years. Would you like me to make you an estimate?' The suit backed down, and the idea has never threatened us again.

"It's the price of every creative profession," The Professor concluded. "You wind up creating good art for consumers who don't understand what you do and who don't even know why it's good." He lifted the screen, pulled out his cup, and raised it in a mock toast. "Here's to trying," he said.

"Clink," I replied.

I JOINED THE ROUTINE. We'd come in every morning, do the usual chat and exchange of news around the coffeepot and watercooler, and then sit in our cubicles and the pall of silence would settle, broken mostly by Blues talking on the phone to his wife, or—more often—Max Stentor conducting all his administrative business in his bullhorn of a voice. Other than that, it was *clackety clackety clackety*, with occasional runs to the printer over in the Computer Area, or a session at the light table in the corner if someone needed to do some sort of construction. At lunch, the group I thought of as the core—me, The Professor, Edgar Allan, and Blues—would go to the Crown Room to grab some food, and then come back together to watch *The Simpsons* or *Seinfeld* or whatever tape someone had handy.

One day shortly into my tenure, no one had brought any lunchtime viewing, so we went with a standby: the video library contained *Fawlty Towers*, the classic seventies British sitcom starring John Cleese. When the episode was over, I said, "I never get tired of that. And what amazes me is, as good as it is, I don't understand why no one has ever tried to copy it."

"You must be joking," said Edgar.

"What do you mean?"

"*Frasier*. It's got all the same dynamics. The absurdly pretentious main character, the slow burn, the descent into farce and slapstick. Sometimes I watch that show and I could swear they must have been taking entire plots from *Fawlty Towers*."

I had never been so quickly and thoroughly schooled before, particularly in an area I thought I was expert in. I walked away deeply impressed with Edgar and all the more grateful to be on this staff. Frankly, because of my tendency to use words like *wherewithal* and *inasmuch*, people in offices often assume I'm deeper than I am, and my observations had long tended to go unchallenged. That all ended when I joined Humor. That was, in fact, the best thing about working in the department: learning about humor from other serious students of the craft. It had been years since college, when I'd dabbled in stand-up. I'd sort of dropped it when I met Jane and started spending all my time with her. I'd forgotten how much I missed the professional camaraderie.*

I got brought up short again a week or so later. I had been thinking about the tendency in pop culture comedies to give doctors lame puns for names, like "Dr. Acula" or "Doc Umen-

---

* In fact, the reason I'd never gone beyond open-mike nights in four years of performing stand-up in Tucson is that I actually liked constructing and discussing jokes more than I liked getting onstage and telling them. You could see it in my set. I once performed a joke that went: "These two observant Carthusian monks are walking down the street, and one of them turns to the other and says, 'Wait a minute. Aren't we supposed to be cloistered?'" It's funnier in a library.

tary." And I suddenly stood up and announced, "Hey, everyone! I've just come up with the very worst possible fake doctor name of all. Are you ready? Doctor Zappointment."

Edgar Allan, who was catercorner to me, just looked up, baffled. "Dave," he said, patiently, "you're not supposed to *try* to suck." I made a note: not every joke is worth saying aloud. And what's great is that I didn't feel humiliated or embarrassed; it was just like Edgar had noticed me napping and nudged me helpfully. Here I was playing the best kind of tough crowd—smart people who could see clear through a gag's structure—and it sharpened everyone's game.

I felt particularly happy one day when the troop of us Humor guys had filed in late to a meeting in the main building. We were skeptical about meetings as a group, but we knew we had to go, and as we sat in the back row listening to some suit from Packaging gas on about a bunch of changes in wrapping paper that couldn't possibly affect us, and which could have just as easily been sent as an e-mail, I looked down the row of us and realized we were all bored out of our skulls.

I had a game for just this occasion. I had invented it in church with a friend of mine who, like me, drew cartoons. When our pastor got going on his sermon—which was always slow and peaceful and never particularly interesting—we played a game we called "Cartoon Ping Pong." One of us would take a classic cartoon cliché—the guy on the desert island, the dog fetching a man's slippers—and try to think of a new variation on it. We'd hand it to the other guy, who had to respond by drawing his own version of the same joke, then a new version of a different cliché, which he'd send back to the first person, and on and on it would go.

And now I was at a completely different kind of dull meeting, with a row full of (counting) three or four bored and authority-resistant cartoonists! (We weren't all cartoonists, but several of us were.) This was literally a Hallmark moment. I ripped a piece of paper from my notebook, wrote a quick explanation of the game, and added, "I'll start off easy. My first volley is a *New Yorker* classic: two people talking at a party." And I quickly drew a cartoon (see Figure 4).

FIGURE 4

"OH, YOU'RE A POET? WHERE DO YOU TEACH?"

I passed it to The Professor, who read it and shrugged—I knew he didn't draw, so what did I expect?—and he passed it to Edgar, who read it and shrugged and handed it down to Blues Man, who shook his head and passed it, and it got passed and passed all the way to Black Peter at the end of the row, who looked irritated and sent it back, hand to hand and finally back to me. No one even wrote, "Nice try!" I realize the drawing was a little shaky, but still, that hurt. It was my first wholesale rejection by every single member of our staff, and I realized that even here, there were probably limits to what I could expect to get an audience for. I wasn't in church anymore.

I still had lunch with Deedee every week or two. It was great to be around her, because I've always liked hanging out with women better than with men, and in Humor I was starting to starve for female company. But it was also nice to have our meetings be public, scheduled forays. I found I worried more about her influence over me when I pictured those days in the wings, working together, feeling her constant presence. She was safer as a vacation from my regular life than as a regular intimate part of it.

Deedee had a boyfriend now and, because he was apparently the jealous type, she couldn't have lunch with me one-on-one anymore. ("Does he work here?" I asked. "No," she said. "But he'll know.") So she began inviting me to small-group lunches with all her female friends, who I thought of as "the gaggle." These included artists and line designers and even one Humor writer from way over in Shoebox. They were all technically single, but they all had boyfriends, and that was what they talked about.

One day Jillian, a bug-eyed, chirpy-voiced cartoonist (also from Shoebox), said, "Can I say the one thing that freaks me out about William is his"—she mouthed the word *penis* silently, looking furtively at other lunchers around us in the Crown Room. "It's not just uncircumcised, but it's *curved* and it's got all these *lumps* and I just . . ." She mimed a shudder.

"I dated a guy like that," said Melanie, who was the eldest of the group, an elegant but severe-looking Season artist of about thirty-five. "It—you know—curved *left*. I actually had to get out my *Kama Sutra* and refer to it for real until we could figure out a position that worked." She took a bite of a sandwich, reflecting, "If he'd been even a little bit longer it wouldn't have made that much difference. But he was a short guy. What can you do?"

"Jerry's not circumcised," announced Deedee. "I got used to it. But the first time I went down on him I had to close my eyes and—" She looked at me. "Oh, look, everyone! Dave's blushing."

"That's so cute," said Jillian.

"I'm sorry," I said. "I grew up surrounded by conservative Christian women. I've never heard a conversation like this before. Not even among my guy friends."

"Wow. Were you all gay? Just kidding," said Melanie.

"Well, this probably isn't appropriate lunchroom conversation anyway," said Jillian.

"You started it," said Melanie. Then she pointed at Deedee. "And you made it worse."

"That's me," said Deedee, obviously amused. "Slut. Whore. Keeper of the gutter."

"I'm afraid I have to go," I said. "But let's do this again really soon. I mean it."

AFTER THIS CONVERSATION, where I felt like my eyebrows had been forever burned into a shocked arch, I stumbled over to the Idea Exchange to question Josh Broward about it. We went out into the hallway where we could murmur, and I explained what had happened. "I don't understand why they would talk so . . . provocatively, you know, with me right there. And one of them said I was cute when I blushed. I wonder . . . do you think they were all flirting with me?"

Josh laughed. "It sounds to me, Dave, like you're every woman's gay best friend."

"Huh," I said. "Well, as long as I'm safe . . ."

"Oh, you're quite safe, I'm afraid," said Josh, and he said it with such certainty that I almost got angry. Was I that harmless? I didn't mind a little safety—I was, after all, committed to Jane— but it would have been nice to have it be my choice.

I WASN'T ALONE in my effete harmlessness. It was all of Humor. One time Blues came in and said, "Hey, guys. My car won't start and I think it's the spark plugs. Does anyone here know how to change spark plugs?"

Dead silence. It hadn't even occurred to me, personally, that spark plugs might need changing, though now that I thought of it, it made sense. "Anyone?" said Blues, and I started to feel really bad. I suspected that changing spark plugs was actually pretty easy. I was just glad I could afford to go to Jiffy-Lube for such things. Blues laughed and said, "Wow. At least now I feel better about myself."

It wasn't just cars. About two months later, Blues came in— Blues was, I guess, the most traditional guy-type guy on our staff—and said, "Hey, did anyone see the game last night? It was really good, and I wanted to talk about it." Again there was silence—and even at the time, I had no idea what season it was or what sports event might have just happened. "I'm sorry," said

Edgar Allan, and The Professor said, "I couldn't tell you." Blues looked around at the rest of us and laughed. "Of course not," he said. "I'm the only man here. My god." He retired to his cubicle, we went back to work, and testosterone quietly gnawed off its own leg trying to escape.

ON A PROFESSIONAL LEVEL, I started learning the little secrets every card writer knows. For example, you almost never write a sentiment that says, "I thought you'd like to know . . ." when you can simply say, "Thought you'd like to know." That way, the card can be sent from an I or a We, and you never know who might be buying. That's also why so many cards have cartoon animals on the cover—we call them *spokescritters*—or cartoon humans of no discernible gender or race, which we call *neuters*. People won't buy a card that looks like it should be coming from someone they can't identify with. If you make the speaker a white male, only white males will tend to buy it. Yellowish cat things sell better every time. One by one, I internalized these rules until they became second nature.

At the same time, I also tried to find ways to contribute to the overall group, to have a particular social and professional niche. I had volumes of humor essays at home by everyone from Mark Twain to Merrill Markoe, so I photocopied a number of my favorites and left them in the magazine area so we'd all have something a little more apposite to read than *Entertainment Weekly*. (We subscribed to *The Onion*, but there was only one, and someone else always had it.) I made a cryptic crossword for Max, which he solved overnight and handed back to me the next day. "Thanks. This was great. But I feel bad that you're spending all this time writing a puzzle that only I got to see."

"My fiancée is in another state. What else am I going to do with my spare time? It helps keep me sane."

"Whatever. It's your nickel, I guess." He tapped the paper. "If you've got the inclination, I'd love to see a cryptogram-style cryptic. I love ciphers, and cryptic crosswords almost never use them." I went home that night and obliged him with a cryptogram cryptic. To this day, it's the only time I've actually filled a custom puzzle request, and I did it with a happy heart, the way two Civil War enthusiasts might trade expensive replicas because they're just so happy to be able to talk about their obsession to each other. But I didn't feel like I really belonged yet. I didn't have a professional identity. I wasn't "the guy who does that one thing." And I wasn't sure what to do or how to get noticed for doing it.

THEN ONE FEBRUARY MORNING the Weather Channel had something I'd never seen before: a Frostbite Advisory. The temperature was 20, but the wind chill was zero, and the advisory said, "Avoid prolonged exposure of skin to the cold air. In case of frostbite, get medical assistance immediately." *Frostbite!* I hadn't heard of frostbite since I was eight, when I read in the Boy Scout Handbook that you should cover the affected area with something warm until you could see a doctor. If you weren't careful, you could lose part of your ear. At the time, I lived in Tucson and saw no reason to bother with a Winter Survival merit badge. I skipped ahead to knots and Morse code and had never thought of it again till now.

Thank you, Weather Channel! I prayed. *You saved my earlobes from disfigurement.* I called work to say I'd be a little late ("There's a weather advisory," I pointed out on my message), and then I wore every piece of armor I had: Long underwear. Snow pants. A face-covering ski mask. A big blue puffy polyester jacket—and of course I flipped up the hood and tied it on tightly. Feeling like the bubble boy, I drove up Grand, passing a little park, where I saw a young man in shorts and a T-shirt, throwing a Frisbee to his dog. *The hell? Didn't this guy hear the warning? This is* frostbite *weather.*

On my way out of the parking garage I passed several people in mere sweaters and scarves, and I started to think I'd made some error in judgment. Did people here routinely ignore cold advisories?

Then it hit me: of course they did. Just as I had once routinely ignored heat advisories in the desert. When it got really hot, you were warned to hydrate, to wear sunblock, and to stay out of the sun to ward off stroke. But it never actually hurt anyone except the very young, the very old, and the otherwise infirm. Maybe a frostbite warning was the same way.

It was too late, however, so I waddled into the Humor Department, just as everyone was standing around talking over coffee. Max whooped and cackled. "A weather advisory! Oh my god, Dave! I didn't realize you were serious!" I sighed, and explained what I'd learned about weather today. But even after the joking calmed down, Edgar Allan kept looking at me, disbelieving. "You know what, Dave?" he said. "If this department were a sitcom, you would be the wacky neighbor."

I didn't correct him, but privately I thought, *You don't mean "wacky neighbor." You mean "irrepressible wunderkind."* It didn't mat-

ter either way, though. Here I thought I'd needed to establish a
particular persona, and it turned out I already had one that people were noticing. It wasn't like being, say, the Disney expert or
the pop-up ace. But it was a sign that I was starting to belong,
and that was enough.

THE NEXT DAY I WAS sitting in the window near Blues, musing
thoughtfully and scratching down the odd idea. I know it was
February because looking out the window became a hobby for
all of us then. It wasn't exactly intentional—it's just that Hallmark was, you'll recall, built on a steep natural incline. As a result, the 2440 building where we were happened to look down
on one of the steepest roads in the city—Gilham Road, which
runs at damn near a forty-five-degree angle for several hundred
feet. In winter months, since Kansas City, Missouri, was chintzy
with the road salt, you could look out the window at almost
any time—but especially at lunch—and watch cars come off
the main road at the top of this hill, take a slow right turn, and
suddenly start skidding terrifyingly down Gilham, some swaying,
some fishtailing, car after car after car. They all made it as a rule,
but the cars never looked stable. It was like some sort of new
sport: extreme steering. It terrified me, and reminded me how
much I hated winter. And I don't think I was alone: all the guys
would actually stand for minutes at a time, shoulder to shoulder,
and look silently out the window as the cars sledded away. I
think we were all holding our breath.

One day while we were doing this, one car didn't actually
steer for once. It just came off the top of the hill and charged
straight down. It sailed along in a straight line, veering a few

degrees, then wider, then wider—and when it reached the bottom of the hill, it smashed into a telephone pole as if it had been aiming for it deliberately. No skids, no brakes, nothing; just whoosh-and-wham.

Here we really did catch our breath.

"Jesus!" said Edgar Allan.

"Oh my god," added Blues. Max came over, and The Professor filled him in. It was weird being above this accident, having seen the before and after, taking in the whole thing like gods. We tried to find something to do.

"Can you see the license plate?" said someone. We couldn't. "It's a white . . . maybe Lincoln? Station wagon."

"He must have had a death wish," I said. "He drove straight for the pole."

"He chose the right road for it," said The Professor. "That thing scares the bejeesus out of me."

"Man, I'd hate to die in a car wreck," said Blues. "If I was going to kill myself, I'd just . . . get a gun or something."

"I always pictured you as the autoerotic asphyxiation type," said Edgar Allan. And we all laughed—the brief, barking laugh of people who need to laugh but know they shouldn't.

"Well, there's nothing we can do now," said Max. "Just get back to work and I'll check the news tonight and see if they mention anything." We wandered back to our stations and tried to write more jokes about how much it sucked to get older. *Another birthday? Look on the bright side . . .* It turns out even greeting cards writers have to learn an instinct for coldness.

9

How to Write a Card

MY IMMEDIATE CHALLENGE OVER THE NEXT FEW WEEKS and months was to figure out how to write a card. The first thing anyone wonders is "How many of them to I have to write?" And no matter who I asked—Max, Josh, my fellow Humor guys—they all said, "Don't worry about it; just do what you can." (Except once, I asked Max, "So if I can do, like, twenty-five jokes a day . . ." and he said, "Well, for god's sake, don't kill yourself." So less than twenty-five was my only guideline.) For the first few months I wondered how a system like this could possibly work.

The answer is: it works just fine. You aren't judged on the number of cards you write in a day. You're judged on the number of acceptances you get in a year. If you wrote only two cards a week, and they both always got accepted, you'd be doing just as well as a guy who writes ten cards a day and gets two of them accepted every week. My own writing rate was around five to twelve cards a day, depending on if I was writing straight jokes or something more complicated, and how easy the caption was. And my acceptance rate was rarely more than ten percent. My guess is that both of these rates are about average, although I heard of one writer who really could knock out twenty-five eight-line poems a day—most of them crap. You just have to find your own best signal-to-noise ratio.

The other nice thing about being judged annually rather than weekly is it allowed the writers to have flat-out blocks on occasion. If I may be permitted to zip forward a few months, my first real block hit me when I was tasked with writing my first Easter cards. It felt like this sudden collapse of creativity came from nowhere, but really there were a number of reasons Easter was such a pain.

1. *It was October.* We generally wrote seasonal cards six months in advance. Which means we're always writing, say, Christmas cards in June and Valentine's Day cards in August. But the biggest disconnect of the year for me was always Easter, where you're trying to write about springtime and bunnies and flowers . . . and you're surrounded by bleak weather outside, as well as paper cutouts of scowling pumpkins, black cats, ghosts, skeletons, and red-and-black streamers in every hallway and around every non-Humor cubicle. It's harder than usual to find the mood.

2. *It's a small-scale holiday.* Easter, while not as bad as Halloween, Thanksgiving, and pissant nothings like Arbor Day, is still, as the company phrase goes, "not perceived as a greeting card holiday." If there weren't Easter baskets, we'd probably sell no cards at all. This means that only greeting card diehards are going to buy the cards, which means you have a smaller number of cards that have to be usable across a wide range of situations and relationships. Which means, in other words, that the "jokes" can rarely be edgy, unusual, or interesting. Every pitch needs to be

slow and in the strike zone—not much fun for anyone who enjoys pitching.

3. *It's an inherently joke-poor holiday.* Christmas is the best holiday ever from a joke writer's perspective. Everywhere you look there's a fun prop to wring a gag from: flying reindeer with funny names, snowmen, stockings, mistletoe, coal, Santa Claus, gingerbread houses, "naughty or nice" lists, familiar public-domain Christmas carols, and of course all those wonderful, wonderful elves.

Easter, by contrast, has exactly three props: eggs, jelly beans, and bunnies. Bunnies subdivide into bunnies in general, chocolate bunnies in particular, and the Easter Bunny most of all (most popular joke: "What's up with a bunny laying eggs?"—with variations on "The Bunny Trail" a close second), so maybe it's as many as five props. Not that small numbers of props is the whole problem. You could work with only five props if they were somehow resonant and flexible. Valentine's Day has only a few props as well—chocolates, hearts, roses, cupid's arrow—but they all speak to some deep craving or happiness, and carry a lot of culture with them. Our hearts beat daily. Flowers always symbolize transient hope. Chocolate is a constant joy and a constant temptation and is convenient shorthand for an entire host of jokes women make about themselves and their bodies. But Easter's props are not only few in number, they're metaphorically thin and utterly inflexible. How often in our daily lives do we ever bump up against colored eggs? Bunnies are nice, but what the hell do they really mean to anyone? And what's resonant about a goddamn jelly bean?

Then there's the religious angle. At Christmas you can joke about shepherds, angels, mangers, and especially the three wise men. But on Easter, all you've got to work with is the Resurrection of Jesus from the Empty Tomb. Even though you could come up with jokes about it, they'd never get turned into cards for fear of offending people, so you're just wasting your time. And in a way that's what the experience of writing for Easter is like, even on a good day: a series of potential brick walls. "How about this? . . . No, wait, that's been done. Or this . . . Oh, right, that's a stretch . . . Or this? . . . No, dammit!" Do this enough and you'll actually feel like you're trapped in a mental hedge maze that someone is making you solve even if you hate it. Easter is so, so, so not funny.

4. *Plus, it gets worse with subcategories.* Within Easter you also have captions that are already difficult even at the best of times: the not-so-close relative captions like Uncle, Cousin, and Niece, where we don't offer many cards, and yet whose people's feelings vary widely about (some folks love their uncles, others never see them) so one card has to be general enough to cover a lot of different sending situations and—in humor—a widely varying sense of what's amusing. At this point the walls of the maze actually start to close in on you.

While writing all this down, by the way, I just thought up an idea for Easter to Niece. So for the rest of this chapter, why not come with me as I write? Let me show you what I've done so you get a sense of the process. First, here's my idea:

[Outside:] Happy Easter—
[Inside:] To "The Niece-ster!"

I'm so well-trained that, at first glance, I don't even notice how idiotic it is. (Or rather, I notice it, but table it as a secondary consideration.) What I mostly notice is that it fits the caption exactly to the point, adding no extraneous information that would give someone a reason not to buy it. ("To my wacky Niece-ster" would result in a lot of consumers going, "It's cute . . . but my niece isn't exactly wacky." No sale.)

The next thing I notice, however, is that there's no emotion being offered. So this is where we trot out the word *special*, which is the hardest-working word in greeting cards—a nag so ill-used that its entire body has long since stiffened into jerky:

[Outside:] Happy Easter—
[Inside:] To my special "Niece-ster"!

Special means whatever good thing the sender and/or receiver want it to mean, and it doesn't necessarily mean "We're really close" or "I like you" or even "You're a good person." But it sounds good. Very useful word, *special*. What a shame there aren't more synonyms like it, but nothing else in the thesaurus quite does the job.

Hallmark has a reputation for being mushy, but its writers actually do write emotionally distant cards—especially for Mother's Day, where only an ogre wouldn't send his mom a card, no matter how awful she is, and in a situation where conflicted feelings often run very deep. And in humor cards, *special* is the way we do it. In this context, a card that says "Happy Mother's Day—To a Special Mom!" might just be the equivalent of saying anything from "I love you so much that I can't even say anything else," to "At least you gave birth to me, you abusive harpy." Precisely because *special* means nothing, the sender who says it has plausible deniability.

So the niece is now special. This adds warmth. But it also

sort of throws off the meter. Plus I'm noticing more and more how wince-inducingly stupid the sentiment is. I really want to make its very stupidity the joke, to turn it into something that has a shot at being amusing to me, the poor card writer. Something like:

[Outside:] Happy Easter to "The Niece-ster!"
[Inside:] Apparently that's how you kids talk these days. I saw it on *Oprah*.

And the immediate problem, as I mentioned earlier, is that not everyone is going to find this joke funny, and that hurts sales, and people don't have a lot of Easter-Niece cards to choose from. (Besides, anyone who's really cool would just give their niece a General Easter card, on the theory that you don't need the word *niece* on the cover to know who it's for. The people who like very specific captions tend to be very literal-minded.) Plus, of course, a sixty-year-old card buyer who has a forty-year-old niece is not likely to call her a "kid." So that's probably going to be rejected by the editor.

Having tried three attempts to make this work, I'm not ready to give up yet—there may still be something in there—but I definitely have to put it aside for now. So I write on my notebook "Happy Easter / To the (or my) Niece-ster" and move on. When I'm brainstorming like this, I like to get as many as twenty ideas down in the first few hours of the day, and then hash them out in detail in the afternoon. Besides, I just thought of another joke, which started when I thought, *What would be a bad thing that could happen on Easter?*

[Outside:] Cartoon of a neuter person looking in horror at their Easter basket: "Yuck! These jelly beans are all licorice!"
[Inside:] The Easter Bunny has a naughty list, too.

Not bad. It feels fresh, plays with common tropes in an unexpected way, and for people who buy and read a lot of cards, freshness is no small feat. The downside: it's definitely not a niece card. So that caption still hasn't been tackled. Also, it doesn't actually contain a sentiment yet. This is a "shared joke" card, which means it skews younger and will probably go from a friend to a friend. Which is fine, except those people are less likely to be in the card stores on Easter. So at the end of three hours, I have two pretty decent ideas, and a dozen dead ends, but I still haven't come up with a card to make the traditional consumer happy.

At this rate, I could still come up with eight to twelve cards in a normal workday, which sounds like a lot. But it's not, because around ninety percent of cards get rejected by the editors who see them. And of the ones that get accepted, probably only half actually get made into cards. (Editors often take good card ideas that they don't need right away in the hope of using them later in another line or at another season. Then, in my experience, they forget all about them.)

Ooh! I just thought of another one! Its connection to the one I just wrote should be obvious:

[Outside:] Cartoon of two neuters looking at their Easter baskets.
Person #1: "That's weird! The Easter Bunny filled my basket with brown jelly beans!"

Person #2, looking dubious: "Those aren't jelly beans."

I've got a joke here, but no inside sentiment. Usually in cards like this, the inside makes a punny reference to the outside cartoon, like so:

[Inside:] Here's hoping your Easter comes out all right in the end!

And I'm done! The card is sort of a long shot—it's a poopie joke, and Easter is a famously humorless holiday—but it seems funny, different, and it actually contains an honest-to-goodness wish. That's a traditionally structured card with a real chance, and on that upbeat note, I can stop this demonstration.

What you didn't see in those preceding paragraphs was the five hours on either side: the two hours of warm-up, and then the three hours of frustration as I tried to make this chapter end with an honest-to-goodness Easter niece joke. But you don't always get the endings you wish for, and sometimes your brain simply refuses to play with the toys you give it. If I'd simply stuck to General Easter, I'd have had fifteen to twenty ideas in the same amount of time. But solving the Easter Niece problem for an editor who needs it solved would be a real feather in my cap.

★★★PAUSE FOR THUNDERCLAP★★★

I was going to add a final section to show that you also write fewer cards when you're writing light verse, so I was going to demonstrate the writing of a silly Easter poem . . . and then, to my own great surprise, I actually solved the Niece/Easter problem! I started with a generic "Hippety-hoppety, here comes the Bunny" sort of verse in mind, and then as I was turning it around, looking for some new kind of angle, *ta-da!*

Here comes Al, the Niece-ster Bunny,
Bringing treats to all the nieces!
Baskets full of Easter goodness:
Colored eggs and candy pieces!
Every stop, from start to finis
Comes with happy thoughts, to boot!
Here's to you from Al and me, niece!
(By the way, he thinks you're cute!)

That just took me ten minutes. And I know that's extremely fast, which is one of the reasons they liked to put me on verse projects. You'd mostly expect that to take an hour, and you wouldn't expect more than four or five such poems in a day. (Of course, this is a rough draft; I need to fix lines five and seven, which are not only kind of a stretch, but also limits the sender: what if the sender wants to say, "Happy Easter from us" instead of "from me"? Finding the right wording could take the full rest of the hour.) So that's another reason "How many cards do you need to write"? isn't always a sensible question. If you were filling a verse requisition instead of a straight joke, you could expect to take all day and maybe only come up with one sixteen-line verse.

But this verse has another happy ending: I am scratching off the "Happy Easter/To the Niece-ster" note—its work here has been done (thinking about it in the back of my mind is presumably one of the reasons I thought of the poem's first line), and nothing I can do with it can possibly compete with the poem, which I love. At least the idea died for a good cause.

But you know what? I can't leave this demonstration without showing you one more card type: the mechanic.

Cards in general took longer to make in Humor than in Main Writing—and longer than they took in Shoebox, too. In Shoebox, they scrawl everything on three-by-five cards—they're almost all punch lines, and the humor is very heavily verbal. In Main Writing, the visuals almost don't matter at all: it'll be whatever background suits the mood of the piece. So those sentiments were almost always typed out as straight poetry or prose without a whiff of cardstock anywhere.

In Humor, though, we had a cabinet full of pre-scored, easy-to-fold blank cards that we wrote and drew everything on, because many of our jokes were visual, and many of our verses needed very specific breaks that would be hard to convey by simply writing straight onto a piece of paper. More to the point, half of our writers were also cartoonists who simply liked having something larger than a three-by-five card for a canvas.

But as long as it took to draw a card normally, it could take forever to do a mechanic. A mechanic is any card that does something unusual when you open it: a pop-up, a turning wheel, a shutter closing; any movement whatever. The crazy thing was, we had to mock up all our mechanics ourselves, reinventing the wheel every damn time. It wasn't enough to simply say, "And then on the inside the skunk jumps for joy: mechanic." We were expected to figure out how to make the skunk jump, and how high. Which makes sense when you think about it: a jump-for-joy mechanic has to look like a jump for joy, not like a balloon slowly rising. If you're trying to sell a card with it, you have to know it can be done.

But Christ, what a pain it was! Like so many other duties at Hallmark, this was a skill that you had to learn on the job—unless, I suppose, you'd spent a dissolute youth obsessed with origami. Our department would buy pop-up books and ruthlessly dismantle them, like pre-Enlightenment vivisectionists pursuing dark secrets. Edgar Allan once turned a Camels cigarette ad he found in *Rolling Stone* into a successful cop-handing-you-a-ticket mechanic; a desperate glance through a kid's haunted house pop-up book reminded me that you could do more jokes per page if the reader simply opened a lot of flaps and shutters. Mechanic cards sell for more and result in more profit, and a brilliant new mechanic was a real achievement anyone would be proud of. Mechanics are the only reason our department had a light table in the corner and a supply of X-acto knives.

The best mechanic I ever came up with was a card in the shape of a cute cartoon dog's head. At its collar, down at the bottom, was the line, "Heard You're Sick!" with an indicator that told you to slide the collar's tag to the right. When you did, the dog's head tilted left, the upper ear popped up, and the tab revealed more words: "Sorry! Get Well Soon!" The text was all but worthless (it had to be; there was no room to write on the dog's neck), but the mechanic! It was everything a good mechanic should be. It showed emotion, it was surprising, it did more than one obvious move, and it had such great toy value that everyone I showed my mock-up to five different people, and they each read it, smiled, and then moved the mechanic back and forth at least three times. It would have been perfect, except for one thing: when the mechanic was sent to the Art Department, the assessment came back declaring that it would cost about $8 per unit to produce. Until head-tilting technology gets cheaper, that poor cute dog will never have its day.

And that mechanic, rough as it was, took me three days to work out. Three days for one card. That's the slowest I ever worked when I was in Humor.

The easiest mechanic, and the cheapest, was the slide mechanic, which you've probably seen. When you open the card, some cut-out something-or-other slides along a narrow slit, from left to right, coming to its final rest in the appropriate position when the card is fully opened. Usually this is used in Love cards or Husband to Wife/Wife to Husband, where the punch line involves two characters cuddling. These were so common, they were practically the only mechanics we were allowed to not mock up: "slide mechanic; two bears embrace" was sufficient. But everything else we had to do ourselves.

I was going to suggest a mechanic for Easter, to show you how we come up with those, but I suddenly thought of something else: the Attachment card, which is the mechanic's less popular cousin. An Attachment is just what it sounds like: a card whose punch line involves having some object taped or glued to the inside: a plastic fork, a fake penny, a paper clip. The most bafflingly successful attachment card I ever wrote was a Disney Father's Day card, with Goofy as the spokesperson, saying:

[Outside:] Thought I'd getcha a TIE for Father's Day! . . .
[Inside:] . . . So I found THIS in the produce aisle at the grocery store!
[Attachment: a Baggie twist-tie]

The challenge here is twofold. First, the joke is always the same: Outside: "I got you this cool-sounding thing for whatever holiday this is!" Inside: "But this crappy object inside is either what I was really talking about, or it's evidence that something went wrong with your present! Get it?" It's very, very hard to escape this structural cliché . . . and the customer might not even want you to.

Second, though, is the additional problem that there are only a limited number of things you can efficiently and effectively tape to the insides of cards. And even when you get a list—and we had a big long list of objects, single-spaced, two columns, just over a full page—you quickly see that many of those objects aren't exactly conducive to jokes. For example, we could technically tape a tiny plastic car to the inside of a card. But I never saw a single card that figured out how to use that for comic effect. I suspect that eighty percent of the attachments we did were repetitions of the same five objects: straws, toothpicks, coins, cotton balls, and golf tees. If there's ever been a funny paper-clip card, I haven't seen it.

Of the top five I just listed, the obvious choice for an Easter attachment is the cotton ball. It's a bunny tail, right? For that reason, it's also probably been done to death, but still—I feel like there's potential freshness in it, and I'm compelled to try.

An hour passes as the author thinks about new variations on the familiar "I wanted to get you a . . ." opening. He tries dozens. Nothing sticks. Pacing ensues. Then he tries to come at it from the other direction: what more or less unexpected thing could a cotton ball represent?

Got one. How about this:

[Outside:] I wanted to get you a lucky rabbit's foot for Easter! . . .
[Inside: cotton ball attachment] . . . But all I could find was this bunny's ass.

Yes, it's rude. No, it probably won't get accepted. But I think it's funny. And you know what else? I hate Easter. I'm tired of it. And fortunately, I don't have to write for it anymore.

10

After the Honeymoon

MY CUBICLE IN HUMOR WAS UNMAGICAL AND UNLOVED. It was also the only choice I had, and it was obvious immediately why no one else had taken it: it was the high-traffic cubicle.

You can picture the Humor office as four quadrants of a giant plus sign. Upper right were the entryway, kitchen, and supply closet. Upper left was the conference room. All the writers' cubicles were in the lower left, and the lower right contained Max's office and the printer/computer area. All the traffic tended to flow along that plus sign . . . and I had the only cubicle that was right at the juncture of both highways.

Within my first hour I could tell this wasn't going to work. The cubicle walls were low, and any sudden movement from someone standing up to go do something would startle me and take me out of my creative trance. It happened so often that it wrecked my whole brain: even when things were silent and immobile I kept bracing because I knew something *would* happen.

The second problem was odder and more surprising: I kept having the urge to lie down. I just knew that if I lay down and no one bothered me, I could think better, but I knew it would be impossible to lie down in full view of anyone passing by from any direction and not have to field comments. So, to avoid the urge to lie down, I stood up and started walking around. Pacing seemed to trigger something in my brain—to turn the world into fuzz where, instead of waiting for the next distraction all the time, the background became a sea of so many distractions that I didn't pay attention to any one of them. If I couldn't lie down, walking wasn't a bad fallback.

I could get away with idly walking in circles around the cubicles for a day or two, but after a while I knew I'd have to do something else. I started tracing a little triangle: sit at desk and don't write; walk around and write and hope not to annoy people; go off to get more soda. If one wasn't working, I'd try one of the other two. Within two weeks I was already starting to feel a little crazy. Why couldn't I just sit in a cubicle and write like everyone else? Black Peter was starting to make a little more sense. Once he was in that conference room with the door locked, I bet he was lying down. What else were those beanbag chairs for? I wished I could go in there, but what right did I have to even ask? He had eight years' seniority on me, and was a bona fide brilliant greeting card writer. I hadn't even written anything that had gotten accepted—and even if I did get an acceptance soon, it would be a year or more before those cards went to market, and even longer before they sold through and I had a rating to my credit. (And let's face it—as I was still learning, my first ratings were liable to be fairly weak.) So how could I have the gall to demand equal conference room time?

"I hope it doesn't drive me crazy," I said to Jane after my first week of suffering. "I shouldn't even be complaining to you.

You've got papers to grade and research to do, and I imagine your life is much harder than mine."

"It's funny you should say that," said Jane. "I only just realized that you're actually serious about this cubicle problem. I can't always tell, you know? It seems like you're always making fun of something, and you do it with jokes, so I can't always tell when a complaint is really serious. But I can hear it in your voice tonight. You need a better cubicle. It never occurred to me that that would be so important."

"Me, neither," I said. "It's crazy, though. I finally got the job I wanted, and it's like they have me working right next to the . . . you know . . . the . . ."

"The flogging room?"

"Or the maggot hatchery. Exactly. Something like that. What good is having a job I want if I can't sit down to do it?"

"In grad school," said Jane, "we have flogging rooms. You just get used to it."

AND THEN, entirely by accident one day, I found a handy solution to my cubicle problem: sitting in windows. It was a nice mix of the solidity of a cubicle and the freedom of walking around, and it had an additional thing I hadn't known was inspiring: I could dangle my feet. Apparently my brain liked that. Many of Hallmark's windows are very wide, with deep sills, as if the architect was accustomed to designing college student unions.

Traditional Humor in particular was all windows, so there were plenty of places to sit. Well—one or two, anyway. I found that The Professor and Edgar Allan were often sitting in their chairs and staring out the windows behind them, and it was unsettling to be in their eye line. But Blues, who had the lower-left corner cube, simply worked intently at his desk and almost never turned around. So I could sit in the window behind him with one leg up, notepad propped on it, and look outside onto Gilham Road and think.

AS I SETTLED IN TO what I thought of as my real job—practically my destiny—I slowly came to realize the ways that being a greeting card writer changes you. The first is relatively simple: once people know you work for a greeting card company, you can never, ever forget anyone's birthday. "How could you forget?" they say. "Don't tell me you couldn't find a card."

My next revelation came a few months in, one Monday morning when I was feeling a little tired and just wanted to stay in bed. I stumbled off the bus, looked at the Hallmark building, groaned a sigh . . . and then realized, *Wait a minute. What the hell am I complaining about? I get paid to write greeting cards! That's my only job!* That's the other painful truth about greeting card writing: you're not even allowed to complain about work. No one would have any sympathy. You can't imagine Willie Wonka saying, "Dammit—another day in the goddamn candy factory."

I slowly learned that even a good job is a bit like a romance: you can't be deliriously smitten forever. Eventually you commit to the long term, and you have to get used to a little bit of boredom and some minor irritations along with the good times. By May, I had gotten over my crush on Hallmark and was starting to figure out how the marriage would work. And so I found ways to complain. The chief frustrations were our consumers—who never got more sophisticated or funnier—and our captions: just when you'd finally figured out a tricky double-rel* card for Valentine's Day, you'd have to do another one for Easter. Properties could be a pain in the ass, too. If, like me (and like many Humor writers), you hated writing for Disney characters, you were guaranteed to hate two dozen requisitions a year. I just kept telling myself, *I'm not homeless, and I don't have to be a printer.* If you'd told me I would need encouragement to write silly poems for money, I would have thought you insane. I imagine even porn stars think, "Once today's sex is over, I'm really looking forward to my needlework."

Underneath all my complaints, I was simply frustrated by my own performance. I'd been told I was part of a revolution that would set the greeting card world alight with brilliance, but all I'd done was perform to expectations and I was starting to wonder if maybe Regina had oversold me to myself. I was good at verse, and everyone knew that—Max once singled me out for praise for an anniversary poem I did with a spades/hearts/clubs/diamonds theme. ("This was a nicely visual poem," he said. "The artists hate it when they get something that doesn't suggest any pictures." I nodded like this had been my plan from the start.) But The Professor was great at poetry, too. Blues and Black Peter were brilliant cartoonists, and Edgar Allan was good at pretty much everything, including pop-ups. I wanted to be "the guy who did that one thing"—I didn't know what that one thing was,

---

*"Double-rel," or "double relative," cards are those that go to a couple you're related to: Aunt and Uncle Anniversary, Merry Christmas Grandma and Grandpa, etc. Cards to two people are four times as hard to make funny. Hallmark prides itself on having obscure captions like "Halloween Birthday" and "Ruby Jubilee" and Grandpa cards that address him as "Pop-Pop." But they never risk being funny.

but I knew I wouldn't be truly happy till it happened. For the moment, it was a struggle just finding a window that was free.

TEN WEEKS IN, AT LUNCH with Deedee and the gaggle, Deedee asked me how it was going.

"I got my first compliment today," I said. "Max liked an anniversary poem I did with a playing-card theme. You know, you gave me a diamond, and now we're in a club, and so on. He said it would be easy to illustrate."

"That's great," said Deedee, and she seemed sincere. I noticed then that I didn't really have anyone besides her looking out for me. (Blues told me once, "We don't have mentors in this department. *Tor*mentors, maybe . . .")

"He's right," said Jillian. "I hate when I get a poem you're supposed to illustrate and there's nothing to draw. I don't know why they do that."

"Also, I had this really interesting conversation." I told them I'd passed The Professor's computer and saw that his screen saver was something in Greek. "He said it was a quote from Epicurus that said, 'Live in such a way as to be forgotten.'"

"Why would you do that?" said Melanie. She sounded disgusted.

"Apparently, the idea is, if you try to be famous or rich or powerful, you're almost certainly going to fail, right? Since most people aren't any of those things. But if you try to seek the simple spiritual pleasures in life—love of your family and friends, contentment with what little you have—you're guaranteed to be happy."

"You sound religious," said Jillian. "Is he religious?"

"Dave here is a virgin," said Deedee, with a naughty grin.

"Really? At your age? Why?" said Melanie. "Are you religious? Because, I mean, why else would anyone . . ."

"That's a really good question," I said. I was religious, but not the fundamentalist they were all suddenly thinking I was. In my new life here, where I wasn't defending myself against conservative Christians or what my family thought, my long-standing plan to stay a virgin until marriage suddenly seemed kind of dumb. I couldn't even remember why it had made sense in the first place. "I'm religious," I said. "But I'm not conservative. I like sex."

"In theory," said Melanie. "Right? Because you obviously don't know."

"I have faith," I replied.

WHAT I DIDN'T HAVE WAS a church. After several good months at the church around the corner—the one with the amusingly crazy basement mass—my attendance became spotty. The diagnosis was easy. For one thing, the odd feeling about the weirdness of mass that I first felt on Thanksgiving had never really gone away. I thought I could just keep going to mass and ride through the spiritual desert, but I hit another snag: it was a pain to get up in the morning . . . and when I managed it, I didn't feel the effort had been repaid afterward. I'd mistakenly expected church in Kansas City to work exactly like every other church I'd ever gone to: join the youth group, hang out, discover new friends. But here in adulthood, there was no youth group and no one hung out, and everyone had friends already. If it was just me and God, I figured He could just meet me at home.

I tried not going to church, too, but that didn't work either. It's a universal experience for anyone who's ever left a fundamentalist church to suddenly feel spiritually empty. This is not because such people actually are spiritually empty; it's because they're less mentally busy with religious thoughts. When you read the Bible daily and guide your every action by its code, and when you picture God watching everything you do, and you scan the world for chances to do some small good or to share a message of salvation—well, if you do all this for years and years, when you stop doing it, you can feel unduly lazy when all you've really done is stopped being a judgmental, hypervigilant ninny. But sometimes you really are lazy. How can you tell the difference from inside your own confused feelings?

What I'd been doing on Sundays instead of church was going to Barnes and Noble's religion section and reading whatever looked interesting. But every time I did, I kept passing by a place called Unity Temple on the Plaza, a nondenominational interfaith church that had been there since 1948. I knew I was resistant to traditional Christianity, but I thought maybe the thing I believed now was something like the radical spiritual Christianity they profess. I looked up the church online. It seemed spiritually very much in my corner: pro-woman, pro-gay, focusing on love rather than on obedience to ancient written rules. In fact, the website overtly stated that the church kept a lot of ideas deliberately undefined and free. That could be exciting. So on Sunday I popped in to give it a try.

Like Visitation, the Catholic church I'd tried earlier, it was about a third full—this was clearly a church on a downward slide from some fifties-era heyday. I sat in the balcony to get more of an all-encompassing view of the proceedings. Of course, it was also a way to stay physically aloof and avoid commitment—I was ready to bolt.

It sounds silly, but what I was mostly bugged by was the familiarity of it all. The church had the same old pews I'd been sitting in forever. They had honest-to-god hymnals and sang "For the Beauty of the Earth" (an almost theology-free song, suitable for even an agnostic). They had announcements and an offering. The bulletin was the same folded eight-and-a-half-by-eleven-inch sheet of paper I'd seen thousands of times before. I had expected something different. I was hugely disappointed.

Perhaps I expected too much creativity. It seemed to me that if you were going to leave behind the basic tenets of Christianity, if you started just from goodness and decency and grew your church from there, then why in the world keep the unrelated accoutrements of Christianity around: the altar, the pews, the hymnals, the same old order of service? If you're spiritually free, and anything's possible, why not do something totally new? Doing the same old thing after being liberated would be like setting your dog free in the wild and then the next day taking the leash for a walk. This church's heart was in the right place, but everywhere I looked I saw empty leashes.

I seemed to want a religion without any clichés. But since a ritual is, by definition, a repetition of something familiar, I started wondering if what I wanted from a religion was actually even possible. I didn't go back. I simply scanned the horizon for something else I could connect to. Nothing came immediately, and yesterday's spiritual emptiness slowly became how life just felt, every single day.

———

ONE DAY IN LATE SPRING, after I'd officially been on the Humor staff almost four months, The Professor did a stunning thing: while I was sitting there in the window, notepad on my knee, he suddenly stood in his chair and then flopped himself belly-down on the cubicle wall he and Blues shared. "You don't mind if I work here, do you?" he said, flailing his arms toward Blues's face. Blues laughed . . . and then they both turned to look at me, sitting in the window.

"Oh, I'm sorry, Blues!" I said. "I hadn't realized I was basically in your light."

"It's pretty obvious . . ." said The Professor.

Blues looked embarrassed. "Yeah, I'm sorry. It is a little distracting, you know. I know the window's nice, but you've got your own cubicle . . ."

"Sorry," I muttered again. I flushed and retreated back to my place. For the next hour I fumed and my face burned. So I'd been bothering people all this time and they hadn't said anything. It made sense. Greeting card people are inherently nice, so of course they'd avoid direct unpleasant confrontation. (I mean, yes, it was also passive-aggressive, but that's how my family was, too. It was a language I understood.) And it sure was nice of my fellow Humor guys to make it a joke and not complain to Max behind my back. But fuck. If the window was out and this damn cube was impossible, where the hell was I going to get writing done?

SO I VENTURED OUT ACROSS HALLMARK, just as I'd done when I was an editor, simply writing away wherever I could: window ledges, stairwells, hallways, snack-machine kiosks. Anywhere would work, but I found windows were the best, with brightly colored offices second. That's how I wound up, weeks later, sitting uncomfortably on the guest couch in the Idea Exchange when the boss of IdEx, Addie Apian, came over to me, frowning like I was a puzzle. "David. What are you doing outside of work?" she said.

"What do you mean?" I asked. "I go home, I watch movies, I call my fiancée."

"But what about your brain? What's it doing? What have you done for it recently?"

I laughed. "I don't understand."

"I see you, and you look like you're always thinking, Dave. You look restless. I know how that is. Do you know that you can take university classes for free? Hallmark will pay for them."

"They will?"

She nodded. "It's like creative renewal. God knows it's helped me. Every time I start crawling the walls here, I just sign up for another course at UMKC. They've got some really good graduate programs."

"Wait—so you can take advanced classes, too?" For some reason I thought there'd be a basic-instruction-only clause, maybe to prevent employees from getting uppity.

"I've got five master's degrees," she said. "And I'm working on another one now."

"Jesus."

She nodded. "Sometimes it's the only thing that's kept me sane. I'd look into it if I were you. I think you could use it. All you have to do is clear it with your manager."

My first thought was, *I could get a master's in religious studies or*

theology. That would be fun. I could even branch out into something completely unusual for me, just for the heck of it, just for
the one class. Anthropology or architecture. Evolutionary biol-
ogy would be a hoot, I bet . . . I don't know how she saw it in
me, but Addie Apian was dead right. The excited part of my
brain had been sleeping, and the thought of a new intellectual
challenge woke me right up and filled me with energy. This is
one reason Addie Apian was such a brilliant manager and had,
to my mind, the best staff. *What a great company,* I thought. *This
is how life should be.*

"I'll be just like The Professor!" I told Jane. "He not only
writes cards, but he actually teaches philology on the side. He
says it keeps his brain sharp. That's what I want to do now—I
can feel it. I've decided to major in theology. I'll finally get to
read Barth and Schleiermacher and Tillich and all these people
I've heard about since undergrad. I've always been curious but I
know it's intense and I never had an excuse to study it all. Maybe
I'll even learn koine Greek."

"You have the best job," said Jane. "And no prelims either.
Can I work for Hallmark when I graduate? Do they need an
academic film archivist?"

"I'll ask," I said.

"I DON'T LIKE IT," said Max the next day. "Theology isn't related
to anything Hallmark does."

I was floored. His refusal hadn't taken five seconds. "But Addie
Apian said it didn't matter."

Max sighed. "I'm sorry, David. Maybe other managers can
justify it. But I have to go and request the money, and I can't do

it if it's not going to benefit the company. You have to be able to show me a specific reason or a specific way that this skill you're getting is going to benefit the company or improve your work. Like business, for example. If you wanted to take some business classes, you can go with my blessing."

Business. I'd gotten a job writing greeting cards so I could *avoid* business. What else would Max sign off on? Maybe accounting, which was also depressing. Or finance: ditto. I couldn't get over the disappointment. It was like I'd been offered a free day in a candy store, and then when I got there, they said, "Sorry—all we've got is black jelly beans."

"What about . . . creative writing?" I asked.

He nodded, smiling. "That I could justify. Sure. You want to take a creative writing class, go ahead. Fill this out and I'll be happy to make it happen." He handed me the forms, and I went to my desk—one of the few times I'd ever actually sat there for more than an hour. Max's smile bothered me, though. He seemed to think that we'd argued and come to a reasonable middle ground. But I already had an MFA, so I didn't need any more classes. They'd be useless to me. Plus, I'd been in writing workshops for eight years, and the thought of going back to do yet another, when I'd been dreaming of doing something completely different, was quite a comedown. But if you'd transcribed our discussion, you'd be forgiven if you believed that it at least had the rhetorical structure of a compromise.

So I took the class. On the first night, the ten of us sat quietly as our white-haired professor cleared his throat and said, "Welcome to the graduate creative writing class. Now: What is a 'story'?" And proceeded to draw a diagram of conflict and resolution that I'd been taught in my sophomore year in high school—and that E. M. Forster had already mocked to its death sixty years ago. I got a story out of it, but that was the end of my Hallmark-sponsored college career, except that I now receive regular dunning from the UMKC Alumni Foundation.

But even this silly experience left me surprisingly smitten with the contact high of being back in college. It had been stupid, but nicely familiar, and I kept thinking what a great job that professor had had. A quiet office. Only a few hours of class a week. Even summers off. I could live with that.

This wasn't the first time I'd thought about maybe getting a job teaching writing. But it seemed impossible. I already had an MFA, so since that was a terminal degree, there would be no point in getting further training. To get a Ph.D., I'd have to go back to school to train in some completely new discipline—but I already knew that writing was all I wanted to do. So I was stuck. The other problem was that I hadn't published anything—and even worse, I had no teaching experience. I had been offered a teaching assistantship back in grad school, but I'd gotten such a huge discount through working for the university, I decided to keep my job with PREVENT and let other people suffer the pain of teaching. In retrospect, that was a mistake, and I could see no way to go back and get the same degree over, differently this time. It just didn't make sense. Again, I was trapped. At least, I would be until I finished one of my novels. I told myself I wanted to be a novelist, but every time I started writing, I got about fifty pages in before I'd get bored, put it away, and weeks later try something else that would also bore me after fifty pages. I was up to four unfinished novels already, and this pattern of not finishing books didn't seem likely to change.

SPRING CAME, and Romeo left the company. I found out when I got to work and noticed an unusual hush. Everyone was standing around and looking as Romeo collected his papers and muttered quiet good-byes. As I watched—a little helpless, since I didn't know him very well—Max Stentor explained: "We're trying to be quiet about this, because he got a job with another card company out in California. Technically, when that happens, you're supposed to call security and have them escorted from the building. But he's a good guy. He ought to be able to say his good-byes without being treated like a criminal. So just keep it quiet today."

Max left, but I remained standing there and found myself beside Edgar Allan, who stared intently at Romeo, looking concerned and just a tad jumpy.

I said, "I can't get over how much paranoia there is about corporate espionage around here. Or maybe it really is real."

"Oh, it's real all right," said Edgar. And then, with significant nods and pauses, he told me what was apparently a favorite story of his. Many years back, a guy in Hallmark's Marketing Department had gotten a call from a stranger. When the Marketing guy didn't hang up, the stranger said, "So, what are you doing?" The guy was polite, and before long they got involved in this long conversation, and they actually hit it off and traded numbers. But later the marketer thought about it and realized that this stranger had asked a few detailed questions about what kind of work he did. ("Oh, you work with greeting cards? What does that involve?") So he reported the call to his manager and asked if he should report this person. The manager said, "No! I bet you anything that's Unnamed Card Company!* If he makes you an offer, take it!" Sure enough, the stranger called back again, and the third time he offered the Marketing guy a little money if he'd inform on the company. He reported this to his manager, the manager talked to his higher-ups, and they started using this guy's contact—this stranger who'd just called out of the blue—to feed disinformation to a rival card company.

Edgar said, "It got to the point where the contact wanted to meet in person to trade some documents, and they actually had this whole setup straight out of a spy movie, with a booth picked out in a restaurant and two guys from the North American Management Team in the booths on either side, listening in on mikes. The guy was wired and everything."

"Really?" I said. "At a greeting card company?"

"It's all business. People do it all over, no matter what they're selling."

"So did they arrest anybody or blow a whistle or something?"

"I don't know," said Edgar. "I've heard the story a couple of times, and no one's sure about the ending. Whatever happened, it's probably not the interesting part."

ONE NIGHT I DID TWO UNUSUAL THINGS: I stayed at work past five, and I was actually working at my cubicle, bent over a cartoon I was quietly penciling into shape. The Professor and Edgar Allan were working late as well, and apparently they didn't see me there, because The Professor walked over to Edgar's desk,

---

* Not their real name.

where he had a number of his old cards on display. The Professor picked one up and said, "This is really good." Then he added, "Of course, if I was Dave, I'd say, 'Oh my god! This is so good! You're amazing!'"

Edgar chuckled and said, "You should jump up and down when you say that. 'Oh my god!'" He flailed his hands in mimicry.

I was only half hearing this, but I thought I'd heard my name, so I raised my head and said, "What?"

They looked at me and froze. Edgar in particular blanched. The Professor cleared his throat and muttered, "Sorry . . ." and they went back to work. I didn't think much of it, finished my card, and left.

As soon as I got home, I received two long e-mails, one from The Professor and one from Edgar Allan, detailing exactly what they'd said, both of them deeply apologetic. "I was trying to be a badass," said Edgar. The Professor noted that he kidded all his friends all the time and it wasn't supposed to be personal.

I actually laughed. I wrote back to both of them and said, "Until you apologized, I didn't even realize what you were doing. But I'm not offended. In fact, I'm actually really happy about it. Just think—most people never know what their friends and coworkers say about them behind their back. I actually got lucky enough to overhear it. And it's not that bad. You made fun of me for being ridiculously intense and enthusiastic. That's exactly what I would have said about myself. If that's the worst thing people say about me, I'm fortunate indeed."

And with that, we were friends again. This more than anything reinforced my belief that Humor was where I needed to be. Not only did my coworkers apparently have the same beliefs about me that I myself held, but if they were ready to write long apologies over an incident this tiny, then maybe they were just as conscientious as I was about trying to be decent to others. Even when they'd been trying to be jerks, they couldn't help but be trustworthy. After that night, we weren't just lunch colleagues. I invited them out to play poker, and we started making it a regular thing. All three of us became friends outside of work. It started to feel like I was surrounded on all sides by a new self-chosen family.

WE NEEDED TO REPLACE ROMEO, and in June, while I was walking through the Humor Department, I noticed a file folder near the magazines that had a cartoon character I recognized: a dumb guy wearing a hood and a cape and not much else.

"My god!" I told Max. "What's the Masked Galloot doing here? That used to run in my college paper. How did you get this?"

"He's applying for a job," said Max.

And a week or so later, Kenneth Riley entered my life. He was the first hire who was younger than me—he had literally just graduated from the U of A art school—and when he arrived he still had some acne. I call that young.

I greeted him as soon as he was free from Max's tour. "I was a huge fan of your strip," I said.

"Thanks," he said. "They weren't all great, though. Sometimes when I had a deadline, I'd write them at the Carl's Jr.—you know that one across Park near Mama's Pizza?"

I did know it, and we talked nonstop for the next hour, and we had lunch together, and we hung out that night, like two

Americans thrilled to have found each other while abroad. It was
fun to be with him, not just because we both needed to remember our homes in this strange new town, but because his energy
was different from mine or the other writers'. Most of us were
ferociously mental. You could see the sort of geeky disconnect
every time we made jokes: the joke would blast forth, but the
body remained stiff, never really losing itself in a giggle or a
feeling. We held ourselves cautiously, perched in our own space,
as if at any point someone might ask us to move to a less-cool
table. Kenneth, by contrast, simply laughed without embarrassment and seemed to completely occupy any place he happened
to be, even if he was just standing and slouching with his hands
in his pockets.

   With the arrival of Kenneth, my social circle established itself.
At work, it was lunch with Kenneth, Edgar, The Professor, and
Blues. After work, it was me and Kenneth and Edgar—the young
single guys who could actually afford to go out. Kenneth made
a welcome fourth for poker night, and when that went well we
started seeing movies and watching *South Park*. Kenneth already
had other friends—he had interviewed as an artist, too, and had
gotten a few phone numbers—and through them I started to go
to pizza parties and birthdays, and I began to finally feel like I
could live in Kansas City.

SUCH A GOOD FEELING couldn't possibly last. And one spring
Monday, as soon as I got in, Max came at me, looking grim.
"We need to talk," he said, and he escorted me into the confer-
ence room.

"David," he said, "you wander around too much. I need you here where I can count on you, so you go to the meetings when they're scheduled. So you're here for the product kickoffs and any visitors we get."

I was flabbergasted. This had come out of nowhere. Friday he had seemed fine, and today I was not only in the doghouse, but I had a long list of priors that I didn't even remember well enough to start to defend. And I hadn't even missed any meetings or kickoffs. Not that I was aware of, anyway. Maybe I'd missed a few and was only getting told about them now. Was he being a strangely unhelpful manager? Or was I actually crazy?

Since I could barely take in all this new information, I grabbed hold of the one thing he'd said that had made sense to me. "But you know I can't work in that cubicle," I said. "Can you move me? Like I could take the cube that just opened . . ."

"I like you in the cube you're in already. It's where I can see you," he said.

"But I need to pace! That seems to be the way it works for me."

"David, for Pete's sakes. You're not that special. You're not so good that you get to be all that strange."

I knew that, but it still stung to hear it. "How about this?" I said. "I'll buy a day planner and I'll check with you to find out what meetings there are. I'll also buy a watch with an alarm so I don't forget."

He chewed his lip. "Okay," he said. "Try that and see how it goes. But David—I don't want to hear about you."

At the time, I thought *I don't want to hear about you* meant *I don't want to hear about you missing a bunch of meetings*. That was

the only conclusion I could draw: that I'd missed meetings without noticing, and that the people who ran these various meetings were doing a mental roll call and noticing I was missing.
What else could Max have meant? *If there was something specifically
wrong, surely he would have told me*, I thought.

And yet, as I reflected once I'd reached my shitty little too-
public cubicle, the whole experience felt eerie the more I re-
played it. *What if it's me?* I thought. *What if I'm annoying the hell
out of everyone, only no one's telling me, like when I sat in Blues Man's
window? Even worse, what if I have something like Asperger's syndrome
and I really can't read people's emotions?* But then I thought it was
crazy to think that an entire company would be as passive-
aggressive as Blues and The Professor, not really saying anything
until they cracked. Especially Max, who was pretty hard to shut
up. If I was just generally annoying, I think I'd have known by
then, because Max would have simply said, "You're really annoying." I hadn't heard that. What I'd heard was that I had specific
things to work on—especially my wandering—and I had promised to focus on those. Closure achieved.

Also, I realized, if I had to decide whether I was crazy or Max
was mismanaging, surely the cubicle problem proved the latter.
Max rode these hobby horses now and then. If his refusal to
move me was one of those, I had just had the bad luck to wander into his sights, and now I simply needed to make nice and
wait for Tropical Storm Max to blow over.

I bought a Franklin day planner, and I set my new watch timer
so an alarm would go off fifteen minutes before any meeting. It
still wasn't foolproof. Often I'd pick up the day planner unthinkingly first thing in the morning, clamp it under my arm, and pace

furiously through the company, my brain circling predatorily around *Easter Snoopy, Easter Snoopy, Easter Snoopy,* completely forgetting that I hadn't set my watch for any alarms at all.

IT WAS IN AUGUST that I got the message. After every sentiment meeting, Max would bring back the cards we'd submitted. The acceptances would be posted in a display sleeve near the filing cabinet, while the rejects would be piled, unloved, on the top of the same cabinet. This was what I loved best about the job: the way you were competing with one another to see who got accepted and who didn't. It wasn't mean competition—no one ever got mocked for sucking. We all knew the pain of rejection. But it was also great to see when you'd scored a solid hit and to track who'd had the best week. This was just for short-term ego satisfaction, since everyone was up one week and down another. But it kept us all sharp, and I loved being part of a crack team of joke writers and seeing how we got problems solved.

But sometimes, depending on the editor, when a season was through, we'd get something even better: sales results. You could see all the actual printed cards in a line with their ratings attached. This was more exciting than merely getting acceptances from an editor. It carried more status, too. It didn't happen often enough.

One afternoon I came in and noticed that everyone was hovering around a sales results display—cards from the just-passed Easter. (I wasn't in it, since it generally takes a year or more for a card to go to market.) The big joke was that the highest-rated card was one Blues wrote that had a photo of a baby bulldog puppy resting its snout near a grown-up bulldog's ear. It said,

"Psst! Hey Dad! . . . (inside:) . . . I ruv roo!" Oh—and the bulldogs were wearing Photoshopped bunny-ear hats. It killed.

We were merciless. "Well, this fine poem I worked on for two days is certainly clever," said The Professor, holding up one of his middle-rated cards, ". . . but of course it's no 'I ruv roo . . .'"

Blues was protesting: "I know. I'm sorry. I don't get it either. I barely even wrote the card. I just stole the dialogue from Scooby-Doo."

I was joining in the merriment when I got tapped on the shoulder. It was Max, back from a sentiment meeting. "Congratulations, Dave," he said. "You're the king of Pooh."

He handed me five cards with "OK" on them. I'd submitted six. My usual hit rate was one in nine. "Wow," I said.

"They really liked the way you handled the emotion. Pooh's different, you know. He's not just jokey, but he's sweet and cute. You nailed it, and not all Humor writers can do that. People noticed."

Max was not one to give compliments lightly. I felt instantly bulletproof in a small, ridiculously specific way. *King of Pooh. Five out of six. I'll take it.* That's all I wanted, it turned out. To be the best for just one day.

I wanted to call Deedee and tell her. Then, of course, I needed to tell Jane after work. I sat in my cubicle and felt suddenly at peace. Success at work. An active social life with great friends. What more could one ask for?

"WHEN YOU VISIT," I told Jane that night, "I think we should actually have sex." She was planning to visit me for Christmas break in December, so there was no reason to mention it in

August, but I had all my rationales worked out and needed to spill them. "I'm not a fundamentalist anymore. We're both liberal Catholics, we'll have been dating for six years, for god's sake, and I don't think it would hurt our marriage any."

"Okay," she said. "Just as long as you're okay with it." In the history of our relationship, I had always been the one setting limits, and she had always gone along with them out of respect for my religious beliefs.

"Okay, then!" I said, and added "Yay!" She laughed politely. Then, since we could both feel tension growing, we changed the subject to other things. How nice it would be for her to meet my coworkers, what the weather was apt to be like. Anything but sex. Neither one of us, after all, knew what the hell we were doing.

11

The Visit

IN SEPTEMBER ON ONE OF MY WANDERINGS, TRYING to think up a few wedding sentiments, I passed by a conference room over in the art area of Season. Dan was in there—a slightly older, mild-mannered Season editor with an easy smile. He'd been at the company for about two years, and sitting in front of him were four young people—obviously either summer interns or new hires. I waved, and Dan said, "Dave! Come in here and meet these people."

"I really shouldn't," I said. "I'm trying to write and you're obviously busy."

"Oh, come on," he said. "I want them to talk to a real writer. You'll be perfect."

So I went in. They were interns. Dan happily introduced me as a writer and wanted to know if anyone had any questions. The kids asked me about what it was like on the Humor staff. I told a few stories, and it felt good—I was an actual authority, teaching eager new students: Professor Greeting Card. Dan said,

"Now, what would you all do if you had to plan a Christmas line? How would you get this writer motivated?"

"We could do pictures or mock-ups of the concept, so they could see and get involved," said one kid.

"How about an exercise, like we do in drama, to loosen up their brains? Like free writing," said another.

"Make it fun," I said. "A lot of editors bring us cookies, and that gets us to the meeting. But if you want to motivate us, give us a challenge that we haven't done before but we're pretty sure we can handle. For example, Dan here did a penguin-based promotion just a few months ago and that was a hoot. We all loved working on it."

"Uh, Dave," said Dan. "This is for the interns to talk out among themselves."

"Oh, sorry. I'll just leave now. Is that okay?" Dan nodded, and I left.

TWENTY MINUTES LATER, I had no sooner opened the door to Humor when I heard "David, get in here!" It was Max, and he was barely below screaming. Eyes dark, he strode to the conference room and motioned me to follow.

Alarmed, I sat down, and Max practically slammed the door and leaned forward on both his hands. "David, I've had it with you! I try and I try, but there's no getting through! You cannot walk around talking to people! I just got a call from Beth in Season saying that you barged in on an orientation meeting."

"That's not true," I said, surprised at my own calm. We never yelled in my family, and I had always been a little curious about what I'd do if anyone ever yelled at me. Not surprisingly, I talked

like my dad, calmly and rationally. "I saw Dan and he asked me
to come in and help. I answered a few questions. Then figured
I'd been taking too much time, so I left."

Max, who had probably been expecting abject apology, actually turned red. "David, that's not the point! You can't just walk
in on people! I'm tired of you going all over the place, inter-
rupting people, taking up their time, and then I get all the complaints! I'm tired of it, David! I've had it with you!"

Complaints? Multiple complaints? *Like how many*, I wondered. Why was this the first time I was hearing about it? So the
problem hadn't been me missing meetings at all. It was me in-
terfering with other people's work time by chatting them up.
And if that was the case, why didn't anyone say, *Go away, Dave. I'm
busy*? I wanted to ask all this, but I felt guilty about my wandering already. It was a necessary evil to get my work done, but I
didn't feel good about it, and this trouble I was in felt spiritually
justified, even if it wasn't logical. It was the world as I knew it:
bite the apple and everything goes to hell; touch the ark of the
covenant and get swallowed up by the earth; doubt the Bible and
get tortured by the Antichrist. There was no logical connection
between action A and result B, but God could be a touchy bastard sometimes. Even as a skeptic, I was still carrying around a
frightened evangelical's interpretive baggage.

Also, of course, when you're getting yelled at for a history of
"complaints," it takes a very strong person to say, "Please—list
these complaints individually so I know just how many people
hate me, how much, and so this chewing out can last five times
as long." That would be like swallowing the gun barrel. I wasn't
that sturdy. All I knew was, I'd gotten one complaint months ago,
had tried to fix it, and had apparently walked straight into wall-

shaking calamity with no further warnings in between. My hope now was to simply fix the most obvious symptoms, and quickly, so this never happened again. For a moment, I even worried that this might cost me my job, but my optimistic instincts said surely not. This was all a misunderstanding. I didn't mean any harm.

"Is that the problem?" I asked. "Not the wandering so much as that when I wander, I talk to people, and then they complain to you?"

"You talk way too much, David. People are trying to work, and—"

"Okay. I'm sorry about that. Now that I know it's annoying people, I won't do it anymore."

Max, only halfway through his apoplectic fury, looked unsure how to take this. "I don't want any more calls!" he said, still yelling.

"If that's what the calls are about, they'll stop immediately."

"Okay!" Max was still flushed. "Because I tell you, David, I can't take much more of this!"

"Right," I said. "No one told me before. Now I know, and I can change."

It's times like this that I wish I were an actor, with some awareness of what my face looked like it was doing. I felt hot and defensive, but I was committed to staying calm, and god knows what expression this mix resulted in. Did I look smug? Standoffish? Overly earnest? Whatever it was, it didn't seem to make Max happy, but we didn't technically have anything else to discuss. So he slowly rose from the table with an uncertain, and certainly unconscious, sneer. And I stayed in the conference room for a while, shuddering. I hate being around rage.

So the thing Magda had warned me about so long ago was

actually true: I did talk too much. So why was this only the second time I was hearing about it? And why didn't anyone tell me to my face to simply go away? For that matter, if I was that consistently annoying, why did I have friends at all? I clung to that obvious fact: Edgar had made a joke about my werewolf beard sprouting out of my eye sockets, so I'd started trimming it. Kenneth had said that unshaved necks made a guy look like a convict, so I started shaving my neck. If I was doing anything truly offensive, surely they'd have pointed it out, possibly in an anonymous note left on my desk, along with an apology for mentioning anything.

I ate lunch with the guys that day and we didn't discuss it. If anyone had had anything to say before, it was too embarrassing now to bring up. The conference room walls were absurdly thin and no match for Max's voice. Everyone knew my whole situation. What's worse, there was nothing they could do to help. I was the only one who couldn't seem to sit still. That really was my fault, and no one knew how to fix it—except for my idea of getting a different cubicle, but Max had already nixed that.

One thing was certain, though. Being yelled at made me want to stay in the Humor area even less. But now the entire company felt unsafe to me. I spent the rest of the day trying to figure out what had gone wrong. It couldn't just be me, because although I'd never been popular with office managers before, I'd certainly never gotten screamed at. The worst thing about me that I knew people talked about was that I was unusually enthusiastic and friendly, and that didn't seem like a screaming offense. There must be something else wrong—some drastic clash between me and some invisible, unspoken part of the Hallmark environment. But what was it?

Had Dan been a total asshole, inviting me in just to complain about me later? Had one of the interns known enough to rat me out in some way? Or had some nosy-ass third party watched me enter the room and decided to make some backstabbing call? Or was my memory bad? Had I been less innocent than I could recall? None of those possibilities seemed plausible, but obviously *something* horrible had happened.

I felt completely helpless. All I knew was that all of Hallmark felt like it was suddenly honeycombed with Judases, and the only guys I could trust were my fellow Humor writers—the coworkers I was wandering away from every day so I wouldn't annoy them.

A MONTH PASSED, and my worries at work continued, though I was true to my promise: I wandered around but didn't talk to anyone, so not even a two-faced hypersensitive weasel could complain about me. There were no further flare-ups, but even the fear of being yelled at again unsettled me. There was only one bright spot, and it happened on my birthday.

I often joked that if you had no money to live on, you could simply wander the hallways of Hallmark and eat three huge meals a day of cake and ice cream. In a company of six thousand people, there's always a birthday on every floor, and everyone brings too much to the party. No matter where you wander in Hallmark, it seems, you can always find some half-eaten cake in a box in some corner, surrounded by brightly colored napkins and paper plates filled with homemade cookies or pie wedges.

Except in Humor. Perhaps because there were no women in Humor, there was also no cooking and no decorations. What happened was that Max would hand you a birthday card with five lottery tickets in it. ("The rule is, if you win big, we split it. One year, someone won fifty dollars.") Then he'd take the whole department out to lunch. Not bad as birthdays go, but decidedly not traditional.

This particular October, on the occasion of my own twenty-eighth birthday, I had a concern, and everyone knew it. The previous week, I had discovered a lump in my neck, just under my chin near my throat, and it hadn't gone away. I had made an appointment with a doctor, but the earliest he could see me was my birthday, so I'd had a week and a half to stew and fret to anyone in earshot. I tried not to overshare, but it was hard to think about anything else with that lump just sitting there. I hoped my friends understood. On my birthday, the plan was to go to the doctor in the morning, and then instead of coming to work normally, I'd simply meet everyone at the restaurant for my birthday party, which would be either really celebratory or really fucking grim.

So when I came into the restaurant that day, I headed straight over to where the entire department was waiting for me. I sat and said, "Good news! Turns out it's just an ingrown hair. I've got drugs and it'll be gone in a few days."

"Oh, thank *god*!" said Edgar Allan. "I was afraid I'd never be able to make cancer jokes again."

We all laughed, because we completely understood why he said it: not that we go around making cancer jokes, but humorists like to have as many tools available as possible. When my mother came down with Alzheimer's, I wrote in a diary I kept at the time, "I promise I will let other people continue to crack Alzheimer's jokes without trying to make them feel guilty." As if this was a moral declaration that any sane person would give a damn about. But it mattered to me, and it mattered to Edgar, and as odd as it sounds, my heart warmed when he said that. *This is why I belong here*, I thought. *These are the only people I know who are like this.* This place would still be my perfect home, if only Max could learn to like me. I looked at him, laughing across the table, and hoped he could remember this moment instead of his irritation. Change from my side was turning out to be harder than I'd anticipated.

The fact that I was able to joke a little around Max gave me courage, so I started looking for other jokes I could bring him. I knew that the best way to do this was to show him a card where the art had gone wrong. For some reason, the writers and artists never actually talked to one another, so Max was constantly sending off finalized copy to artists who screwed up the execution. He loved nothing better than to have some card in his hand that he could show to the higher-ups at some future meeting. For example, Edgar Allan once wrote a card that said, "I was going to put all the candles on your birthday cake myself . . . but I was afraid I'd get carpal tunnel syndrome!" Not a bad sentiment for the mid-nineties, when carpal tunnel syndrome was still a new concept. But the artist who drew the card clearly had no idea what carpal tunnel syndrome was, and so he'd illustrated the sentiment with a picture of a big moving van, with two bears unloading a single huge candle from the back. Max showed it to everyone and then cackled for an hour in his office. He surely stuck it to someone later in the week, and it probably made his quarter. If I wanted to get back in his good graces, a find like that, I thought, might go a long way.

As I mentioned earlier, napkins in the Crown Room were

taken from existing Hallmark product—usually napkins that weren't selling so well, or napkins they had simply overproduced. They weren't, however, *old* napkins as a rule. Anything you found in the Crown Room you could still probably find on the shelf of some Hallmark store if you looked in enough of them.

One day I was eating alone and noticed that the napkins du jour were Marvel superheroes napkins—not any one hero in particular, but the whole pantheon: Spider-Man, The Incredible Hulk, Thor, Captain America, The Fantastic Four; those guys. I had always been a fan of Marvel comics as a child (and, okay, into my early twenties), so I took an extra napkin to look at.

When I unfolded it at the table, I saw that it was pretty much what you'd expect: all the characters sort of charging at the viewer from the center of the paper. What was interesting, though, was that the background wallpaper was a series of random frames taken from various Marvel comics through the years. (This wasn't Hallmark's doing; every property from Disney to Peanuts offers style books that contain not only guidelines for how the characters can be used, but sample wallpaper patterns that you can deploy for whatever projects you might work on.) *What fun!* I decided. *I'm going to squint at the background and read a Dadaist collage comic strip.*

I soon found, however, that the panels were always tantalizingly unreadable. You'd get two words of a sentence, and the rest would be blocked—first by Thor's hammer, next by The Hulk's left foot. I kept trying and failing, trying and failing, and halfway down the napkin I still hadn't read a single complete sentence in any of the back panels.

Eventually, down near the bottom left, I finally found a sentence—the only complete sentence on the entire napkin. The panel showed a generic suit-wearing thug sneaking up behind someone, gun extended, and his thought balloon read as follows:

"You and your accursed experiment shall die within this room! Heil Hitler!"

My hands trembled a little. An accidental Nazi napkin! I could actually imagine a kid squinting at the napkin and asking her parents, "Mom, what does 'Heil Hitler' mean?" This was the gold mine of hilarious printing errors. It was perfect in another way, too: not only did it say "Heil Hitler," but it did so a mere inch above the Hallmark logo; what luck that it had appeared in the worst possible position on top of everything else! What I loved most about this error, though, was that you could even see exactly how it happened—the artist had just used the old-panels wallpaper that Marvel had supplied, and hadn't thought twice about it. After all, who reads the wallpaper? It was a perfectly understandable disaster, and that's what made it human and charming.

Since I had a spare, I ran to Max Stentor and said, with a giddy pride, "This is one for the record books—a new classic to add to your bad-product collection." I explained and handed it off as a loving gift. This was going to get me my long-needed pat on the head.

Max, however, didn't laugh. He stared at it, looked very serious, and said, "Thanks, Dave. I'll get on this right away." He took the spare napkin and, as I walked away, I could hear him making a call. The next day, all the napkins were gone. I imagine they vanished from all the Hallmark stores as well. Possibly overnight.

I still have mine, which is probably the only one left in exis-
tence. Even though it didn't pay off like I'd hoped it would, it's
still wonderful on its own merits. I've held it close to my heart
all these years, and it is now framed on the wall of my apartment.
I may never own anything cooler.

THE BEST THING, THOUGH, happened a month later: Jane was
coming for a week at Christmas break, and we were going to
finally *go all the way* in the biblical sense. For most of November,
my concentration was shot, and whenever I thought about it, I
found myself holding my folder over my pants front like a junior
high school boy.

She came in on Sunday late at night, having had a huge argument with a cabdriver who had gotten lost on the way from the
airport, drove her all the way across Kansas City, and tried to
charge her $120. Since she was nice to a fault, even when she
was getting ripped off, she still paid the guy and gave him a
double-sized tip, and she was pissed about that, too. So as I
helped her inside with her luggage, I could read her scowl and
I knew there would be no sex that night. Jane's bad moods were
storms you had to wait out; they couldn't be cured by kissing.
When she was angry, she didn't even like to be touched. Fortunately, I had that king-sized bed. We were able to sleep on the
mattress all night and not touch distractingly.

Then a funny thing happened on our journey toward sex.
Neither of us brought the subject up. There was a standard blow
job Monday night—in the bed, lights off; Happy Thanksgiving
(Belated)—and then nothing on Tuesday. Then another blow
job on Wednesday, and before I knew it, it was Thursday and

we hadn't talked about actual coitus at all, and her visit was
nearly over. It's embarrassing to even write this now, since it's
obvious we were both terrified. But at the time, I simply couldn't
understand what was wrong. Also, I couldn't find a natural way
to bring it up, and trying to just let it happen had so far led to
no "it" at all.

On Friday, she visited me at work in her usual T-shirt and
jeans, and I dragged her all around the company, introducing her
to Deedee, to Kenneth, to Josh Broward, to my fellow Humor
writers. It was nice to finally have these two worlds of mine
reconciled; they'd been rumors to each other for so long. Everyone was polite, Jane told jokes, we all smiled, and it all went
swimmingly.

But then she had errands she intended to run—she didn't
explain what—and since this would leave me a little bit of time
between work and her return home, I used the day to think
about what nice thing I could do for her that might turn into
actual fucking.

In my theoretical ideas about sex, and based on what I'd
learned from Cinemax, I knew a few things that sounded like
fun: sex on the living room floor, sex against a wall, sex in the
car, maybe even mild role-playing. These vanilla dreams were
quite exciting to me, but at the same time I knew they'd never
happen with Jane. Once, when I'd visited her in Minnesota, I'd
come up behind her while she was washing the dishes and she'd
shrugged me off, saying, "I'm sorry, Dave, but I'm concentrating
on dishes now. We'll cuddle later, 'kay?" And we did cuddle
later—but not in front of the TV. I put my arm around her on
the couch and again she shrugged and said, "I'm sorry, bear, but
I really need to watch this. Just wait till bedtime." And sure

enough, at bedtime we cuddled and she blew me. This, I figured, was what was meant by compromise.

So if she didn't like even being hugged while washing the dishes, anything even more spontaneous was clearly out of the question. But we needed to do something, and fast. I could actually feel myself panicking for reasons I couldn't quite understand. I pictured our sweet legitimate marital sex and imagined it would be wonderful in some vague way. The extra stuff—the sex around the house, which isn't mentioned in the Bible or in Marriage Encounter classes for Catholics—just wasn't in the cards, but since I was going to be allowed to have sex *at all*, surely asking for a specific type was just selfish quibbling. What I needed to do was think of some sort of compromise—something sexy and fun besides just the bed, but something sort of defined and stable that she'd be comfortable with, too.

I had figured out at this point how to think about the emotional needs of the consumer, so I soon came up with a lovely idea. Although my fiancée was clearly not into anything dangerously unstructured, I knew that she loved taking baths. A long leisurely bath had been something she'd set aside time for on every vacation we'd ever had. But we'd never had a romantic bath *together*. Bingo! So in the time before she came back from wherever, I popped into one of the girly boutiques on the Plaza and shortly emerged with a dozen small candles—the low wide kind you burn for saints, only vanilla-scented—along with lavender bath oil and a box of lambent red beads that dissolved in water and contained unicorn tears or something. Each candle had its own little aluminum holder, so I was able to simply set them on the floor and light them. Eight to trail up the short hallway into the bathroom, plus one candle for each corner of the bathtub: it was perfect. (Well, almost perfect; before I could set down the candles, I had to hurriedly clean my apartment, since there were papers and books all over the floor and furniture; it was like I had decorated with kindling.) I ran the bath, made sure it was nice and hot so it would still be warm later, noticed the specks of mold on the shower curtain and removed it completely (I hung it over the closet door in the bedroom). Then I put on some soft music—Bach performed by Isaac Stern—and waited, all the while keeping a nervous eye on the newspapers still visible in the living room. I could hardly stand the suspense.

She returned in fifteen minutes with her arms full of laundry and announced, "I cleaned your clothes, honey!" She was, thank goodness, in a happy mood. She came through the door, looked at the candles lit on the floor, and stopped rustling. "Oh my god!" she said, sounding truly delighted. She ran to set the laundry down on our bed and then came back to me, and I led her along the path to the bathtub. "Wow!" she exclaimed, clearly moved. "Major boyfriend points for you, sweetie!" And she kissed me.

We stood there, swaying in each other's arms, drunk with limerence, and I said, in a sexy voice I'd never used, "I was thinking we could take a bath together."

Instantly her countenance clouded. "Oh, gee, Dave, I'm so sorry. But taking a bath is an extremely . . . private thing for me. It's my way of meditating and getting away from everything, you know? I can't possibly enjoy it that way if you're with me."

I don't think I winced visibly, but I felt her words like a whip-crack to my chest. She wasn't saying, "Not tonight." She was saying, "Never." This was so unexpected that I didn't even know how to react, so I went to my default: suffering with a smile. "That's okay, honey," I said. "You just take your bath."

"I'm really sorry," she said.

"If you're happy, that's all I care about," I said. Even as I said it, I felt as if I'd turned into a greeting card. Who would believe what I'd just said? But being the good boyfriend was my identity, as essential as being the nice guy, the amusing eccentric, the writer, the moral person. Even someone as emotionally detached as I was knew that something horrible had just happened. But I also knew I couldn't put it into words yet, and anyway, how stupid would it be to take this romantic gesture and turn it into an argument? How selfish would that be?

We kissed, she closed the bathroom door, and, looking at the scenario with fresh eyes, I bent over and blew out the candles in the hallway. That's when I started feeling—actually feeling. I noticed my hands and jaw were clenched, and it felt so good I just let them stay that way. On a logical level, this rage—that's what it was, apparently—made no sense at all. I'd just done a nice thing for the woman I loved. She was happy about it and was enjoying my gift. So where was this anger coming from? Had I given her a gift with a selfish motive behind it? And if I had, wasn't it good that it *hadn't* worked, to maintain the altruistic purity of the gesture?

"But Jesus Christ," I found myself muttering, almost loud enough for her to hear. "I just want to take a bath with the woman I love. I'm not asking for goddamn whips and nun outfits. This is like pulling fucking teeth. This isn't fair." And as soon as I heard myself say it, as soon as I'd actually released this thought onto the world, a chill went through me and I knew I was going to have to think this through. Was sex supposed to be fair? Did that question even make sense? What were the rules here, so I could know better than to trust my unreliable heart, my renegade body?

I'd had moments like this before, and I knew it took time for the actual shape of the conflict to seep into my brain in some manageable form. In the meantime, I sighed and put away the candles and stored them in the kitchen with the teacups. I never used them again.

One part of the plan worked, though. My fiancée came out of the bathroom, wrapped in a towel, and she hugged me and said, "I think we should have sex tonight."

"All right!" I said. I was unusually emphatic, either out of anger or to shout the anger down.

"Do you have condoms?" she said.

"Of course." I'd bought them in anticipation of this very scenario. What luck that it was actually happening.

She dried off and changed into her nightclothes, I stripped and showered (quickly, because I had removed the shower curtain, and this was no time to start a side project involving mops), and when I went into my bedroom she was lying on the bed in her T-shirt and panties, smiling. I stripped down to nothing and climbed on top of her. We hugged and kissed and rolled around, and then she took a deep breath and took off her panties.

I had never really seen female genitals before. Not in the softcore porn I'd indulged in, and certainly not in person. The few drawings I'd seen in sex ed were unbodied diagrams, like charts of old sailing ships that show where all the ropes go. I'd felt my fiancée through her clothes, and had somehow managed to do the right things to her rumored clitoris when called upon, but aside from that, my sexual education had revolved around *Playboy* and Cinemax, which is like getting your information about alcohol by drinking Shirley Temples. An actual vagina, with actual labia, was completely foreign territory to me. It struck me at that moment that it had never even played a part in my erotic imagination. Even thinking about the vagina had seemed rude and unchristian.

But tonight I was going to explore this new country, and I'd better love it right away. The window was closing fast. So I backed up, grabbed the condom box, put one on like I'd learned years ago in health class (this was also my first time; I'd never even practiced with a condom before), and prepared to Do the Act.

Looking back on it now, I can think of several reasons why I couldn't keep my manhood up. For one thing, I had never trained myself to be aroused at the sight of a real vagina before—just by what I *imagined* it would be like. For another thing, I was still angry about being denied the romantic bath I'd envisioned. Third, we were both really nervous. The fact that we were running out of time and wouldn't visit each other again for six months surely didn't help. And then let's not forget the years of repression and fear that I'd learned from my religious upbringing, plus the actual fear of sex I had from the obsession I had personally experienced. Fifth (or is it sixth now?), it's difficult to transition from masturbation to conventional penetration even when you're eighteen; I was twenty-eight and had an extra decade of physical programming to unlearn, and I didn't even know that this might present a problem.

And you know what else? Condoms make your dick numb.

I can't even say I tried all that hard. I could tell I was doomed from the outset; I could barely escape my own swirling head long enough to notice Jane, the room, the moment. After a few well-meaning pokes, it was very clear that I was merely al dente. I said, "You know what? I don't want to do this." Then, since that sounded insulting to her and made me sound potentially gay, I said, "I mean, we'll be together forever, we've got all the time in the world. There's no reason we have to do this whole thing tonight." I was a twenty-eight-year-old virgin with a girl-friend of six years, and I actually said, "Let's not be hasty."

"That's okay," said Jane, and we downshifted into the same blow job I'd gotten two dozen or so times before. It's the only time in my life I've ever received a blow job and felt distinctly like complaining.

I've mentioned that it sometimes takes a while for the emo-tional significance of an event to hit me, and I often miss subtle-ties altogether. It was actually as early as the next day, while we were walking through the Plaza, that I realized the big problem: it was her last sentence, the way she'd said, "That's okay." Some-thing clicked and I started brooding. *"That's okay," she said. She's really okay with not having sex. Oh my god—that makes perfect sense. Because my girlfriend has never been a fundamentalist like I was, and yet she's always been okay with my rules! What girlfriend anywhere could put up with a boyfriend who didn't fuck her for six years? Jesus—if it was in a movie, I wouldn't even believe it. And yet we've never even had an argument about it.*

Yet a breakup was absolutely unthinkable. What I thought was, *We certainly have a lot of interesting issues to work through to-gether once we're married.* For all I knew, maybe we'd find, farther down the line, that not breaking the Christian ideal that night had turned out to be a blessing in disguise. Wouldn't that be a wonderful surprise?

There was yet one more idiotic problem. In searching for an explanation for my inability to perform, I actually came to believe—because my sex education was so inadequate—that my failure to get hard with my fiancée was quite possibly a significant warning sign: that it might indicate that I didn't actually love her on some deep psychological level. (I also thought it might be a sign from God. A completely baffling inexplicable one, but a sign nonetheless that demanded explanation; it couldn't just be incompetence.) Looking back on it now, I can confidently state that while it's a tempting diagnosis, the personal history that has followed in my sex life since (ahem) suggests that of course I loved her, and the problem was more physiological than emotional. But I didn't know that at the time, and it lit a horrible fuse.

JANE LEFT MONDAY MORNING, and before she went, she kissed me and said, "You didn't notice the dishes."

"What?"

"I did all your dishes. And I cleaned all your laundry yesterday. That's how you know I love you. It's what I love doing for you."

I could only say, "Thanks." What I wanted to say was, How about fuck the dishes and you let us take a goddamned bath together?

Feeling uncertain about the weekend we had just had, I went back to work and fished for compliments from my friends.

"SHE WAS REALLY NICE. And smart," said Edgar, when we gathered in the conference room for lunch. "I can see why you like her."

"Thanks!" I told Edgar. "She liked you, too."

"Good luck on your marriage," said The Professor. He sounded like he meant it.

AT HER COMPUTER in the Everyday wing, Deedee agreed. "I just think it's great that you've found somebody. Like a soul mate."

"Well, I didn't just find her, of course. We've been together almost six years."

"Right. It was great to finally meet her. So did you guys have sex?"

"Um . . . we're still kind of working on that."

"Jesus Christ, Dave. Fuck her already. You know she wants it."

OVER LUNCH, KENNETH SAID, "I liked her. She was cool. But it was a little weird how she didn't seem all that thrilled to have you touch her. I mean, like, every time you tried to hold her hand she pushed you away."

"Oh, that. She just doesn't like public displays of affection. She thinks it's rude to do that when you're around other people. I keep forgetting, so she quietly reminds me."

Kenneth nodded whatever. "My ex-wife was like that. I hope you got some alone time."

"We did," I said. *And the less said about that, the better.*

JOSH WAS THE LEAST IMPRESSED. "I don't know," he said. "I just got a real lesbian vibe from her."

That amazed me. "You must be joking. Trust me. She's definitely straight." *If she was gay, I think she'd have wanted her pussy
licked by now.*

"I have to be honest. The whole time, I just felt really concerned for you. You didn't look happy."

"What do you mean? I was thrilled to have her here. To have
you meet her."

"I mean you looked so fucking happy you were exhausted.
Like you'd been *doing* happiness instead of just relaxing. I've
been happy, Dave. It's just a thing you enjoy. It gives you energy;
it shouldn't make you worry."

That was the oddest comment of all, because he was dead
wrong about Jane—how many lesbians like giving blow jobs?—
and I knew from experience that he was dead wrong about my
being happy. But he'd described something else about me perfectly: the anxiety that had come from nowhere and still hadn't
left. If Josh was wrong about his diagnosis, he'd still caught the
symptoms. But what the hell was causing them?

IT WAS MY FIRST TRULY GRAY WINTER. I went to work and did
my thing, and time passed. It was still nippy one day in early
February when I was wandering around Main Writing and
some older woman I don't even remember—a writer—said,
"Hey, I hear you're going to be working here next month! That's
great! Congratulations!"

"What?" I said.

"Yeah! It was just announced at this morning's meeting.
What—didn't they tell you?"

"It's the first I've heard of it."

I went immediately back to the Humor Department and told Max what had happened. He looked pained.

"They shouldn't have announced it at a meeting. We weren't ready. That was dumb. And you shouldn't have found out like that. I'm sorry."

"But you're moving me?"

"You've been promoted. They like your serious copy, and they want you up there."

"But you said I'm being promoted. So I'll be a Writer II?"

"Well . . . not yet. But a move like this usually happens before a promotion. They like what you do enough to ask for you. Show them what you can do, and . . ." thumb up, he raised his fist skyward.

There seemed nothing else to say. In theory, I could have complained. I hadn't been asked if I wanted the move. But this was proof that I'd been wrong: Max wasn't just temporarily irritated at me because of a complaint here or there. Apparently, Max really hated supervising me and really wanted me gone.

In Max's pleasant spin on the decision, as in almost every conversation I ever had with a Hallmark supervisor, it was completely unclear how much of the official story to believe. Maybe Main Writing *did* really want me. I didn't want them, but since Max wasn't warming to my style, it was maybe for the best. Better to be with people who were predisposed to like you than in a situation with a boss who wanted you dead. Careerwise, it would be the smartest thing.

Still—Main Writing. That was where all the dull cards were cranked out. Even when I'd been an editor, I'd hated reading them. My eyes just slid right off them like they were tax forms. And this was what they wanted me to write now?

The only way I could think about it happily was to think that (1) it probably wasn't going to be as bad as I thought; (2) it would lead to a promotion, which would put me the next step closer to moving to the Idea Exchange; and of course, (3) it was inevitable, so I may as well get used to it.

Yet way down under my confusion was a tiny kernel of doubt and fear: a theory-only intimation that, just possibly, the good times were over forever.

PART FOUR

Cope

My Year and Change
in Main Writing

12

Works Well with Others, If They're Not Touchy

ONCE I KNEW I WAS MOVING TO THE MAIN WRITING staff, I accepted it with a sort of desperate hope, optimistic that maybe, in some way, this new position would surprise me with its challenges and differences. At the same time, a cynical part of my brain said, *Dave, you've read the sorts of things they write up here. Unironic paeans to a Very Special Daughter. Card after card featuring some design variation on watercolor flowers in a vase. This isn't your place and you know it.*

Not that there's anything I could have done about the actual transfer or the shape my job had suddenly taken. But if I'd listened to that voice, I think I might have faced my Main Writing tenure with less frustration. But I was hampered by two things. First, I was a recovering fundamentalist. Conservative Christians learn, almost as an instinct, to ignore their own tastes and preferences, since desire is inherently grounded in sin and selfishness. So the very fact that I wanted something didn't necessarily make my own desires nonnegotiable. Second, I really was tragically optimistic about my own creative malleability. I was nice! I was people-pleasing! I was young and full of energy and inspiration! How could my muse not get along in any circumstances, no matter how pastel?

I wasn't the only one complaining. Kenneth, who had moved to Shoebox to be an artist rather than a writer in Traditional, was facing challenges of his own. "It's so . . . weird," he told me that day over lunch. "This is alternative humor, that's what they call it. So they'll tell me to draw a spokesneuter—just a guy, really, talking on the front of the card—and I do it and submit it and they send it back and say, 'We need something more alternative.' So I do something really out there and they return it and say, 'That's *too* alternative.' I thought alternative was, like, experimental. But it's actually this very specific consumer and they aren't explaining her very well."

"This job," I replied, "is a weird thing for people to do."

Anyway, there was one good thing about the move. When the cohead of Main Writing, Constance Blandish, told me in an almost gushing excited-girl voice that I would be joining their staff, she also noted that Evan Wilson would be my mentor.

"Evan Wilson!" I couldn't help but exclaim. "I love that guy."

Evan was generally described to visitors as "that guy who looks like Santa Claus," and while the writing staff had pictures of famous writers all along the walls—Poe and Woolf and Shakespeare and Twain—it was surely no accident that his cubicle sat under a picture of Papa Hemingway. The best thing about Evan Wilson was that he was a legend in light verse. He was so good—able to pitch a line at any age, any gender, and to keep it light and clever and winning, no matter what the topic— that, as I heard the story, he rose to the top of the profession,

Writer V, so quickly that he got bored. He detoured into management but didn't like it, and when he came back to the Writing staff, they created a brand-new rank just for him: Master Writer. There have been Master Writers since, but he was the first, and he'd been the best for decades. This was my mentor.

"You should feel honored, too," said Constance, who was selling my new workplace really hard. "He's been at Hallmark over twenty-five years and he's never mentored anybody. He's so shy, he just hates to do it, and of course we just let him do what he wants. But he's been noticing your work and he made an exception for you."

Amazed as I wanted to be, I thought this had to be a hyperbolic sales pitch, since it was pretty clear that I was dubious about the move. But then a few days later when I actually met with Evan in a tiny conference room, just the two of us, he was also visibly excited, and he said, in a voice that seemed all the more earnest because it was so quiet, "I've never mentored anybody, but I'm going to retire pretty soon, and I see you as my legacy. I want you to be able to carry on in the tradition I've sort of made for the company." I may have developed a bit of a man-crush then.

I was still dubious about the move, but one thing was certain: Main Writing wanted me. And as long as Evan was in my corner, it felt like things could turn out all right. Somehow. I'd just have to figure the details out later.

"I'VE GOT A DATE TONIGHT," said Deedee to all of us in the gaggle at lunch, and her eyes were practically welling up with musk. We'd been hearing about her last boyfriend for several weeks now—he was crazy, he was controlling, he was gone— and she'd just found this new guy online. "He's tall and he's gorgeous and he's one of these dot-com millionaires. I mean he's literally a millionaire. Not good at meeting women, but god, so cute." She exhaled to the chandeliers. "We met this weekend, and we hit it off so fast that we've already got this next one planned."

"Did you do anything?" asked Jillian.

"He's a gentleman. Isn't that cute? I told you he was cute." She touched her face self-consciously, and I felt envious that anyone could have that effect on Deedee. I'd never affected any woman that way. "I tell you one thing, though," she continued. "If he doesn't go for it tonight, I'm just going to attack him. We're going to a movie, and we're sitting in the back row, and I'm going to wear the lowest-cut top I've got." She shook her head, dizzy with hope. "I cannot *wait* for this man to touch me."

"Please," said Melanie dryly. "Talk about it some more."

"Wait a minute," I said. "You mean in the theater?"

Deedee looked startled. "Haven't you ever made out in the back of a theater? It's exciting because you have these limits, you know, like you can't go too far or you get in tr—"

"Yeah, but . . ." I was trying to puzzle something out. "You said you couldn't wait for him to touch you, and you meant in the theater. So do you . . . do you *like* having your breasts touched?"

"Of course!" she said. "All women do."

"Not *all* women," I said.

"Oh, you poor man," said Deedee. She looked genuinely sad.

I looked around the table. The other women all confirmed it: breast touching = good. I felt acid in my lungs. *You poor man,* she'd said. Was I? After the romance, the storybook engagement, the years of support and care we'd shown—after all that, was I really a figure of pity? I could take a few people not liking Jane. We had our own relationship style and not everyone understood. But to have people think I was in a *bad* relationship . . . that I could do *better* . . .

It took me the whole rest of the day to get used to the idea. Women like having their breasts touched! Why didn't they teach this in sex-ed class? Or did they, and I hadn't been paying attention? How long had this been going on? When I got home, I walked through the Plaza, and for once actually sauntered through the high-end boutiques with their perfume counters and makeup mirrors. I passed woman after woman and thought, *She likes having her breasts touched, and so does she, and that one, and that one, and probably both of them over there . . .*

This is such a silly thing, I kept telling myself. One sexual preference more or less hardly mattered when stacked next to me and Jane's nearly six years of love and friendship. But I couldn't stop thinking about the irony. I wasn't a particularly freaky guy. I just wanted to touch my partner's breasts and have her enjoy it. And yet the only woman I had ever loved, the woman I'd committed my heart, soul, and future to, was apparently one of the only women on the planet who found it absurd. I told myself I was okay with that. But some part of me that I hadn't listened to my whole life was squatting in the back of my brain with a clicker and a calculator and muttering, *No living room sex, no bathtub, and now you don't even get* this *much, you sorry motherfucker.*

WHEN I FIRST TOLD Josh Broward that it looked like I was moving to Main Writing, he told me a cautionary tale about a mutual friend of ours. This friend—an ebullient, irrepressible, gorgeous (but married) woman I'll call Joy—did a six-month rotation in Main Writing from another staff. She was widely loved, had lots of friends across the company, and spent a certain portion of her workday on the phone: talking, laughing, and expressing other human emotions.

Two weeks into her rotation, she came to work and found, in her mailbox, an anonymous slip of paper containing nothing but the definition of *silence*. The entire definition, from etymology through 1.a. and all the way to the end, taken from *Webster's Third New International Unabridged*, which is a pretty windy dictionary. It had been hand-copied. And this was the first hint she had that anyone might have wanted her to quiet down.

When Josh told me this, he added, as if smiling through the pain, "What gets me about the story is that they *hand-copied* it. They didn't just Xerox a page and clip it out. This person thought about what they were doing. They got really involved. The painstaking obsessiveness of that gesture just creeps me out." They never figured out who was responsible. Presumably this person was still there on Main Writing somewhere, hiding behind a cubicle wall, quietly judging, judging, judging.

AS IT HAPPENED, HOWEVER, my early days in Main Writing allayed my worst fears. I did the rounds and discovered at least four good eggs I seemed to get along with immediately. Everyone was happy to see me. People brought me welcome cards and baked cookies. If this was passive-aggressiveness, at least it tasted great.

Make no mistake, however. Main Writing was a huge change from the sort of ugly bachelor apartment of Traditional Humor. In Trad Humor, I'd been working shoulder to shoulder with eight twenty- and thirtysomething men, all sort of geeky and overeducated and utterly skeptical of everything. When The Professor had come back from a trip to Italy, the next day at work he'd brought in a commemorative plate with the Supreme Pontiff on it, which he hung just outside the conference room, where it hung, quietly kitschy and disdainful, for the next several years.

You could never have done such a thing in the Main Writing staff. My new coworkers were more than two dozen women in their forties to sixties, half of whom were unmarried and childless. They loved nothing better than to work on condolence and grief cards. If you stood in the hallway outside Main Writing, you could practically smell the Zoloft. All this leads to a stark change in creative culture, and nothing epitomized this change more than the Crying Room.

They didn't technically call it the Crying Room. It was called the Quiet Room—from outside it was just a label on a door between the conference room and the soda machines. When I asked what it was for, Constance just waved her hand and said, "Well, you know, sometimes the work we do can become sort of . . . overwhelming." She didn't elaborate, and I got the hint. I never asked again. It had been rude to even bring it up.

It was indeed a very quiet room, and I found myself going there a lot—not to cry, but just to get out of my goddamned cubicle. The room—about the size of a walk-in closet—contained a rocking chair, a table, and a rolltop desk. There were books of poetry and inspiration along the desk's top, a few handmade pillows, and track lighting on a dimmer switch. Any time you wanted to, you could close the door, hug a pillow to your chest, and rock quietly in the dark. Or you could turn the lights way up and do a little research, reading a little handbook of Shakespeare's sonnets or a 1959 collection of humorous verse. I preferred, however, to dim the lights, because if you turned them too high, you'd notice that it was still obviously a standard Hallmark room, with the off-white unornamented walls and the sturdy eighties-era carpet.

I should add that while the Quiet Room is fun to talk about anecdotally, in actual practice I hardly ever saw it used. So it's not like everyone was having constant emotional breakdowns. Or if they were, it's possible they simply wept quietly at their desks. The cubicles on Nine were built too tall to peer over, and many had plastic doors you could close.

FOR THE FIRST TWO WEEKS of my tour of duty, I wandered and chatted mostly with the funniest or most friendly people on staff. Laughter ensued. Polite good-byes were shared. Except for my newfound habit of being distracted by breasts, everything seemed to be going fine.

At the end of my second week, however, Evan came by and said, with an embarrassed look, "We have to talk." He led me into the Quiet Room, closed the door, cleared his throat, and said, "Dave, you're using too many literary allusions in your casual speech, and people are complaining."

I defy you to quickly come up with a sensible reaction to that statement. My first instinct was to ask, Was this about my cards? But of course it couldn't have been. He'd said my casual speech. I was flummoxed. "What does that mean?"

He shrugged, looking even more embarrassed than before. "I was just told to tell you."

I had to say something, react in some way, so I said, "Uh, I'm sorry. I guess I'll have to work on that." And Evan Wilson, my mentor, changed the subject—"How are things going creatively?"—and five minutes later our meeting was over.

It's a measure of how insecure I was that I didn't press the issue. Part of my passivity was just because it was clear any straight answer was going to be hard to get to: some unnamed higher-up had told Evan to tell me this one weird thing that other vague unnamed people were saying. Obviously, accountability wasn't at a premium. But even if there had been a clear chain of provenance, I don't think I would have pursued the question. I thought of Hallmark as literally the only job I had skills for—the only job I could ever have that I wouldn't utterly hate. If I was fired, then, I had no options except a life of misery doing something else I would face with actual pain rather than occasional weirdness. And since I hadn't worked out in Humor, and hadn't liked editing, this stint in Main Writing was essential to my survival. So when my meeting with Evan was over, I also felt as though, by agreeing to change and by nodding with a show of comprehension, I had waived my right to go back and ask, "What the hell does that even mean?"

The only information I had to go on was that single sentence

of warning, and for the rest of that day I turned it over and over
from every possible angle, trying to glean sense:

You're using too many literary allusions in your casual speech.

Literary allusions? What literary allusions? It's not like I was
going around saying things like, "My god, that meeting was as
dull as the Customs-House chapter of *The Scarlet Letter*!" or
"It's been a *Metamorphosis* kind of morning—and I mean Kafka,
not Ovid!"

But even if I had been that kind of pretentious ass, it left
other questions unanswered. What were the unwritten rules I
was breaking here? Was this a ban on literary allusions, or was
pop culture also judged and wanting? Is opera a literary allusion?
How about Monty Python? Would it be rude to name all the
dwarves? For that matter, what if I said—as I often did, fully
aware that I was in Kansas City—"Oy vey"? Was that counting
against me?

Then there was that phrase "too many," which suggested not
that my literary allusions were annoying, but merely that I was
indulging in them at a level that exceeded local standards of
taste. How many was that?

Problem was, I could think of only one bona fide literary
allusion I'd committed. Three days earlier, I'd wandered into a
conversation with two other writers, one of whom was complaining, "It's so frustrating! I not only have to do eight lines of
verse, but the editor is actually demanding a specific rhyme
scheme! I've never seen that before!"

I'd never heard of such a thing either, but I said, "Well, you
never know. It might help. I don't know if you can have art

without limitations. G. K. Chesterton, in his book *Orthodoxy*, said that the essence of every picture is the frame."

I admit that was excessive. But it was the only literary allusion, *qua* literary allusion, that I could point to in my entire fortnight's tenure. Is one literary allusion in two weeks excessive? And where did they get off judging my frequency anyway? With only one allusion on the books, the next one might be months off! How could they be so damned sure another was due?

I also want to point out that the reason I cited G. K. Chesterton was out of intellectual honesty. I could have simply said, "The essence of every picture is the frame," and it would have been faster. But it would have left the impression that I'd come up with the line, or—worse—had read it on a T-shirt. Chesterton, an author I love, deserves better than that, and if I slighted him in this I'd know my sin and I'd have to live with myself. So I mentioned G. K. Chesterton—and as soon as I did it, I thought, *My interlocutor might not know who G. K. Chesterton is, so I'd better mention the book so they know he wrote books.* Besides, Chesterton wrote dozens of books, and I'd hate for someone trying to track down the quote to have to go vainly through volume after volume of *Heretics, The Everlasting Man, The Club of Queer Trades*, etc. I like to save people time.

So I wasn't trying to be pretentious. I was just offering helpful and considerate footnoting. That's some responsible goddamn scholarship right there! If I'd been them, and I hadn't gotten the reference, I would have thanked me for the extra help.

But they didn't. Which led me to the second half of the accusation:

. . . and people are complaining.

It was spooky. Not just one person, but *people*. Faceless, gen-
derless, misty, and omnipresent, like Mr. They in "They say . . ."
I could never confront my accusers or gauge their sanity, because
they barely existed. Even the warning had come to me indi-
rectly, reporting not on a specific incident and such-and-such a
time. It was more like a weather report informing me that the
atmosphere had changed. I had two options: dress differently or
die of exposure.

This is the part that most amazed me: *people are complaining.*
I'm no stranger to office politics, and goodness knows I've complained about my coworkers before. But this statement meant
that people had gotten together—at lunch, in meetings—and
someone had said, "God, that Dave and his literary allusions! He
makes me so upset!" And someone else had said, "I feel exactly
the same way!" And a third person, maybe, said, "Isn't it intoler-
able? Something must be done—and quickly, too, before another week passes, because I don't like this situation's current
trajectory!" And they—whoever they were, in whatever numbers—decided that this problem (me saying things) was so out
of control that it could only be handled by upper management!

Or else—and I'm just blue-skying here—they were spine-
less hypersensitive weasels so utterly helpless that they relied on
their superiors as proxies for their own attenuated social skills.
Try as I might, the friendliest spin I can put on the story is that
maybe—maybe—people thought the behavior was annoying,
but were also afraid of hurting my feelings because I seemed so
guileless and tender-skinned, so they made the criticism oblique
in order to not make me cry. But even when I try to see it that
way, it falls apart: that sentence is a threat, not a helpful hint. This

was something a little more territorial: the old cats hissing at the new one.

In any event, I didn't have to think very long about it before I realized two things. First, I was in actual trouble—enough trouble that my boss had apparently seen fit to point out that I was playing a dangerous game not even a month into my second-chance position. Second, whatever the problem was, it couldn't possibly be what I had been told it was. Literary allusions as a bad habit made no sense however I dissected it. I wasn't sure what the real problem was, of course, because these professional greeting card writers, alleged experts at the marriage of words and feeling, had failed to clearly express themselves. The only thing I could think of was that I must be doing something really annoying that felt, to an inarticulate person, like something they might plausibly describe as "too many literary allusions."

I mentioned this to Josh Broward, and he shook his head and said, "Welcome to the ninth floor," with a look that was equal parts smile and wince. I talked to other friends in all corners of the company, and they all professed to share my bewilderment and my high dudgeon. But they could offer no advice.

In the meantime I had to go to work each day in a new department, not trusting anyone, wondering who hated me and for what petty reason, terrified to say anything for fear that one distant echo of Poe would bury the needle and make the boiler explode. I found myself wandering away from the ninth floor and spending my days working elsewhere: the Crown Room, the lobby, the glass walkway to 2440. I exiled myself at my own job.

I had a notebook with me—a habit I've had since high school—and I found myself writing in it not only when I had a card idea, but whenever I felt the urge to say something that might be taken as a literary allusion; something I thought I maybe shouldn't say but blurted out anyway. With notebook in hand all the time (rather than in my pocket), I began stifling myself by writing down what I thought instead of saying it to someone.

When a week passed, I did an assessment and I discovered that I wrote five to ten completely work-irrelevant entries every day. And most of these related to puzzles or word trivia. "CHANGE-LESS is ANGEL inside CHESS!" "MARTHA STEWART is MART plus HASTE plus WART." I ran across an unfamiliar word—*neoteric*—in a review of a U2 album in *USA Today*, and I wrote not only the definition ("modern") but noted also that it was an anagram of "erection." And so on.

I wrote down only one actual allusion. Someone said, "I don't think people can really get along if they don't have the same level of intelligence," and I bit my tongue and did not say what I wrote: "In an interview, Alma Einstein once said, 'I don't understand relativity, but I understand Albert.'"* So this review of my methods complicated my situation because, on the one hand, it was obvious that literary allusions really weren't the problem. And while I found that writing down these urges was soothing, and made the urges retreat, the fact is that most of my urges were wordplay related, and I almost never share any of the wordplay trivia I notice. *If these people hate my literary allusions*, I thought, *imagine if they knew all the stuff I'm not saying*. Disturbing though this was, I vowed to continue taking notes and re-

---

* This quotation, by the way, turns out to be apocryphal. So it's a good thing I didn't speak up and perpetuate a myth. What would people think?

viewing them each week, on the theory that eventually some helpful pattern would emerge. But in the meantime, I felt distinctly freakish.

The one place I felt safe to be myself was among my fellow Humor writers. Not because I wasn't a freak there, too—I was, after all, the wacky neighbor—but because they knew me and, except for my old boss, seemed to like me anyway. Of course, I wasn't technically a Humor writer anymore, and they weren't my fellow anything. But I still went to lunch with them and hung out when I could. In a company that had suddenly and unpredictably turned on me, it was the one place that seemed to make sense.

In the second week of my note-taking experiment, I was walking to lunch with a group of the Humor guys, including Blues Man, Edgar Allan, and The Professor. We had just crossed the glass walkway into 2460 when Blues Man stopped and said, "I was just thinking. We do a lot of monkey cards, and we call them monkey cards. But they're always using photos of chimpanzees. And I don't think chimps are monkeys, are they?"

As it happens, I had done a report on apes in fourth grade, and for some reason I had remembered it. So I said, "Actually, chimpanzees are apes, along with gorillas, orangutans, and gibbons. They have no tails and they're not exclusively arboreal, although they still have those long brachiating arms. And you know what's weird? In the *Planet of the Apes* they don't have any gibbons, and they never explain it!"

A silence fell over the group, and I knew I should stop. But I had more to share, and when would this subject ever come up again? Quickly, Dave! "But you know," I continued, "my real favorites are these weird primitive monkeys they call prosimians— the lemur, the tarsier, the galago or bush baby, the kinkajou.

Really cool, strange-looking animals. If they had a movie called *Planet of the Prosimians*, I would totally watch that movie!" Whew! Done!

The silence furthered. Then Edgar Allan laughed and said, "Hey, Dave, speaking of animals, would you like to see the rat's ass that I give?" Then everyone laughed, and we continued on to lunch. And I thought, *Oh. It's stuff like that, I bet. That's my vice. I inform people against their will.*

That's when I felt cold dread seep in. Because although I could possibly change my behavior in little ways here and there—take extra time to iron a shirt, keep still for an entire meeting, etc.—stopping my exuberantly irrelevant brain was a hopeless task. I was obviously already clamping down on it as much as I could bear to. But what was worse, that moment of actually using and sharing the information I knew had given me such a rush of joy, made me feel so connected, somehow, to both the books in my past and to the friends who had agreed to put up with me, that shutting it off would be misery. And if I wanted misery, wouldn't any job do? I began to fear that, while I had friends at Hallmark and people who understood me, none of them were on the ninth floor: the best that floor could offer was polite endurance. So within a month, it was quite clear that moving me to Main Writing had been, and was, a terrible idea. All that remained was for the doom to play out.*

---

*I feel compelled to add that, in talking about apes to my friends, I was misremembering the facts. Apes may be "not exclusively arboreal," but so are some non-apes, like baboons. And apes may be tailless, but so is the Barbary macaque. So the only real distinction between apes and monkeys seems to be genetic—which is why people get them confused. Also, I'm embarrassed to point out that despite what I said back then, the kinkajou isn't a prosimian. I should have referred to the pygmy loris instead. In my defense, I would like to point out that "kinkajou" is really fun to say.

13

How to Not Write
a Serious Card

MY FIRST WEEK OF TRANSITION INTO MAIN WRITING, I
didn't write anything. I'd look over the requisitions—"We'd like
a sixteen-line prose piece telling a daughter how much she
means"—and I would think, "Well, I'm still unsettled and thinking like a Humor writer. I'd better read some archived copy to
get a sense of what I'm doing." By the second week, when we
needed four-line verse about angels for an encouragement/cope
promotion, I still didn't feel moved, like I needed more time and
more research. Before I knew it, a month had passed and I hadn't
written a single requisition. This was starting to look bad.

I talked to Evan Wilson and said, "I'm having trouble really
getting into the writing up here. Do you have any ideas?"

He looked at me, utterly buffaloed. "You just . . . write. I
mean, it's four lines, maybe eight damn lines. You don't need
to *feel* it in your *soul*, for god's sake. We aren't writing Shakespeare here."

What a great point! How silly I felt! I actually laughed aloud
and apologized for the dumb question. Then I returned to my

cubicle and faced exactly the same resistance I had before. For some reason, my brain simply refused to do the work at the moment. And now I wasn't sure who to talk to.

Since I'd fought writer's block before in my writing classes in college, I knew the solution: I just had to figure out what was causing the resistance and find some way to make the pain of the guilt of not writing worse than the pain of writing. Of course, since much of the guilt was ready-made—I was being paid to write greeting cards and I wasn't writing any; I had been a complete fraud for a month now—clearly the stress pushing *against* my writing must be great indeed. But what could it be? I took a quick survey of my life now and compared it to my life in Humor.

1. *The Environment.* The entire environment was much more insular. The rule of silence was strictly enforced, both by executive fiat and by shushing. The cubicles were all very high—too high to look into—and they all had doors, which meant we worked in the equivalent of monastic cells: it felt like twenty-six little offices, not one unified staff.

2. *The People.* The staff on Main Writing was overwhelmingly female (four men, including me, and more than twenty women), and I was the only writer in my twenties. (We had three thirtysomethings. After that, it centered around fifty-year-olds.) While there were several sweet people on the Main Writing staff, they generally weren't in my demographic. That is, they were either women in their fifties and sixties, or they were in my age range but uncomfortable with my verbally rambunctious tendencies. They were all incredibly quiet. Also, as I had already discovered, many of the writers were hypersensitive and even

simply batshit crazy, and it was impossible to tell which was which, since they did all their complaining by proxy.

3. *The System.* One of the great things about Humor was being part of a crack team who all got a specific assignment, worked on it, and got the acceptances posted publicly. That didn't work on Main Writing. (Constance said, "We used to do it that way, but it got . . . very competitive, very negative.") Assignments were sometimes quietly dropped by your door, and you had no idea who else was working on them, and there was no one deadline that everyone was striving toward. What's more, no results were publicly posted; you got your rejects sent back quietly in your mailbox, and to find out what had gotten accepted for, say, the Angel Themed Cope Promotion, you had to look at a weekly printout that listed every acceptance by every writer in every department, and figure out from there which ones were probably Angel Cope acceptances. In other words, you had to calculate it yourself, which I had a hard time caring enough to do—particularly since no one talked about their work, so this would never come up in conversation later. You certainly couldn't mock someone for writing "Ruv Roo." What was everyday banter in Trad Humor would have exposed raw skin on Main. It was not a place where jokes flowed freely.

4. *The Subject Matter.* This, of course, was the killer. Main Writing handled everything that wasn't Humor or the Idea Exchange, and so, in addition to paeans to the New Graduate, we also had to write hangtag copy for a new snowmobile ornament ("Race your way into a memorable Christmas!") or come up with the name for a gardening teddy bear figure or—this was the worst—come up with 120 words about marjoram for a "Year

of Seasonings" calendar. This felt like the exact opposite of humor: it was a demand to take stupid things seriously. How anyone can do this happily is beyond me. I could barely manage to do it at all.

So really, when it came right down to it, the problem with Main Writing was *every single goddamned thing about it.*

The only thing I could think to do was to keep writing humor. Main writers had a bit of leeway to choose what to work on, and they were just as able to submit humor requisitions as anyone else. (And they often did. Ditto for the Idea Exchange; when they weren't brainstorming brilliant new paths for the company, they were submitting pieces everywhere.) So for a few weeks I simply ignored the non-humor requisitions and just pretended that I was a Trad Humor staffer in exile. Constance, who really did read the weekly summaries of acceptances, noticed what I was doing and took me aside. "You can't just write humor," she said. "You really have to try to learn the serious side, too." I nodded and thought, *Just wait. You'll see that my humor is better than my serious work, and you'll be forced to send me back where I belong.* In the meantime, I made a good-faith effort to try to write non-humor sentiments. *I have my own serious side, too,* I told myself. *So when a non-humor requisition comes along that grabs me, I'll take it on without trying so hard.* I looked for the next several days, but no such magic requisition appeared. Instead, what would happen was something like this:

1. I would pick up a requisition for, say, "Brother Birthday," and let's say the requisition said something like, "This is for an older brother where they maybe don't see each other very often but they're very close when they meet.

HMYM and TYDS have been very successful in this caption."

2. I would then think of what serious things I would say to my brother, and I couldn't come up with much. My brother and I talk about movies, and video games, and how is everybody. We don't do General Wish. I couldn't really write a card that said, "I saw this great episode of *The Simpsons* yesterday," so I had to think broader.

3. When I thought of more general things to say, they were as follows: *Happy Birthday. You're a great brother. It's a shame we don't see each other more often.* Not only are these hardly worth saying, but they don't even work for the caption— this is Brother Birthday, not "Close Brothers Who Don't See Each Other Very Often Birthday." It's supposed to be *suitable* for them, but not limited to *only* them.

But even if I could use those simple, straightforward sentiments, the only way to make them into actual cards would seem to be to add bullshit—to make them needlessly longer, as if they were a term paper in college that had to be fluffed up to ten pages. "When I think of all the good times we had growing up together, brother, and how much fun we still have when we talk on the phone, it's a shame we don't see each other more often." That's a card, maybe. But it feels less honest to me than the original straightforward statement—you can practically smell the way it's straining to make itself longer—but even then, it's probably have-sim.

4. *Fine*, I would think. *Let's try another tack. Let's look at those theme codes. How Much You Mean and Things You Do and*

Say work, so let's think. Universal specifics. What could they be? "Brother, you . . . have always been there for me." "Brother . . . I like talking with you."

5. And I would instantly think, *What boring fucking sentences. With fifty years of writing on file, surely they already have cards that say something this dull. What do they need me for? Jesus.*

6. *So maybe,* I would think, *I should come up with something in light verse instead of prose. Well, not LIGHT verse, of course, because that would be humor and wouldn't fit the caption. But verse of some sort. I'm good at verse!*

7. I would no sooner lift my pen than I'd have to pause. The problem with writing verse—at least the way I do it—is that you need to have a punch line first, so that you get a sense of what the meter is going to be. If your punch line is going to be, "YOU are the brother I like making mischief with!" (a terrible idea, since nothing good rhymes with *with*, but let that go for now), then you're going to need anapestic tetrameter. (DUM-da-da DUM-da-da DUM-da-da DUM-da-da. . . .) But without a punch line—not necessarily a joke, but just a main point to get to—there was no structure and nothing for me to work with.

8. So, in search of a non-joke punch line, I'd think about my own brother, and what memories we have together— sharing a bunk bed, playing Dungeons & Dragons, going to church camp—and I would notice two things instantly: first, that none of these can be directly alluded to because they all limit the sender (not everyone shared a bunk bed or went to church together), and second, that

the first thing I want to do with any of these memories is to share a joke. (Remember that time you fell off the top bunk without waking up? Remember when we each ate an entire pizza and suffered stomachaches for the rest of the day? Man, we were idiots!) I had occasional other memories—for example, we had both gone to Canada and visited our aunt and uncle, and had picked fresh strawberries for the first time—but I couldn't think of a way to turn that into a birthday-type sentiment. I couldn't even imagine how I'd even bring up that memory to my brother: "Hey, Dan—remember when we visited Canada and picked fresh strawberries? . . . That was nice."

9. Now I'd find myself with *two* things I couldn't do. The first was to say, "Even if I could use the strawberries as a launching pad, writing about the sensual details of the juice running down our wrists and the sunlight on our backs or what have you, I couldn't really talk about it warmly because I remember it merely as some stuff we did. I don't go into raptures very easily. Not over strawberries, anyway." The second was to say, "Plus not everyone picked strawberries together, so that's a dead end regardless."

10. I would write something general in a verselike form, trying out a line here and there—"Happy Birthday, brother dear! Guess it's been another year!"—and I would scratch them out instantly. (Ick. And too humorous, anyway.) Or I would finish a complete verse that I hated and submit it while wincing. Which also wasn't fun and didn't make me want to leap nimbly to the next requisition.

11. I would look up and see that three hours had passed, and
     I had not only not written a goddamn thing, but I didn't
     even have any good ideas. I was exactly where I'd started
     three hours earlier, with a blank wall of a requisition and
     no seeming way to gain a toehold.

I was able to squeeze out a few serious sentiments for Love by
thinking about my fiancée and expressing myself as directly as
possible. ("When you're not here, I can physically feel your ab-
sence, like a breath I always need to catch. . . . ") The editors
would tweak it so it was less specific, or used less interesting
words, and I'd get an acceptance out of it. But right out of the
starting gate, I could tell I was running at about a quarter of my
usual speed or less, and instead of rattling off jokes and gimmicks,
I spent most of my first few weeks in a state of bafflement—
staring at requisitions and shrugging, or going to the archives,
looking at the crap that sold, and wondering why the top sellers
were considered good, and what the hell they needed me for.

When I asked around for help, I got three kinds of advice.
First was Evan Wilson's, which was "Just suck it up and don't
think about it so much."

Constance Blandish, who looked at me very sympathetically
at first, said, "Sometimes when we have a hard time in our personal lives, it makes it hard to write certain types of copy. Just
give yourself time and trust that the writing will emerge."

This was mirrored in Josh Broward's advice to me, which was,
"When I find that a requisition doesn't move me, I skip it and
get another one that does. Of course, where I work we get lots
of interesting requisitions. In your case, good luck."

Edgar Allan just threw up his hands and said, "If I were in your situation, I'd be screwed. Serious cards just aren't my thing. I'd go quietly crazy and then have a public meltdown. Then maybe they'd move me into management."

The Professor added, "Maybe you should start by trying to be happy where you are. It's not like you've got a choice."

And Deedee said, "It sounds to me like you need to start drinking."

THERE WAS ONLY one good thing about Main Writing: I could lie down. The cubicles were head-high and they all had doors, so it was a simple matter to recline when I felt the urge, which was pretty often. What I most liked was curling up under the desk and tucking myself completely out of sight. A friend of mine accused me of having claustrophilia, and maybe there's something to it. For some reason, when I was wedged into a single stiff position, I could feel my brain loosen a little and ideas start to come. They were all humor ideas, but still, they were something.

There were only two problems: the first is that, when I was lying on my back in the dark and thinking, I had a tendency to fall asleep . . . and then I'd snore. I got two warnings from my neighbors, and then I started bringing something pointy with me—a pen or some dull scissors—so that if my head drooped I'd poke myself and wake up. That worked, but it also made my curling-up time a bit more tense. The other problem was that even lying down didn't work all the time, and I'd feel a need to run around, jump, or just pace, none of which could be done in

my cubicle. So I started wandering again, too, walking right back
into the habit that had gotten me in trouble before. I couldn't
seem to find a happy balance.

One day on a fruitless wandering journey into the artist's area
of Season cards, I had that urge to lie down again. I found a
conference room, way off near the back where no one ever
went, and closed the door. It was a midsized meeting room, with
a table that could seat maybe twelve, and I had to decide to either curl up in the corner or go under the table, since there
wasn't enough open floor for normal sprawling.

I went with under the table. My theory was, someone could
come in. If they saw me in the corner, they'd go tell somebody
and I'd be in trouble. If I was under the table, no one would see
me and I could wait them out. So I kicked some chairs out of
the way, turned the dimmer switch low, and slid under the table
with my notebook in hand.

It almost worked. That is, it felt like it should work, because
I felt snug and happy and comfortable. The problem was still the
piece I was writing—serious Sister Graduation—and nothing
was coming offhand. But I felt creatively comfortable for the first
time in ages. *Sister Graduation*, I thought. *Sister Graduation* . . .

When I woke up, someone had flipped on the lights. I had
a moment of panic, then remembered where I was. A pair of
women's feet padded to the back of the room. She was humming
something idly. I heard her sniff and clear her throat. She stopped,
and her flouncy skirt swung a little as she surveyed the room or
something. I held my breath, and after a moment, she walked
right back out of the room.

Relieved, I rolled over on my front like a cougar and made as
if to pounce out the door. But I knew I couldn't just burst out

right after she left. That would look odd. Also, she might be coming back. So I had to time it carefully. Wait thirty seconds for her to go back to her desk and maybe get something. One . . . two . . . three . . .

On twenty-two she came back, this time dragging an easel. She leaned it in the corner and started straightening the chairs one by one. From the math, I guessed there was going to be a meeting. Possibly very soon. And since she was straightening all the chairs, it might be well attended.

When you're in a brand-new situation, it's often hard to accurately weigh your options. I could think of four ways to play this:

1. Stay perfectly still and hope no one kicked me or looked under the table.
2. As above, only with the backup plan; if caught, I'd pretend to have been sleeping.
3. Think up some excuse to announce myself now, when there's only one person looking instead of ten.
4. Wait for her to leave again and really rush out this time.

The last was obviously the safest, so I waited . . . and my heart skipped as I saw her go to the doorway again. But she stopped and called out, "Carol? Just bring those samples when the time comes, okay? They're right on my desk."

Thank heaven. I knew that voice. It was my friend Mia, an editor in Season. She knew me, she knew I was a little strange, and from her I could get forgiveness. So obviously I had to say something now. All I needed was the proper opening line.

I didn't come up with much except to try to keep it mild and quiet. And to avoid attracting attention, I waited until she was back at the head of the table away from the door. I heard something being shuffled, and then little handouts started thumping above me: *Thwap. Thwap. Thwap.*

I breathed in, crossed myself, and called out, "Hey, Mia . . ."

Her scream was like a fire alarm: high, monotone, piercing, endless. (I never asked, but I'm guessing she sang soprano.) Since it was too late to avoid attention now, I clambered hurriedly between two chairs and into the air again. "Oh, hi, Mia. I was just—"

"Dave! What are you . . . ?"

"Um, resting, and . . . you know what? I'll just take my notepad, and we'll talk later."

Before she could protest I was out the door . . . and I saw, arrayed before me, the entire artistic staff of Season, who were standing in their cubicles or paused in the hallway, looking at me, concerned.

"It's, um, actually a funny story," I managed, then skedaddled. There was no point in actually telling the story. The rumor mill would take care of that.

I NEVER GOT REPRIMANDED FOR THAT, but the scream alone was enough to keep me penned in my cubicle for the next month. In that whole time, I still couldn't write and I hated myself more every day. I got only one break: the Religion editor wanted me to look at our Christian Humor line and help make it, as she said, "less cute and more ha-ha." She'd heard that I'd performed stand-up comedy as a Christian and figured I'd be ideal for the job.

"I'm not exactly a Christian anymore," I said, though I really wasn't sure what I was. I hadn't even thought about it in what felt like months.

"That's okay," she said. "You speak the language. You know what you can push and what's too far." I agreed: it was an excuse to write humor again; I'd be a fool not to take it. So she handed me a few Christian comedy CDs, a Christian humor book, and a book called *The Power of Prayer*. "You should read this," she said. "It's really good."

I tried not to roll my eyes. I've never understood the point of books on Christian prayer—you either believe it works or you don't, and if God's all-powerful, what else is there to learn? It's not like leaning this way or doing it at a certain time of day gives Jesus better reception or makes him nicer. But she'd asked, so later at my desk I politely flipped through it—and I read something that blew my mind.

The book was filled with testimonials from this woman's life as she risked asking for bigger and bigger things. Two-thirds of the way into the book, she asks, "Can prayer change the weather?" She tried it. Her Texas homestead was undergoing a terrible drought, but the Lord had been faithful for a hundred pages already, so she took a gamble and prayed to God to help . . . and a few days later, rain came. And what rain! It rained so hard, in fact, that the water rose and threatened to flood the house. Uh-oh! And then, in an amazing sentence, she said, "And so, rebuking Satan, I prayed again. . . ." The rain stopped; the house was saved.

My jaw actually dropped. *Wait a minute,* I thought. God makes it rain, but Satan makes it rain *too much*? How does that make any sense at all? But I also knew that I had prayed dozens of times using exactly the same chop-logic: to the person praying, the move can make perfect sense. I thought, *So wait a minute . . . what if, when we pray, we're really just expressing anxiety over things we can't control?* As soon as I thought it, it clicked into place: we pray to pass tests or to find a parking space. We don't pray that aspirin will work. I started reading religious cards, and listening to people talk about God, and sure enough, prayer and God were always used either to settle the uncertain ("God's in control") or to add meaning to what might have been a mere coincidence ("It was meant to be").

The next morning I woke up and thought, *If there's no God, then it's just me and my thoughts and there's no one watching.* And I realized it felt exactly the same as when I'd talked to God; it was like an imaginary friend. I bought a bagel and thought, *Why don't I just steal and kill this very minute?* It turns out that I'm a decent person who respects the lives of others, and that's a better motivation than fear of hell. So now I was living life as I always had, only without an imaginary friend *and* with a better motivation to do good. The more I tried on the theory, the more the dominoes kept falling. I hadn't intended to make any huge life changes, but by the end of the week, I realized I was an atheist. And that I'd been living like an atheist for quite some time.

I had momentary worries—especially when I thought, *What happens when I die?*—but they were actually short-lived. Because for me, the evidence was in, and if anything, becoming an atheist simplified my life tremendously: I could simply sidestep all forms of superstition, and love my neighbor because he or she was a human being worth respecting. John Lennon was right: it isn't hard to do.

I also decided, however, not to go the whole other way and

try to assassinate all forms of god-talk and god-think. If my suspicions were correct, our brains are sort of wired to be religious, and talking as if God existed was still useful. I still admired Saint Francis even though I didn't believe in stigmata anymore. There was something beautiful about the church, and about our human longing for meaning, even when I believed these rituals were just symbolic. And by tapping into that—into the good parts of the life of faith I'd lived up till now—I was able to finish the project.

By the way, the religious cards I eventually wrote were quite successful. Josh Broward told me he saw televangelist John Hagee receive one on TV for his birthday: "Top Ten Hymns for People Our Age."

"My mom called me about it," he said. "I recognized it as your work. So John Hagee read your card out loud to America, Dave. Congratulations, I think."

"Thanks," I said. "I didn't believe a single word I wrote." We laughed, ruefully.

14

Saint John

MY CONVERSATION WITH DEEDEE CONTINUED TO HAUNT me for weeks after, and its salient idea—all women like having their breasts touched—seemed to paint all women in bright colors I'd been blind to since birth. Thinking abstractly about breasts and nerve endings led to other thoughts, and for the second time in my life, I started feeling dangerously out of control of my own desires. I spent my days surrounded by women who were lively and enthusiastic, and I would think, *I wonder if she likes sex, I wonder if she's aggressive* . . . and each new possibility was so alluring, so shiny, that I could sense what felt like some desperate bird inside me, batting against my rib cage. It scared me with its intensity, and for a month or more I stewed and worried. I strongly suspected that if I didn't have some sense of the road not taken, I might be tempted to take it. I'd fallen into sin and perversion before. I didn't want to do it again.

So, as with my old voyeurism problem, I knew I had to solve it in a religiously unorthodox manner. But this time, porn wouldn't work. I was curious about real women, not siliconized actresses, and I wanted to know how they felt. And unlike my voyeurism, this time a woman I loved was involved—she was, in fact, part of the pressure. Essentially, I felt like normal people were owed some life experience as far as women were concerned—maybe two or three actual relationships—before they got married. And as I saw things, it was just my dumb luck that the first woman I ever dated turned out to be The One I'd wind up marrying. I felt cursed by my own great success in love, because if you tried to fix something that's already perfect, wouldn't that make you crazy? What do you do when the best thing in your life causes you the most confusion?

I finally mentioned my concerns to Jane, and when she asked what I intended to do about these feelings, I was forced to think rather weirdly. I knew I couldn't date anyone, didn't want to cheat, and didn't want to let these feelings bust up our approaching marriage. So I suggested, "Maybe I should hire a prostitute. Not to have sex with, but just to look at and touch, the way Georges Rouault used to hire them as models." (I invoked Georges Rouault because he was a famously religious Catholic artist. If Georges Rouault had done it, surely it couldn't be evil!) Jane was a very creative thinker, a determinedly liberal, prostitution-legalizing feminist, and she knew me well enough to trust me. So she gave me permission. "I don't want to know about it, though. Just get whatever it is out of your system. I love you." Jane had always been my model for normalcy, and our relationship was the best thing in my life. For our entire relationship, I had been the geeky out-of-mainstream fuckup who needed to be taught how the world outside the Bible worked, and up till now I had felt stronger and saner with every passing year. The idea that Jane, or our engagement, might be somehow flawed never even crossed my mind.

THE VERY NEXT weekend—payday—I went shopping. The prospect terrified me. For someone who thought getting blow jobs from his girlfriend was naughty and excitingly shameful, doing something actually illegal and actually sexual seemed like opening the pits of hell. I wasn't sure enough of my balance that I wouldn't slip and fall in. But I took deep breaths and told myself, *I'm doing this for us; for our future. I have to do it.* And so I went looking for call girls.

There's no school for this sort of thing, and I wanted to keep it completely secret, so I had to learn the entire process in real time. I ruled out streetwalkers—they were dangerous, too public, and probably less pretty (which mattered, since I was trying to defuse a distracting fantasy by letting myself experience it perfectly just this once), and the only real advantage they had was price. (Which, by the way, is why Georges Rouault used streetwalkers as models; he was poor.) I was making greeting-card-writer money, so I went for the ads in the Kansas City arts weekly. There were six different companies with ads in the back that all promised an "escort" or "private dancing." So I started with the "AAA Top Models and Companions" and made the call.

"I'm looking for an escort," I said.

"I'm sorry," said the voice on the other line. "We do private modeling shows."

"Oh!" I said. "My bad." And I hung up.

The next two places also did modeling shows, and as I hung up, I thought, *Damn! Why do they advertise as escort services if they don't actually use call girls? Where are the real escorts hanging out?*

The fourth place I called, I was wary. "Do you guys do, like, modeling shows? I mean, who are you?"

And the woman said, "My name is Jen, and I'm five foot two with brown hair and a C cup. . . ."

"But . . . do you do . . . I'm new at this and I'm kind of confused. What kind of 'shows' do you do?"

"We do private in-home fashion shows where I model some lingerie, and sometimes I wear just balloons . . ."

A strip-o-gram? How silly!

"Well, gosh," I said. "That's not what I'm looking for."

"Oh, that's a shame!" she said. "You sound real nice."

I hung up and thought about that last phrase. *You sound real nice.* Not the kind of thing a mere stripper would say. It struck me that maybe these really were *all* escort services, only I hadn't been able to crack the code. So I went back to one of the earlier phone numbers and tried a new tack.

"Look," I said. "I'm looking for . . . companionship. And I thought I might find them here in these escort ads. But for some reason every place I call just seems to do modeling. Can someone tell me what the fuck is going on?"

The woman on the other end was silent for a while, and then she said, "Why are you calling up places and asking for a call girl? That's illegal. If someone did that, they might get arrested for soliciting."

The subjunctive mood! The traditional grammatical structure of paranoia. I got it. Or thought I did.

"So, uh . . . do you have any . . . uh, models available?"

"You want a fashion show in your home?"

"Yeah, whatever. Who do you have?"

"We have Crystal, who is a brunette, five foot five and a hundred and ten pounds. She's a thirty-six C and—"

"I need . . . uh, I'd like real breasts."

She paused for two quiet beats. Then: "We have Melody. She's. Well, she's the only one available right now who matches your—"

"What does she look like?"

She was blond, and that was good because the whole point of this experiment was that I fondle someone who looked different from my auburn-haired girlfriend. Melody also had more of those thirty-six C breasts—the C cup being, apparently, the official cup size of the Kansas City call girl.

"I'll let you talk to her," said the woman, who I guess was either the madam or the dispatcher. And I was patched in to Melody, who was on one of those newfangled-in-1998 cell phones somewhere.

"Hi!" said Melody, sounding comfortingly enthusiastic. I immediately felt at ease. "I understand you want a show. What time did you need me? I mean, is this for tonight, or . . . ?"

"Tonight. Really, whenever you can get over here."

"I've got a . . . thing I'm going to right now. How about nine?"

Nine it was. She asked where I lived, and I told her. "It's easier to come through the back way."

"Oh, I'm really not comfortable with that, because of, well, you know. You have to meet me in the lobby."

She had a thing. She was afraid of well, you know. This is the price of trafficking in the demimonde. All of your threats and fears are ghostly and yet present, like Schrödinger's cat. All our conversation skirted around this darkness.

Before she hung up, I asked, "How much?"

And she said, "A hundred and twenty."

I didn't have that much on me. "Do you take credit cards?"

She laughed and said, "No, honey. You've got some time. Go get the cash."

I bundled up, crossed the street to my bank kiosk, took out one hundred and sixty—I figured I might want groceries later—and by the time I got back to my apartment it was seven-thirty, so I had an hour and a half to wait and think about what I wanted. I really wasn't sure. On one hand, the idea of hiring a prostitute was supposed to be freeing; to let some steam escape from the walls-closing-in feeling of my impending marriage.

And yet I definitely didn't want sex. That would be cheating. But what was this woman coming over to do? Did I want to get to first base or third? It struck me how crazy this all was, and I kept turning it over and over in my mind. How the hell was I supposed to know what I wanted? Pretty much my entire sexual life had revolved around receiving blow jobs. It's like my entire sexual lexicon contained only one word. (Well, two letters.) With such a poor vocabulary I could scarcely begin to articulate what I wanted in this tiny sanctioned interstice between my past life of superstitious abstinence and my upcoming life of principled abstinence.

And this whole time, of course, I was also wondering if I really had a call girl coming, or if I'd wind up somehow spending $120 on a fashion show.

As it happened, I had longer to consider this than I thought, because she called me at nine and said, "I'm lost." I lived basically at the corner of two of the most prominent streets in town. I lived right across the street from the Plaza, which is really the only reason to visit Kansas City in the first place. It's also one of the richer parts of town, which made it seem unlikely that she wouldn't know her way around. I mean, Christ: the Marriott was just two blocks away. Don't tell me call girls don't know where the hotels are. But I assumed there was something else going on (that darkness again) and I just guided her in without asking questions. She finally buzzed the front door at nine-forty.

I thought for some reason that, out of politeness, I ought to offer her something like a romantic environment. Candles seemed over the top, but how about music? I looked over my albums and realized I only had one non-rock-and-roll, sort of high-class album: Handel's *Messiah*. It was September, but I thought, *What the hell. It's less of a buzz kill than Christian rock.* I settled on a decently low volume—below conversation, above the ambient hiss of the heater—tossed a few errant clothes in the closet, and went to meet my fate.

Here I am, going to pick up a hooker, I thought, as I ambled to the front lobby. *I wonder if anyone will know. I bet this is the kind of thing that could get me thrown out of the building. What the fuck is wrong with me? How have I come to this?* The very halls of my apartment complex seemed to frown at me, though I was relieved to note that I passed absolutely no one in the halls, and there were no old ladies sitting in the lobby, which was where they usually lurked.

To my surprise, Melody was dressed like a hooker. I had obviously been romanticizing this whole thing. For a hundred and twenty bucks, you don't get Gigi. But as hookerwear went, her suit was pretty fun: she had a white form-fitting dress, white stockings, and the tallest, fuck-me-est fuck-me-pumps I've ever seen. (And even with the pumps, she was smaller than me. And I'm only five seven.) She was carrying a huge gate-mouthed brown handbag that not only didn't match but it looked really heavy. I thought, *Of course. Tools.* And I decided then: *I'm not sure what I want, but I know I don't like cold metal objects touching me, and I don't like being naked near electricity.* The tools would stay in the bag.

"Hi," she said, and we shook hands. "Are you Dave?"

"Yes," I said. Though tonight I wasn't sure.

When we got back to my place, some tenor was singing "Every Valley Shall Be Exalted." I took her jacket. She didn't say anything about the apartment, which was nice of her. Whenever I'm alone, my living space becomes an undifferentiated series of clothing and book piles, and the only way you can tell which room is which is by guessing at the furniture. I moved some books off a chair (*the chair my girlfriend's dad gave me!*) and invited her to sit. I imagined there might be a warm-up chat, like I saw in *Pretty Woman.*

"Thanks. Do you have an ashtray, honey?" she said, setting the bag down with a quiet clatter. I didn't. When you have as much paper as I do lying around, a single cigarette can destroy your whole credit rating. I went to the kitchen, rummaged for a bit. All I could find was a saucer.

"Here," I said, setting it down on the arm. "I never drink tea anyway."

We talked a little. "And the Glory of the Lord Shall Be Revealed" was intermittently audible during our chat. She didn't comment on the music, so I assume it was a passable choice. I had a little wine, too. I'd bought it and a corkscrew months earlier to feel classy, but hadn't opened it until now. This was my chance to seem worldly, so we drank that while we talked. I told her about my job, and she was fascinated. She asked me all the usual questions, and then I was finally able to ask her about herself.

All she said was she was a nursing student, working her way through school. "I've got two rules," she said. "I don't kiss. And if you see me outside anywhere, you don't know me. I'm serious. I'll fucking kill you. In my job, this is . . ." She tapped the ash off her cigarette with casual finality.

"Don't worry," I said. "And thanks for the information. I'm completely new at this."

Suddenly she got up. "Can I use your bathroom?" she said.

I nodded, thinking, *Is this on the clock? Did she just drop the flag?* She emerged a few seconds later wearing a green satiny dress. "Sit down," she said, gesturing to the couch.

So I sat, and she started humming. "This is the fashion show," she said. "Hmm, hmm, hmmmmmmm . . ." She strutted for maybe five steps, twirled, and ended with show hands: "Ta da!"

Then, looking relieved, she stepped out of the dress (wearing white lingerie underneath, which was pearly and overfrilled), and said, "I did the show, and that's what you're paying me for. Everything that happens from here on out is just a spontaneous thing between two consenting adults. So . . . should we go back to your bedroom?"

"Uh, no," I said. "The bedroom's a mess and I didn't bother to clean it. I don't really want sex or anything. I just . . . I just want to see your breasts and, you know, touch them, if that's okay."

She stopped short. "You're shitting me."

I tried to explain my situation, but even before I started,

something in my story must have triggered distrust. "Is this some
kind of joke?" She started moving around the room, looking. "Is
there a camera somewhere?"

"No, no . . ."

She opened the closet door. "God, I just know there's a guy
with a camera in here. Hello?" She moved the jackets aside; nothing. She looked at my bedroom. "Are they in the bedroom? Is
that why you don't want to go in there?"

"No, I swear." And I opened the door, and while she scanned
the room (it was a disaster) I told her the whole story.

"Your girlfriend said this was okay?"

"As long as I didn't have sex."

She shook her head. "I don't know how you guys do that.
Long-distance doesn't work. You mean you've been together six
years? And you've been apart for over three of them? And in that
whole time you've never cheated on her?"

"No."

"Well, she's definitely cheating on you. Trust me. I know how
these things work."

And I knew, just as certainly, that she didn't understand us.
This, more than anything, convinced me that what I was doing
was wrong. Not morally wrong, per se; just psychologically
screwed up. A person in her line of work never met people like
me and my girlfriend. In a perfect world—or at least in a world
where my religion's story about human nature was accurate—
this wouldn't have been happening at all.

When no third party appeared, she agreed to my request.
"What do you want to do?" she said, and she even sounded
uncertain. I decided I didn't want to do anything below the
waist, so that Jane's would be the only labia I would ever see. So

I just asked her to take off the bra and let me fondle her breasts.

"That's all you want?"

I said it was.

"Fine," she said. "It's your money, baby."

It struck me that maybe I should request a discount, but I figured she had a flat hourly rate she was accountable for, like they do at an auto shop, and I didn't want to bother getting her into trouble. So: fondle fondle fondle. I just stood there, and she clearly didn't know what to do. She just waited there patiently. And while I knew, looking at myself as if from a third-person perspective, that what I was doing looked absolutely silly—even pathetic—I have to say, she was beautiful. So beautiful, in fact, that I really did try to memorize the feel of her skin, the pressure of her breasts, the contours of her face, the stiff prominence of her nipples. Her breasts were, in fact, much prettier than my girlfriend's, a fact that fascinated and scared me. *I need to remember this*, I told myself. *This is the only other woman I'll ever know.* The intensity of the sensation was enhanced by its onetime novelty. To be touching a woman at all—particularly a new, different woman of distinct loveliness—felt like winning the lottery. Mostly, though, I felt hopelessly hungry. Touching Melody made my heart surge like it was the most important act my body needed, and yet it wasn't enough. So I kept running my hands over her face, her neck, her shoulders and breasts, maybe with the hope that if I kept it up long enough, it would be sufficient; the way you can eventually feel full even if all you're eating is Styrofoam peanuts.

Suddenly I became aware of a new problem. Melody, my hooker, was clearly getting bored. Since the whole point of this

exercise was for me to be with a woman who actually liked having her breasts touched for a change, my heart sank and I saw a
hundred-dollar bill sprouting cruel wings. I once heard a theory
that prostitutes go into the business in order to act out on themselves over past abuses. If that was the case with Melody, the mild
treatment I was administering was clearly not meeting her needs.
She started to get antsy. This pulled me out of the dream, and
the stereo made an oddly familiar vamp, which distracted me
even further as I worried. Which side of which disc was this?
Were we about to be interrupted by "The Hallelujah Chorus"?
Nope. It sounded like "Behold, a Virgin Shall Conceive." Embarrassing, but at least it was only side one.

"You should feel my ass," she said. "I'm serious. I have a
great ass."

"What?" I said, but it was clear what she wanted, because
she pulled down her pants (frilly girl-panties! Jane never wore
those . . .), then turned sideways and dragged my hands to her
butt. I wasn't an ass man at the time—remember my one-word
lexicon?—but since my own mission had now failed, I felt guilty
about bothering her, so I felt her ass, just to make her happy.
"Very nice," I said. Nowadays I would have paid more attention,
but her ass just went to waste beneath my ignorant monosyllabic
hands, and she could feel it.

She knelt down. "Don't you want me to jerk you off or
something?" she said. "You could come on my tits. You'd like
that, wouldn't you?" *No, I'm about sixty-five percent sure I wouldn't,*
I thought, but she didn't even listen to hear me decide; she just
unzipped me and reached into my boxers like she knew what was
good for me.

I said, "Wait! . . ." But I honestly didn't have much time to formulate an argument. I really didn't want to come on her tits; I didn't want to associate this stranger with me coming at all. Yet she was so insistent, and I remember feeling bad for her. She so obviously wanted to do something that interested her; maybe she just had a strong work ethic. So by the time I was in her hands, I was of two minds as to whether to let her continue.

My decision was made for me in about five seconds. Perhaps it was simply a function of loneliness and hunger, but Melody's grip was indescribably intense. I've never experienced anything like it since, but Melody, who had known me for about twenty minutes, was not only better than my girlfriend of five years, *she was better than me.* Let's hear it for specialized skills. I really didn't have any volition at this point; I was simply in the grip of some ineffable force, like a tidal wave or a very friendly vacuum cleaner. So I came on her tits, and she made a big show of saying, "Wow!" and spreading the stuff all around, which, at the time, I just thought was weird and unsanitary. But I just smiled and said, "Thanks. That was great." And she smiled back, in her first truly satisfied expression of the night, and excused herself to the bathroom again to sponge off.

Myself, I was confused. I felt like a fool. This absurd experience hadn't done anything at all for my relationship with my girlfriend. It felt like a detour that had wound up in exactly the same neighborhood I'd been trying to leave. It struck me then that it was this attitude of my girlfriend's that was the problem. I wanted someone else to actually hunger for me; I wanted to feel physically desirable. This whole experience might have been helpful to me—to my curiosity, to my relationship's future—if the woman had been someone I'd met at a bar, some vivacious young thing who just couldn't wait to tear off my clothes. I could see then that I didn't want sex, per se. I wanted spontaneity, excitement, and mutual sexual desire. I even started to think—very gently, like a stray unserious theory—that this sort of happiness might be something that even a sinful guy like me actually *deserved*. Tonight's illusion didn't work precisely because it had been clouded over by money.

Speaking of which: while she was in the bathroom, I opened my wallet and thought, *Are you supposed to tip prostitutes?* It made sense; it was a service industry job, after all. But what would be appropriate? Ten percent, like an agent? I tip waiters twenty. Finally I realized that the math would be simplest if I simply tipped exactly fifteen percent: $140.

"Here you go," I said.

"Thanks," she said, and tucked it into her bra. "This was really interesting. Which way's the back way?"

"Don't you want to go out the front?"

"I trust you now," she said, patting me on the cheek. (Hey, guys, I think that prostitute really liked me!) So I showed her to the back entrance, and before she left she said, "Have a great night."

"You, too," I said, before I knew what I was saying. God knows what she was headed into.

"This was really interesting," she said again, and clop-clopped off in those absurdly high pumps. I watched her until she reached her car (a small white Honda of a certain age) and then went back inside and tidied up—by which I mean I picked up my ashed-on saucer and dumped it in the sink. I almost turned off the stereo, too, but it was on "The People That Walked in Darkness," so I figured what the hell, I'd just ride it out.

Interesting, she'd called this encounter. I wondered if that was a backhanded insult. I could imagine that I might be exactly the sort of client that prostitutes complain about among themselves. I pictured her back at work, in the employee lounge, maybe, stubbing out a cigarette in disgust. "I mean, Jesus. Why did he even call a prostitute if he didn't want to fuck?"

"I knew a guy like that once," I imagined her friend replying. "A weird French artist named Georges Rouault."

"Catholics," Melody said. "They're so fucked up."

15

House of Cards

"SO WHY DO YOU SAY YOU FEEL LIKE A 'FREAK'?" ASKED Dr. Gray, my new shrink. A berry-shaped black man with a calm demeanor, he was sitting in his chair with his head tilted in curiosity. I was sitting on his couch, my body huddled into a C of tension. It was deep in the afternoon, and the light was dying. I felt like lying down.

"Well, I'm a twenty-eight-year-old virgin, for starters," I said. "And I've got this perfect relationship and yet I seem to hate it. Also I hired a prostitute to get to second base. I don't think that's normal. For that matter, she didn't think so either. The prostitute, I mean."

Dr. Gray took a calming breath in the silence. "It's hard to transition from a religious upbringing. Of course you're going to find yourself conflicted. What's great about these mistakes you're making is that the collisions can bring everything into focus."

I relaxed. Dr. Gray had been raised religious like me, and that's why I'd settled on him. I wasn't sure where we were going, but not being alone in this was a huge advantage all by itself.

THE INCIDENT WITH the call girl hadn't helped, and I told Jane that I still felt like I needed some kind of sense of what was out there. Not sex, of course, but some datelike thing. I wasn't able to articulate it very clearly, but again, Jane trusted me and said, "If you want to date other people, without having sex with them, I guess that could work for as long as we have to be apart."

This new plan brought a new relief that lasted exactly as long as it took me to hang up the phone. Because in actual practice I couldn't figure out how such an arrangement would work. As I thought about what I wanted, the scenario was something like this: I go to a bar, I meet an attractive woman, we like each other, and after talking a bit we go off to some corner (or her car—even then I figured my car wasn't a draw), and then—fondling! Then, feeling silly, we part ways agreeably, and I am soothed: I know what's out there, I can freely choose, and I choose my fiancée—who is, after all, the person I know and love the best, other women's boobies notwithstanding. Thus my problem would be solved. I had tasted the forbidden fruit, done my own minor rumspringa, and come out on the other side a more morally contented person.

The problem I kept running into was my inability to lie. I couldn't picture myself talking to this hypothetical b-girl without picturing me saying, "Look, I'll be honest. I need help, and my fiancée and I have this arrangement—so I'm free to date, but we can't have sex and it can't really go anywhere serious, but I really need some kind of noncoital sexual experience before I get married, and I've got like a nine-month window." Marvel at my innocence: I actually wondered, Who would bother to date a guy with that kind of opening spiel? What woman would be interested in a no-strings short-term relationship with no risk of pregnancy or disease? It also never occurred to me that maybe this could be something we could agree to deal with later, within the context of our marriage. There was no logical reason for me to be this willfully naive: I was reading Dan Savage's "Savage Love" column in every issue of *The Onion*, and he was discussing cuckolding fetishes and open relationships every week. And even back in 1997, Craigslist was just a click away. If I'd bothered to scan those personals, I would have at least felt less exotic. I guess all of that was easy to ignore because in my heart I knew I was a simple Nilla wafer trying to get home.

Instead, I was convinced that everyone was just like me— longing for a romantic connection, taking sex seriously and even religiously—and I imagined that any woman I met would be as disgusted with my request and all its subclauses as I was with myself for apparently having to make it. Why couldn't I just be happy? I was convinced that what I wanted was something inherently unrealistic and childish, like a porn fantasy—the frottage version.

The only other option, then, was to be deceptive: meet a girl, string her along, get my boob jollies, and then break it off mysteriously and hope she never found out I was engaged the whole time. But I couldn't live with being a cad, and being even remotely dishonest felt evil. (While it's tempting to blame my church for this hyperconscientiousness, I think it was more a brain-driven anxiety that many nerds suffer from, and that my church simply enabled.) So the impossibility of this, too, made it unworkable. For the first time, I thought I had a sure fix for my growing anxiety, yet there seemed to be no ethically consistent way to achieve it.

So, with no obvious way out, I did the only other thing I could: I went to a counselor. So far, the main thing I liked about Dr. Gray was also the thing that scared me: he made me realize that my impulses were normal, that I should listen to my instincts, and that the healthiest way to think was to realize that a breakup, while unfortunate, might not be completely out of the question. Just by having the option on the table, I felt like maybe I wasn't insane to think of it.

I should point out that there is a much simpler way to describe my whole problem: I wanted sex to be fun and spontaneous and not a huge crushingly meaningful deal, and that's not how it was likely to be with Jane. (After six years, asking for our first sex to be *spontaneous* was a non sequitur.) But it was literally a year before I could even think this thought. I had been so well trained as a Christian that it was actually impossible for me to believe that fun sex might be important. Certainly it couldn't be important enough to break up a relationship over. That would be nothing but shallow, unspiritual hedonism. Every Christian sex-ed class emphasized this over and over again: you're friends first, and spiritual partners, and you're committed to each other, and then, later, once you're married, after everything is over, you also get to have sex. In the train of any relationship, sex was supposed to be the caboose. It might be a great caboose where everyone wanted to hang out after work, but the train would run just fine without it.

And if your own train stopped running, despite following the directions . . . well, you must be screwed up somehow. Have you tried praying harder?

AS THE TENSION mounted within me, Jane and I began to discuss her next visit. It was near the end of the semester, she was studying for her prelims, she was really stressed out and exhausted, and she wanted to make her after-school-year plans as soon as possible to improve her mood. The problem: while she wanted to see me, she also wanted to visit her brother in New York City. Since she only got a few weeks off a year as a teaching assistant, she needed to make a decision. Should she visit me, visit her brother, or divide up her vacation, and if so, in what order?

For my part, since we talked every day and this topic had appeared before and would appear again, I just kept talking and telling her everything I was thinking, stream-of-consciousness style. After all, we had no secrets. That was the healthy way to proceed, right?

"So are you still feeling conflicted? How are you doing?" she asked.

Blurting theory instead of thinking smart, I said, "Well, yeah. I've figured out that dating other people won't work as long as we're engaged. That would hang over everything, and it would, you know, sort of ruin the experiment before it could even start. We need something just a little more radical. Here's what I've been thinking. We've got a year until we get married. Maybe we could, like, break up for a year, look around, and come back to each other after that?"

"Oh," she said, and she sounded seriously disturbed for the first time in these conversations. "I couldn't do that. Our engagement is really important to me. I'll cut you a lot of slack, do what you need to, but I can't do that."

Well, that sucked. Because I actually had this really romantic idea planned. As I mentioned, I'd been writing my fiancée poems for years. It started at a poem a week, but although it had since scaled down to one a month, I'd maintained it for all this time, and I'd occasionally do a burst of extra poems—like, for example, I once bought her a complete set of Horatio Hornblower novels, and I wrote a poem on the inner cover of each book, eleven poems in one gift. All told, I figured I'd given my fiancée some fifty or sixty poems over the years, and I'd planned almost from the beginning to collect them all in a book I'd title *Poems from a Love Affair*—with a possible sequel, *Poems from a Marriage*, since I intended to keep writing her a poem a month forever.

My big romantic idea was that, although the idea of temporarily breaking up was really scary, during the year apart, I'd be secretly writing her a poem a week again, and when we got back together I'd present her with this huge sheaf of poems, saying, "I never stopped thinking about you." What would be even cooler, I thought, was if I could somehow get hold of all the poems she already had from me in various scrapbooks, so I could literally give her all my poems at once: to finish this big dangerous break with a gift of memory and history, and a promise to never part again. That would be a story for our grandkids, and maybe even for *USA Today*. I'd convinced myself that not only was this a perfect gesture, but that my fiancée deserved nothing less—our love called for an actual headline, just like when we'd gotten engaged.

It was an intoxicatingly lovely idea to me. I just hadn't worked out all the details. But it definitely involved us breaking up temporarily. So when my fiancée finally refused this plan of mine, I was a little rocked. She'd been okay with my hiring a prostitute, but not with breaking an engagement? Since when was that anything more than an agreement? Was she planning to sue me for disappointment of promise, like in some nineteenth-century novel?

"Look," I said. "Honey. This thing I have, this problem, there's no way to actually fix it if I'm engaged. That interferes with every solution we've talked about. If you agreed with me that I needed to hire a call girl, to sort of get out and experience other things—not sex, we agree on that—why can't you see that this is important, too?"

"Are you deranged? It was completely different. The call girl was a financial transaction. It was a paid-for solution to a physical problem. Now you're asking for emotional . . ." Her voice trailed away, then came back more determined. "You know, Dave, I think I've already been *very* open-minded about your whole deal."

"I'm not saying that. I'm grateful. But . . . look, you've been with me through every problem I've had. Remember how when we first started dating, when we watched movies I'd close my eyes during sex scenes, and you'd tell me when I could open them? Well, we got past that, right? We found out that closing my eyes didn't work as well as just not being stupid and learning to relax around nudity did, and things have been better, right?" She said nothing, so I pressed on. "So as you know, I tried the call girl, and I know you don't want the details, but nothing happened, but it didn't work precisely because it was a transaction. There was something missing, a kind of . . . excitement? Maybe? I'm sorry, honey. I don't even know what's missing. I just know that I can't fix this panic I have, not with one call girl or a hundred. It's the wrong thing. Like closing my eyes; we need to change strategies."

"You need to listen to *me* now, Dave," she said. "Our engagement is important to me. You don't know what it's like here. The work is insane, the politics are complicated, and it's lonely and cold and miserable. And when I'm surrounded by all this bullshit, our engagement is something I really cling to. It's this constant in my life, and I don't want to give it up."

"I don't want to give it up either, honey," I said. "I don't want to. I just don't see how to get out there and fix the—"

"You keep saying 'fix.' What do you picture happening? In your dream scenario, why does something that happens make you feel better?"

I tried to picture it. Me, at a party, meeting some attractive woman. No match for Jane in the brain department, but sexy in her own, different way. We'd wander off to some quiet corner, do some necking, and I'd figure out . . . what? I remembered Deedee's comment that we date in order to make mistakes. "I feel like I've never made a mistake," I said, trying it out even as I said it. "Like if we get married, I won't have had a choice. I hate the thought of meeting other women. I know they'll disappoint me. I don't want to date anyone because I know I'll be bad at it. But I think I need to do it—not sex, but something date-like, like we've said already, something sort of romantic—so I can come back to you from a position of strength, of knowledge. In a way I guess I feel like—you came along just when I needed help, like a miracle, and everything has gone along so perfectly ever since . . . it's almost like God chose you, not me. But I want to choose you. I want to know what that's like."

She was silent for a long time and I wondered if I'd said something hurtful by accident. "Look, honey," I said. "This isn't anything we need to settle tonight, and if I think about it some more, or talk to my shrink, maybe I'm just being insane. Let's just . . . we can talk it out some more when you get here, okay? I love you."

"Dave," said Jane slowly, "are you breaking up with me? Because there's no point in my flying down there to visit if you're just going to break up with me."

I hadn't expected this obvious question, and I let silence hang there for longer than I should have, trying to think of what I actually wanted. "No!" I said. "I mean, I don't want . . . I just mean, temporarily, in like a harmless . . ." I trailed off, though, because as I was talking I felt the walls start closing in again. *Oh my god*, I thought. *I do want to break up with her. I couldn't do it forever, because being without her would kill me. But I really do want a break. Why would I want something like that?*

"Oh my god," said Jane, as if the idea were just striking her. "You're trying to break our engagement. You really don't want to be my fiancé anymore."

"Not 'anymore' . . ." I tried feebly, hoping to parse some optimistic distinction between *anymore* and *not for a little while at least*. But she started crying, and I realized my mere desire, my little brainstorm, had hurt her worse than anything I'd ever said. I also knew that, precisely because we'd been honest with each other this whole time, if I went back on my word now and tried to act like I hadn't been serious, she would know I was lying.

"Oh, fuck," she said, sobbing. "Fuck. I can't talk anymore."

And she hung up. I felt I'd been kicked in the stomach. No, worse—I felt like the guy in your standard film noir mystery: the innocent man who wakes up with his hands covered in blood and spends the rest of the movie trying to figure out how things wound up that way.

I WISH I COULD SAY that that was the breakup, and that it never got worse, but you can't break off a six-year relationship just by accidentally saying a few incautious things over the phone. You have to talk about it, painful as it is, and for the next three weeks we shared a mutual agony: not being able to bear to call each other (after talking nightly for an hour for six years), then finding our separation too painful and risking another call where we tearfully tried to work out a solution, which would end with another depressing breakup. I developed a theory of relationships that has served me faithfully ever since: no relationship can end until staying together is consistently more painful than the alternative. Nowadays when friends ask, "Should I break up with him?" my stock answer is, "The fact that you're asking for advice is a sign that the breakup is coming. But the fact that you're asking for advice also shows you're not ready yet."

The only thing that sustained me, in the three weeks of excruciating back-and-forth that came in the aftershock of our first rift, was the hope that maybe this wasn't permanent. She'd come around and see I only meant it temporarily. We'd get past this somehow and things would work again and I wouldn't lose the best friend I'd ever had. And behind it all was that dream of the big, beautiful, loving, restorative gesture: my gift to her of all the poems I'd ever sent her, assembled together in *Songs from a Love Affair,* where the first new poem on top would be called something puckish and rueful, like "The Break Didn't Take."

Reality wasn't cooperating. Instead of the polite temporary breakup I'd planned, it looked like my fiancée was actually thinking this was permanent for both of us. And I was actually afraid that she might do violence to the poems I'd sent her, *and I needed them for the manuscript.* I didn't have copies—they were all hand-written—and they were essential for any hope I could place in a romantic happy ending. So one night of painful attempted reconciliation, while we were hurt and sniping at each other, talking about how one of us was unreasonable and the other was cruel, I managed, through a constricted throat, to ask, "Well . . . can I at least have the poems back?"

Jane gasped. "What?"

"I . . . I need to get the poems back. Can you send them to me?" Even as I said it, even as I heard her gasp, it seemed like a basically reasonable request.

"Fine!" she said. "Un-fucking-believable!" and slammed down the phone. I realized then that I'd done something very, very stupid. I held the phone, frozen, waiting for a miracle, for this not to have happened. Could I unsay what I'd just said? If she took me back, wouldn't that sliver of knife tip still live under the skin? As I hung up on my end, I actually closed my eyes. I couldn't bear to see myself release the receiver. Even with my eyes closed, I held on to the phone for several minutes, because I knew when I let go, we had officially split up. In the days that followed, I would sometimes look down at that right hand of mine, the one that had let go of the phone, had committed this murder. It felt strange and cold to me.

Even that wasn't the end, of course. There were still details to be worked out—for one thing, I had to send her her father's furniture—and at one point in the denouement, she said, "You know, Dave, I don't think you realized how much I loved those poems. I loved them! I cherished them! I went to them every day. And now, every time I miss you, or I feel bad about the breakup, I just think about how you asked for those poems back. That makes it easy."

She sent them, too. By the time I got them in the mail, I realized how amazingly foolish and monstrously hurtful it had been to ask for them. She had even torn the title pages from each of her Hornblower books. I made photocopies dutifully, a zombie miming a ritual, but once it was done I looked at them and couldn't think straight about what to do with them. I realized that she probably didn't want to see them anymore. I also felt bad keeping them. I was the asshole in this relationship; why should I get to keep all the cool poems?

I threw them away. I still wince when I think about the needless pain of it all. If they ever invent a time machine, that'll be the first thing I fix. I hurt the woman I loved more than anyone I've ever hurt for a simple stupid reason: I was so focused on the romantic greeting card dream of dramatic, eternal love against the odds that I completely ignored her real feelings. I should have at least confided in Josh Broward or Kenneth Riley and asked for advice, and maybe the poems, at least, might have been saved. She should have kept them. I'm more sorry than I can say.

THE BREAKUP WAS like an unremitting fire that burned through every muscle in my body. I winced when I even moved my arms to raise food to my mouth. I've never felt worse in my entire life, and with any luck I'll never suffer that much again. I reported to Dr. Gray through those agonizing weeks of breaking-and-fixing-and-breaking-once-more, and he kept saying, "Think about what you want, not what you *should* want." It was an alien concept to me; I wanted to want what I should want. When the break seemed truly final, I came into his office looking and feeling shattered. Me—the guy known for his calm demeanor and sunny disposition, the guy whom powerful emotional goblins try to scale but can't get a crampon into. I'm a born essayist, intrinsically detached and bemused; it's in my very cell structure. When you're a guy like that, an actual heart-wrenching is doubly agonizing for the same reason that introverts are the most miserable people at a crowded, noisy wake—they're facing two stresses, one outside, one in. This wasn't just sadness; it was a sadness so profound it did actual violence to my nature, and I felt it like a metal band around my heart that punished it for daring to swell. If I found myself admiring a joke, or taking pleasure in the sunshine, the moment would barely register before I'd remember, *Oh, fuck, I almost forgot that I'm dying*, and the band would tighten again, as if my heart were a dog that needed to be broken to a new and crueler leash.

I wanted to scream, but no one has that much screaming in them. I could barely even bother to lift my arms in the shower. When I limped into Dr. Gray's office, I'd been dizzy for days, fighting to keep it all inside. I must have looked like a fugitive.

Dr. Gray was sympathetic. He said, "Breakups after a long-term relationship are one of the most devastating things we encounter. So what you need to do right now is be good to yourself. Do something you enjoy. Your spirit needs to know that it can still feel okay."

Something I enjoy, I thought. *Good idea*. So I ventured out that Friday night, with the flight-ready caution of a driver who's just been through a collision at this same intersection. I liked old movies. That was the first thing I'd come up with. So I figured I'd rent something—obviously a comedy, and one with no romance in it at all. Maybe the Marx Brothers or W. C. Fields. All the way over in my car I was mulling my options (something safe that I'd already seen, no musicals, no beautiful women stars even), then walked into my accustomed video store (An all-guy cast, yes! Maybe an action comedy like *Gunga Din* . . .), walked toward the "Classics" section . . . and smacked right into *Casablanca*.

To this day, no mere emotion has ever caused me such real and sudden physical pain. I literally reeled, like I'd been hit. My legs buckled and I actually sat down in the middle of the aisle to catch my breath, ignoring the people around me, keeping my eyes cast firmly at the floor and shading them with my hand so I wouldn't see the accusing cover again. *Casablanca*. Jesus. My favorite movie of all time, the movie that had underpinned our relationship at every point, that had been a symbol of the happiest moments of the last six years . . . and I had ruined it forever.

I also thought, *Dr. Gray, that was some awful fucking advice. What the hell were you thinking?*

The pain didn't get any worse, and I eventually rose to my feet, but I realized I couldn't risk the Classics section. Even if I rented, say, *Duck Soup*, I'd see that one of the minor actors was Leonid Kinskey and I'd think, *Aah! He's the guy who played the bartender Sascha in* Casablanca! *I've completely ruined my life!* Clearly I'd have to go very modern, some movie made after everyone in *Casablanca* was dead.

So I looked around at the New Releases wall and thought, *What's something that'll distract me that I won't care about at all?* I settled on *Extreme Measures*, a late-1996 Michael Apted film that had come to video a few months prior. It's essentially *Coma*. Scratch that: it is *exactly Coma*, only without any critical or financial success. A kind of dumb, fitfully smart thriller about doctors and chicanery and secret forbidden experiments, it was Hugh Grant's first mainstream American shot at a serious drama (*A Really Big Adventure* only played the art houses here), and America collectively looked at the marquee and said, "When's it going to video?"

Now that I realized that I was more vulnerable than I'd thought, and that I couldn't do it alone, I called Kenneth and asked for a big silly-sounding favor.

Several years earlier, when I was still an undergraduate, four members of my college Christian youth group had been killed in a terrible auto accident. We had four funerals in a month, and I started to notice a few things about grief. The most interesting thing to me was the way in which you get *tired* of grieving long before the grief is through, tired of being the grieving one, of having to talk about grief and having everyone look at you and ask what's wrong. You start to want a different job, even if only for one night's rest, and even if it's more of a sinecure than a real occupation. Back then, I noticed the things that I found the most soothing and filed the information away in case it ever became useful again. Tonight I needed those notes and tried to remember what I'd learned.

"I know this is short notice, but here's what I need," I told Kenneth. "I just rented a mediocre movie and I need to watch it to take my mind off of the . . . off everything. But I might not get through it, you know? I'm so . . . So I, uh, I need you to watch it with me, and I need you to invite a few people over, too. I also want you to, like, just, talk among yourselves and feel free to ignore me if I don't feel like talking. And, finally, if at some point in the movie I just break down or whatever, I need you to just stop the movie and wait until I'm better, talk if I need it, and then start again."

And Kenneth said, "Sure. Do you want pizza?"

I don't remember anything about *Extreme Measures*, and in this, I'm exactly like the people who saw it in the theater. But I do remember stopping the video three or four times, always apologizing, but never hearing a word from Kenneth. (He didn't bring anyone over, so the talk-among-yourselves part didn't happen. But that was okay.) I cried, I worried aloud, we stopped the film, he listened politely, and then we got back to watching. And the evening worked. I think I got through the worst of my despair simply by being around someone who cared enough to accommodate my difficulty, and I did it on an evening that at least *felt* like it was moving forward instead of circling for the millionth time around the same bleak thoughts I'd been turning over for days. I talked about this later, and Kenneth said, "I knew it must have helped, because before you left, we hugged for a really long time." If you ever have to go through grief, I highly recommend my system. But it really helps to have a friend like Kenneth around.

16

A Flash of Brightness

BY THIS TIME, THE ONE THING THAT HAD BEEN SORT OF working for me in Main Writing—writing love copy by thinking of my fiancée—was anathema to me. And of course nothing else was getting easier either. When I was on the ninth floor, I was suffering. When I left, I suffered less but also got less done. The whole thing is nicely summed up in a cartoon I drew around this same time (see Figure 5).

FIGURE 5

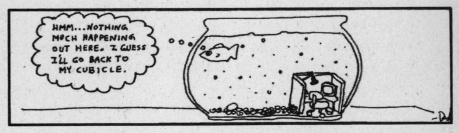

So after months of fighting my writer's block—trying to care, sweating through the hatred, and coming up with nothing—I decided to simply shut down. Since I wasn't getting writing done either way, I figured I may as well at least reduce my suffering. I'd already had enough of that with my love life.

Speaking of which, I still felt pretty numb, but maybe numb was the first step to normal. At least I wasn't in constant pain. One day when I had walked to Deedee's office—I had a daily routine now, and Deedee was the first stop—I told her, "You know, I'm starting to think I could date again."

"Really," she said, and there was an unusual tone in her voice. She turned to me with a sideways smile and stroked her chin dramatically. "What I was going to tell you is it's over with Randall."

"The breast guy? I mean, the millionaire?"

"Not a millionaire. A liar." She wheeled in her chair and then pointed at me impishly. "I think we should go out."

My oxygen vanished. I could hardly believe it. The one person who I was most attracted to in all of Hallmark, a woman I thought I never had a chance with, was actually asking me out. "Yes!" I said, and one half of my brain said, *Hey, didn't that hurt just a little?* and the other said, *Shut up, shut up, this is the chance of a lifetime.* "Um . . . when's good?"

She laughed, and it really did seem like music then. "We both work right here. Why don't you just come by at five and we'll go to dinner across the street?"

"Great idea," I said, and I felt that brave pain again and shoved it back down.

She giggled. *I had an effect on her!* "You know, I've been dating so many assholes, just yesterday I looked around and thought, there are so many great men in my life already, why don't I date someone I actually trust for a change, you know? Someone where there's a future."

I turned cold. At the word *future*, my entire libido shattered like a nitrogen-frozen, science-class banana. I was strong enough to stand on my own. To meet someone harmlessly. In short, I felt ready for a fling, something that wouldn't possibly hurt me. Leave it to Deedee to decide at that moment to finally stop being casual and start implying forever. The irony was annoyingly perfect. It was fucking "Send in the Clowns."

I had to at least try, though. I waited all day for my heart to come around to the great luck Deedee represented. But, damn it all, my heart looked up at that steep-ass hill and said, "Fuck it; I'm not running anymore." My flesh was willing but my spirit was on strike.

Even then, I refused to give up. I came by and got her. She hugged me, and it felt great, but she kissed my cheek and I flinched. We walked to the restaurant without accidentally touching or bumping shoulders the way real daters might. But I was so far into my head the whole time, I can scarcely recall a single scent or taste or thing we talked about. I remember the restaurant was French. I remember for dessert I had ladyfingers.

During a pause in one of her stories—and god, she looked gorgeous in the candlelight—I broke down and said, "I'm really sorry, Dee, but it turns out I'm not ready yet, after all. I'm so pissed about this, but what can you do?"

"That's okay," said Deedee. "I've been there. You need time. Stay positive!" She patted my hand, we split the check and went home, and I didn't swing by her office for a week and a half.

Afterward I puzzled this over and had a revelation. When my heart had rebelled from this offer of easy bliss, it had felt exactly like my own writer's block: the same instant, perversely stubborn refusal to budge where once it had moved freely and with joy. My heart had lover's block. Not a single part of my life seemed capable of motion.

WE FINALLY HAD one of those writers' retreats that I'd longed for ever since I'd first read Josh Broward's poems. This day's seminar—an exploration of modern poetry—was being led by an actual prizewinning poet who was the head of a creative writing department at a big southwestern university. About twenty of us clambered into a van, which drove forty minutes out of town to an honest-to-god farmhouse. It was a two-story cottage, bedecked almost exactly as you'd expect, with flowers in vases and rustic objects bolted to the walls inside and well-kept gardens outdoors. There was even a duck pond and—if memory serves—a tire swing. All it lacked was a swimmin' hole.

It should have been a relief to simply lounge as we did on actual couches, reading photocopied packets full of interesting new poetry I'd never heard of, eating catered sandwiches, and trying to write our own poems, which were inspired by what we'd just read. The professor who was leading us was a great teacher who loved his craft, and all day we were being invited to enter into an actual relationship with literature. We didn't have to say anything was *special*, there wasn't a birthday in sight, and we were free to be honestly expressive and even somewhat dark and sarcastic. I needed that.

But even when we split up at noon to do our writing, I recall sitting in an upstairs window, in the soporific warmth of the May sun, and looking down at the front of the house, where two women from Main Writing were sitting away from each other,

sharing the extreme ends of the porch swing, and I realized I
didn't trust them. I thought about everyone curled up and staring
at walls all through the cottage and I knew I didn't trust anyone
here except Josh, because no one from Humor had shown up.

Our lecturer was fascinating: as an actual academic creative
writing teacher, he was like a living example of my road not
taken, and I wanted to ask him what his life was like back in that
desert climate. Do people complain about you behind your
back? Do they make you do things you suck at, and then yell at
you when you fail? And even with all that bullshit around you,
is it still fun anyway, just to be able to be as creative as you like,
and to write and read anything that interests you?

But I didn't talk to him except to say, "Thanks for this packet."
I was afraid someone would be listening, that I'd make some
reference to Shakespeare, it would reported, and I'd have some
mysterious vengeance visited on me later. In a way, though, I
knew already that the answer to all my questions was yes. Dad
had taught me how much evil can surround you at a university.
And I knew in my heart that I might just love it anyway, that I
might even be teaching in college now if my past had turned
out differently.

On the way back to town, in the van, though, after a day of
surprisingly exhausting work, I looked around at my coworkers,
many of whom were silent or napping, and my heart softened.
We were all just people, after all. Probably my situation here was
no different than it would have been at a college. In fact, it was
better here. In college, you had to publish or perish. You had to
keep your work respectable. At Hallmark, all you had to be was
funny. I'd always found *funny* easier to pull off than *respectable*.
With any luck, Hallmark would let me do funny again soon.

I HAD ONE ALLY I was sure about on the ninth floor—my cubicle neighbor, an African-American woman named Flora, who dressed like the elegant mom she was: hoop earrings, bright patterned dresses, thick wavy hair. We bonded in our unhappiness. She kept writing cards, for Mahogany that the higher-ups wouldn't accept,* and was subject to all the little indignities that happen to any black person in a whites-heavy white-collar job. I was apparently understanding, and she vented to me freely. (She told me once, "There's a woman up here—I won't mention her name—who every time she sees me over at the mailboxes, she stands there and watches until I leave. As if I'm going to steal a memo or some copy of the acceptances list, which, by the way, we all get. I swear, one day I just kept her hovering behind me for eight minutes while I pretended to write something. I don't understand these people.")

She knew I couldn't write and knew I was getting desperate. One day I actually said aloud what I'd been formulating at the retreat as I felt the walls close in. "If I'm doomed here, I've got no job skills. The only thing I could think is to go back to school, but I already have an MFA in creative writing. They won't let you into a Ph.D. program if you've already got a terminal degree."

"Really?" she said. "I didn't know that."

The very next day, Flora walked over to my cubicle and said, "You know, I called UMKC yesterday, just because I was curi-

---

* Mahogany was constantly frustrating to our few black writers. In one classic example, a Mahogany thank-you card that said "Good looking out"—an African-American idiom that the African-American editor okayed—was nixed by the white higher-ups, who said they couldn't understand it.

ous. David, you're crazy. Of *course* you can get into a Ph.D. program. They don't care. Just go get your GRE scores and go do it."

I checked. She was right. Not only that, but there were actually several places in the country where you could get a Ph.D. in creative writing, which I'd never heard of. It felt like a backward move, but I decided to apply for the GRE exam, so that just in case the worst happened, I'd have some kind of backup plan. I had no savings, and no idea how I'd get money to move on, and I wasn't sure creative writing was such a smart thing to major in anymore. And yet, as soon as I wrote the testing date on my calendar, a little wave of—what was that feeling called? Oh, yes—*relief* sent a temblor through my body. When I went to bed that night, I felt like a prisoner who suspected the parole board might be friendly the next time around.

I'VE SAID THAT I COULDN'T WRITE, but that's not exactly true. I would occasionally manage to squeeze out a sentiment or two. But since I hated it, it never actually felt like writing; I never got the release I got from delivering a truly fun idea, so that potential joy stayed strangled inside me. You could perhaps think of it as a very intense writer's constipation.

In fact, in a certain sense I was writing as much as ever. The problem was that the things I was writing a lot of were mostly irrelevant. My strangeness to the staff led me to notice the strangeness of office work in general, and for some reason this was inspiring me to write a whole series of poems about work and business, none of which could possibly work on a greeting card. To take only two examples:

I come in at nine and sign papers,
Then I forward them on until ten.
I go to a midmorning conference,
Then push a few papers again.
I lunch, then I have some more meetings,
And at fiveish my workday is through.
It's a really good job and I'm happy.
I'm just not really sure what I do.

Since Casual Fridays are hip now,
Our office is taking the chance.
Just remember—it's "Casual Friday."
It's not "Come to Work Without Pants."

I was also drawing cartoons aplenty—but I found, just as had happened with my crossword puzzles, they were growing increasingly odd and noncommercial, as evident from Figure 6.

FIGURE 6

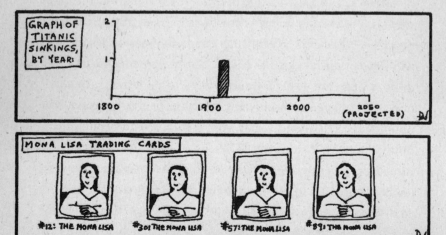

GRAPH OF TITANIC SINKINGS, BY YEAR:

1800   1900   2000   2050 (PROJECTED)

MONA LISA TRADING CARDS

#12: THE MONA LISA   #30: THE MONA LISA   #57: THE MONA LISA   #89: THE MONA LISA

To survive with actual submissions amid all this flotsam, I got a lot of the useful writing I could do, not by filling regular requisitions, but by leaving the ninth floor entirely and going to the "brainstorms" that the Idea Exchange had once or twice a week.

They worked like this. Some editor would drop in with a special, specific, last-minute request. They had an idea for a promotion and needed some sample copy to sell it. Or they hadn't gotten enough copy for one or two particular cards in their line and needed a focused push. Something either unusually urgent or unusually small and odd.

The Idea Exchange conference room was, I suppose, the same size as all the others, but it felt much tinier. Partly this was because, in keeping with their antique-desks-and-hanging-windows motif, the table itself was a long, massive rectangular thing, scored and gouged from decades of hard living. In addition, the conference room was also a storage area for papers no one much cared about, and it was clear there had been a long-time pattern of not caring. The room, then, was crowded in on all sides by chest-high towers of computer printouts, rubber-banded stacks of three-by-five cards, empty manila folders, and—beyond all this—a smattering of odd things that apparently hadn't made the cut as official decor, but which no one had bothered to toss out. A model airplane. A bag of marbles. A few cowboy and Indian figurines. And—for some reason—a single metal panel from the back display of an old pinball machine, with a picture of a clown and a label reading HIGH SCORE. This did not make the room look actually playful, like a child's room. It looked cluttered, like a grown-up's attic. And so walking into the Idea Exchange conference room often required sliding sideways behind other people's chairs, bumping against teetering stacks of dusty papers, and the whole place had a slight submarine energy.

When I say these lunchtime meetings were called "brainstorm" sessions, I don't mean to suggest that they were actual traditional brainstorms. If you thought that, you'd no doubt be picturing a bunch of people sitting around a table, while one person says, "What about doing it this way?" and then another says "Hey, yeah! And then we could do this other thing!" A third says, "But we need to consider the impact of some other vague whatever," as the conversation boils to some exciting compromise or conclusion, with everyone taking part in the overall idea. In almost any definition of brainstorm, that's what you'd be led to imagine.

The problem with this impression is that, at the time, Hallmark had an absolute horror of interaction, for a simple reason: its reward model for employees was based on number of ideas contributed to the company. So literally every sentiment, every hangtag, and every helpful notion tossed to an editor in the Idea Exchange had to have an author. Let two people talk, and suddenly they'd both be claiming authorship for the idea that resulted, or you'd wind up giving out half credits and third credits, and where would it all end? Best to keep it simple. So at an Idea

Exchange "brainstorm," there was no talking. The visiting editor, whoever she was (most editors were women), would usually stand at the end of the table that was near the door, while up to thirteen people filled the other seats. Everyone had a handful of three-by-fives, and there was a hat in the center of the table. The editor would say something like, "We need a sentiment for this drawing that shows two robots holding hands." And then, in absolute silence, everyone would scribble an idea, toss it into the hat, and write another idea, toss that into the hat, and so on. There was no shouting out, no back-and-forth. For maybe five minutes all you heard was the *skritch-a-skritch-a-skritch* of pencil, and the occasional leaflike falling of a card into the hat. It was just exactly the same as writing quietly in your own cubicle, except that you had to do it faster, and there were other people to look at. When it was over, the editor would read all the ideas aloud—why, I'm not sure, since what we thought of the senti- ments didn't matter, though it was nice to get the table to laugh. And then it was on to the next assignment. Every idea was also anonymous, the premise being that this freed you up to write truly crappy ideas without fear. What this meant is that you often had to wade through a lot of truly offensive jokes in order to glean the few usable ideas from the pile. It was this kind of brainstorm where Josh first made his "giving blow jobs to Satan" joke, and my own attempts weren't always much better.

For me, though, in the middle of my writer's block, there was one truly great aspect of these brainstorms: it reintroduced com- petition, made me once more part of a crack team working on a project, kept my fellow writers small and seeable, and gave me a clear deadline and the immediate gratification of knowing if something was good or not. In a single stroke, the Idea Exchange brainstorms restored everything that had motivated me in Humor, and which was entirely missing on the Main staff. Here, I couldn't help but write. If only they'd had these sessions every day, instead of once or twice a week.

I heard the silence of these brainstorms broken only once. Stan, the editor for Mahogany, said, "We've got some art we'd like to get writing for." And so a dozen of us white writers waited quietly to come up with a sentiment that would speak to the black community in a black voice. Stan held up the first illustration: it was a cartoon of a black cupid, hovering over what looked like part of a slightly run-down urban house. "Go," he said.

There was no skritching. Where normally people just started writing and flipping, writing and flipping, here you could see everyone just frowning at their cards. I know I felt completely daunted. Everything I thought of was crap and I knew it. *Why write anything at all?* I thought. *Don't black folks say Happy Valentine's Day just like everyone else?* I tried "Happy Valentine's Day, Man." Too seventies, too gendered, and too much like what a white person might think a black person might say. I started writing, "Hey, Bro—" then erased it. What were black folks' lives like? "Happy Valentine's Day—from My Hood to Yours!" Yeesh. No way. How about . . . I couldn't think of a single thing. I looked again around the table, and there was still a lot of frowning and erasing. There were only five cards in the hat.

A sudden WHAM! rang out. Over at the end, Josh Broward had just pounded the table with his fist. "God!" he said, disgustedly. "I am such a *racist* sonofabitch!" We all laughed, wincing. It was true. We shouldn't even have been doing this. I wrote one single horrible idea just to get one in—something about Bowz in the Hood—and then couldn't wait to get home and shower.

MY GRE DATE APPROACHED, and even though I wasn't taking college all that seriously, it seemed wise to be careful this time around. I'd always been a good reader, with a head for facts, and back in high school when I'd taken the SAT I had refused to study, convinced that my great genius (which all my teachers had praised) would be sufficient to buoy me to Harvard. That hadn't happened, and while I enjoyed my time at my state school, I thought that perhaps now a little humility and discipline were in order. So I bought three GRE study guides and carried them with me throughout the day, lugging a backpack like I'd done back at PREVENT. One of the books was to help me ace the literature GRE, and one was just for the basic stuff: English, Math, and Logic. The third was a book of sample exams, which I kept plugging away at after reading the other two. As a result, my brain started mixing everything together even worse than usual. So I read, for example, the quote from Hamlet where Hamlet says, "I am but mad north-northwest. When the wind is southerly I know a hawk from a handsaw."

I know a hawk from a handsaw, I marveled. Not only was that a fun expression, but it suggested a really tough GRE question:

hawk: handsaw :: ?
a. ass : elbow
b. ass : a hole in the ground
c. shit : Shinola
d. all of the above*

---

* Answer on page 369.

It was yet another joke that was basically impossible to share with anybody. I was smart enough nowadays, however, that I didn't even try to push it on anyone against their will. But Jane would have liked it. What a fucking shame.

Jane remained on my mind, in fact, all throughout this process, since she was the only person I knew who had gone to grad school. She'd found it really hard, even as brilliant as she was. So when I bought the GRE books, I also looked through the literary theory books, found a big huge one—*Literary Theory: An Introduction*—and took it with me. I figured I'd read it after the test.

I was busy. Even though I probably only needed a good Verbal score, I studied Quantitative (that's math) and Analysis (that's logic) with equal vigor. Math I felt pretty good about. Logic was giving me trouble, since the puzzles seemed to involve long-term consequences of moves and remembering where you'd put things. Mostly, of course, I was counting on Verbal to win me the love of the Educational Testing Service.

The test had changed since my SAT days. I was sent to an address on the UMKC campus and put in a room with a computer. No more filling in bubbles with a No. 2 pencil; no more folding over pages in a booklet. The whole test was on-screen, and you couldn't go back and erase things later. For the first time, I really felt the disconnect. *I wonder if I'm too old to go back to college now. I still remember the smell of mimeograph paper.* Jane stayed in the back of my mind the whole time. Back when she'd gotten her GRE scores, I'd written her a celebratory poem that read, in part:

So now we can see
That a Yale Ph.D.

Next to you has the brains of a gerbil.
Your Analysis—whoa!—
Was a seven-six-oh,
With a perfect 800 on Verbal.

I really wanted to get an 800 on the Verbal myself. I'd been a word freak all my life, had read dictionaries, had written puzzles . . . and how many chances do we really get to have this very specific skill set assigned an actual number? I'd hate to say that I wanted to beat Jane, but I really did feel like I was defying her the whole time, as if outscoring her would somehow banish her ghost. I concentrated furiously for hours. When I finished I was actually sweating.

Then, with that over, I dutifully opened *Literary Theory: An Introduction*, and a funny thing happened. I got interested. Every section was filled with original selections from essays under the topics of Marxism, Feminism, Queer Theory, Structuralism, Post-Structrualism, and it was like *Charlie's Angels*: I couldn't choose a favorite. All these articles were unlike anything I'd ever read: incredibly difficult and loaded with jargon, but genuinely engaged in questions of literature and culture that I hadn't realized I cared about. And as I cared, I found myself catching on—learning new uses for words like *reification* and *hegemony*—and it was like my brain had gotten up from years of lounging and was trying out the new Exercycle. That book was over a thousand pages, must have weighed ten pounds, and I started carrying it with me everywhere. Even when I was walking to the lunchroom, I'd read the book while in transit, looking up occasionally to avoid whacking into poles or people.

I was torn, though. Dad had warned all of us kids about academia. It was a lot of airy nonsense with no practical value. And just by carrying this volume around with me, it must have looked like I was pretending to be oh so smart and rubbing everyone's nose in it—particularly since if someone asked me, "What are you reading?" I didn't have any really good answer. If I said, "I'm reading about Antonio Gramsci's take on Marxism, which is a little more subtle and interesting than the vulgar Marxism we got in high school," I would surely be accused of overinforming and being pretentious. If I said, "Um . . . it's probably more than you want to go into," I was being pretentious yet again. The answer I finally settled on when someone asked "What are you reading?" was "Academic bullshit." People would laugh or shrug, and I'd be off the hook. The only problem was, it was dishonest. I didn't actually think it was bullshit. But I was finally learning a really handy survival skill for the business world: to make small talk, lie about what you're actually interested in. Be yourself on your own time.

I started to feel readier to date. Not enough to risk full-on commitment yet, but I was confident I could get through a meal and a good-night kiss without crumbling into sobs. Deedee, alas, had already found someone else. (Timing is so important in these things; it's part of what makes the whole system idiotic.) But one day Kenneth came by, biting his nails nervously, and said, "Dave. There's this new girl interning for the summer and I've got to meet her. You've got to help me." Intrigued, I said, "Okay. We'll do a walk-by." *This must be important,* I thought. He'd come all the way from Shoebox, where he worked now.

We walked by and met her. Her name was Angela, and I was smitten as well. She was fresh out of college, and she was just my type, insofar as having one girlfriend establishes any type at all:

she had fiery red hair, wide bright eyes, and an air of calm creativity. Even when she sat perfectly still, you could see her thinking; the air around her fairly swirled. I took one look at her and
thought, *Friendship be damned, Kenneth. I'm going after her myself.*

I started slowly. The three of us went out a few times, and
every time Kenneth left us alone I'd make jokes to win her over.
("Planting seeds," we called it when I was a fundamentalist.) The
day I decided to finally ask her out officially, I called her place
and Kenneth answered the phone. "Oh, hi, Dave," he said. "Angela and I started hanging out after work, and now I'm over here."
They didn't even admit they were dating for another two months,
but it was clear to everyone. This time my spirit was willing, but
my flesh was apparently unappealing.

TO MEET WOMEN OUTSIDE WORK, I started attending the Young
Friends of Art, a service organization that works with the Kansas
City's Nelson-Atkins Museum of Art, one of the finest museums
in the Midwest. The Nelson-Atkins did a mind-blowing video
installation by Nam June Paik, whose TV-and-light collages are
fascinating (as well as dangerous to epileptics—they had a sign
and everything). When King Tut was on display in the 1970s and
traveling from New York to L.A., the only place it stopped mid-
way was the Nelson-Atkins. You can count on it quite reliably
if you're ever curious about what's new and interesting in the art
world.

The museum is great, but I found no haven among the Young
Friends. These people should have been exactly my demographic:
under-forty professionals with good educations and refined cultural taste. All I know is that at one of my first meetings, we were

discussing possible upcoming fund-raisers, and when someone suggested a dress-up 1930s evening, I joked, "Or we could do a simulation of a night at Warhol's Factory. Does anyone have heroin?" They all looked at me like I was spattered in blood.

A girl at the end raised her hand strenuously and said, "Could we have a wine seminar? Where like a wine expert could teach us about wine drinking? You know, like, what goes with what, and what to taste for, and all that stuff we need to know?" Everyone around the table nodded—what a brilliant idea! They were actively excited! And that's when I figured it out. *These people* like *wearing suits. They can't* wait *to be grown-ups.* There was some core unspoken desire around this table that I simply wasn't getting: the joy of belonging, perhaps; the soothing bouquet of order and control.

I started noticing my own behavior from the outside and I began to figure out some of my problems. One time, for example, in my wanderings, I was on the stairs from Nine to Eight and saw an artist I knew casually coming up as I was going down. We nodded in passing. Two hours later, while down on the seventh floor, and coming down yet more stairs, I saw him again. *My god*, I thought, bemusedly. *It's like one of us is omnipresent.*

"You again," he said, chuckling.

And I blurted out the first joke I thought of: "Yeah. I'm just working on my Omnipresence merit badge."

He continued to smile with his mouth, but his eyes froze, and he nodded quietly and we passed in silence.

My initial reaction was to say, *Goddammit, that was a good joke! Why didn't he at least laugh?* But the more I thought about it, the more it seemed that it had been almost mean of me to spring that on him unawares. He was just saying hi and making social noise, and I had essentially asked him to suddenly process two distant cultural references and respond appropriately, and I'd done it unthinkingly, instead of just saying, "Ha ha." While it would have been nice to have had a great audience for that joke of mine, it did strike me then just why certain people in the Young Friends of Art might be hostile, and even why my fellow writers on the Main Writing staff might have complained about my alleged "literary allusions." What if being around me was a challenge? What if it was a challenge not everyone felt they deserved to be faced with? Is this why Young Friends of Art resisted my every playful sally? Did I ever have a chance?

And yet I kept going to YFA meetings and began to feel I was bemusedly tolerated, if not warmly understood. It's where all the beautiful single women were—but none of them found me interesting at all, and I wound up making more and more platonic friends for reasons that continued to baffle me. In the meantime, though, and with few social options, I kept coming to the relationship poker table, putting up money and time, and walking away with nothing. In that respect, they were very effective at fund-raising.

I REMEMBER EXACTLY when I got my first powerful sign of thaw. It was the first weekend in July—the first truly beautiful day we'd had in weeks. I woke up feeling miserable as usual, did my morning routine, dead and zombified, and although I wasn't in constant agony anymore, there lay in my chest a sort of ashy dread that would twinge if I moved too thoughtlessly. On this day in particular I felt ready to brood about Jane and my grim future and what was wrong with me. But I also knew that this was probably unhealthy, so I might as well force myself outside while it was still day out. Maybe I could get a shake at Panache Chocolatier on the Plaza. Even as I thought this, I knew that this milk shake, the most amazing milk shake in the world, made with homemade ice cream and sprinkled with still-warm shavings of fresh chocolate, would taste like sand to me. I also felt trapped. It was better than doing nothing. So I togged up and went out.

The summer so far had been a disappointment, but as I walked from my apartment to cross the customary bridge to the Plaza, I could see that the world had been transformed. It was a few minutes before noon, there was an all but cloudless sky, humidity set just so, and the sunlight itself seemed to make everything extra-yellow, in a bid for popularity. On the bridge where I was shambling, there were even flowers poking out and blooming, with actual butterflies fluttering over them. And yet I saw all this with the sad resignation of a foreigner looking at a home country he can't revisit. A breeze kicked up—a warm breeze, surely—but I actually couldn't feel it. It was like my skin had learned to resist even tiny threats of pleasure.

If anything, the beauty and outright joy of the day made me feel all the worse by contrast: a frigid little beetle of a man with a shriveled soul and a stomach as dark and empty as a coal-scuttle. What right did I have to even blight this absurdly pretty scene? I remembered my fiancée, remembered what I'd done, and did a little math. I had never met anyone like her. I would probably never meet anyone like her again. Therefore, at the age of twenty-eight, I had destroyed my life—I would certainly never be as well matched in love again—and I didn't even know why I'd done it! Was I really that stupid? That willful? Was my happiness like my muse, a fickle impulse that didn't even know a good thing when it was laid right before me? What the hell was I even looking for?

Without realizing it, I had paused on the bridge instead of crossing it, and I was staring up at the sun, thinking, *Try your best, you dumb bastard. I can't be warmed one joule*, when a large dark van drove on the bridge and slowed to a stop beside me.

Someone needing directions, I guessed, and I had just enough time for a stray thought—*Sometimes helping others makes you feel better about yourself*, chirped my neglected inner bluebird—when I saw the window roll down, and a lovely young woman of about twenty actually leaned forward, far out of the window. She was wearing a bikini. She was smiling at me.

"Hey . . . LOVER!" she announced, and she whipped off her top. I just caught a glimpse of her naked breasts dancing in the sunlight as she jerked herself back inside and out of sight. The van revved up and sped away, and I could hear two women squealing with laughter as they drove out of sight. It was so startling, I didn't know what to do. Just before they turned the corner, I had just enough presence of mind to blow them a kiss and wave. I don't think they saw it.

There was no one around, but I had to tell someone, so I simply spoke out loud. "Wow!" I said. "What a . . . *lovely* world this is!" After years spent feeling guilty for even looking at porn magazines, here came a pair of beautiful breasts that just showed themselves for free. For the lark of it, the sheer, daring fun. My bad mood vanished—it turns out it was a frame of mind and was susceptible to disruption—and I was left instead with a puzzle. What the hell had just happened? And how had it happened here, in Kansas City, Missouri, of all places? I knew that there were wild women out there—crazy women who flashed at Mardi Gras and Spring Break and all points south. I'd seen them online. But I'd always thought they had to get drunk, or there had to be peer pressure, or there had to be a special occasion—a concert or something—to serve as an excuse. To have this happen to me clean out of the blue, in broad daylight on the corner, just because it was a really nice day, was contrary to everything I thought I knew about women.

I didn't have it figured out at the time—as I said, it was a year before I knew why I'd really broken off my engagement, much less what I wanted instead—but it didn't matter, since you don't need to understand aspirin to cure a headache. What had happened was that an example of the kind of woman I really wanted had just appeared to me, and I hadn't even realized they actually existed. They did! And they were hot and funny, and they didn't take things too seriously, and they thought that sexiness was a hoot and something worth celebrating, and they didn't care if anyone watched while they made out in the middle of the theater or held hands in the street. With a woman like that, sex itself would be not an armistice, but an adventure.

I didn't know all this at the time, of course, in my confused, monosyllabic, boob-startled brain. But on a deeper level, and for no logical reason, I suddenly felt ineffably content and optimistic. Damn *right* I was gonna have that milk shake!

It was over the milk shake that I remembered something I'd learned in one of my Religious Studies courses. I'd taken The Sociology of Religion with author Andrew Greeley, which used a book he'd written called *Religion: A Secular Theory*. It began with a series of propositions, to wit:

1. There exists in the human heart a propensity to hope.
2. Life and its trials bear down on us, however, and we need that hope to be periodically restored—something that usually occurs when experiencing the love of our family and friends, or engaging in activities we enjoy.
3. Every so often, however, we experience a sudden renewal of hope that is completely unexpected and that is often overpowering and mysterious.
4. That, for the purposes of this book, is the beginning of religion.

In the book, when describing this moment of renewed joy, Greeley uses examples like when a butterfly unexpectedly lights on your hand, or when a stranger in the street suddenly smiles with real warmth. But I have to say, give me two lovely bare breasts flashing by on a summer day and you can keep every butterfly that ever lived. In that moment, my hope was restored, even though I didn't believe in God or even capital-G Grace anymore. It was just nice and unexpected. That was enough.

17

Laying Plans

THE WOMAN BESIDE ME AT THE BAR DREW ON HER cigarette. "I'm smart," she said, "but I'm not, like, book smart. I mean I don't need to know the"—she gestured a little drunkenly at the screen in front of us—"capital of Guatemala or whatever to be smart, you know? I've lived. I don't get fooled. That's smart to me."

"I agree wholeheartedly," I said, then kicked myself. "Wholeheartedly" sounded too geeky. I should have just said, "Yeah." Why was I so driven to use interesting words, when I knew perfectly well what it cost me?

Probably the stupidest thing I did to try to meet women was go to T.G.I. Friday's at a local mall and play the on-screen trivia game. I was good at trivia, I enjoyed it, and I thought, *Maybe some woman will be impressed by my knowledge and then somehow sleep with me!* I hadn't worked out the middle part. I didn't need to, though, because it turns out that the people who play on-screen trivia were mostly lonely single guys like me.

And yet, by some miracle of persistence, I found myself now sitting next to a woman my age and having an actual conversation. Her name was Meredith, and she was a paralegal. I had watched her drink for her while she'd gone to the ladies' room, and when she came back, we'd sort of stumbled into a discussion about personal growth and dating and a few other things. She was leading the stagecoach all over the place.

She drew on her cigarette—this was back when you could actually smoke in bars—and said, "I can tell people. Like you, for instance. I can tell you're a sharp guy who doesn't put up with a lot of bullshit."

"Thanks," I said. *Better, Dave. Keep it ordinary.* I leaned back and swirled my rum and Coke casually, like I'd been drinking for longer than a few months, like a guy who actually got drunk instead of quitting after two servings for fear of the alcoholism his church always warned him about.

"That's so great to find," she continued. "You know. Like, I meet a lot of guys—well, not *a lot of guys,* don't get the wrong idea! Ha ha!—but I like met this guy a couple weeks ago. A cute kid. Met him online." Puff. "So we're talking, and he's younger than me, he's twenty-four. And it turns out he's a *virgin.*" She nodded to me significantly. "I mean, Jesus. What does that tell you? Let's just say the date did not go well." She smiled knowingly and stubbed out her fag.

I smiled bravely, but I felt like I'd been hollowed out. She seemed to like me, but if that twenty-four-year-old virgin had been a loser, what did that make me, at twenty-nine? I was—quick calculation—about twenty percent more pathetic than he was. I tried to sound calm as I said, "Well, maybe he had some sort of religious convictions that prevented him from, you know . . ."

"Oh, please," she said, rolling her eyes. "You *are* a card writer; so nice! No, seriously. If a guy gets to be twenty-four and he hasn't figured out how to fuck yet? I mean"—she waved away some lingering smoke—"I've *been* to college. I've *had* the bad sex with those boys who don't know how to please a woman. I'm sorry, but I don't want to give lessons anymore, you know? I want to be with a *man*."

My testicles were shriveling by the second. I put her at twenty-six, maybe twenty-nine at the outside. If I'd been normal, I'd have maybe lost my virginity at eighteen or nineteen, and I'd have had ten years of experience by now. I might even be jaded, like her, and have actual taste in what I liked and didn't. What a relief that would be, to have had so much sex you could actually be bored by some of it! But here I was—a year past my breakup and no closer to my first sex than I'd been before. It was so frustrating that I knew if I thought about it too long, I'd just plunge into depression. "Oh, look! Another trivia round!" I said.

"I'll play with you," she said.

You wouldn't like me, I thought. *And maybe you'd be right.* "Oh, wait," I said. "I have to meet some friends. Look—I'll be back here next week. I'll buy you a drink next time!"

"I'd like that," she said.

I never went back. In fact, I stopped playing trivia entirely. It seemed like I had a much more important problem on my hands, and trivia was literally distracting me from the main goal. I was almost twenty-nine, and I really needed to end my virginity already. It was all I could think about. After all, so far twenty-eight hadn't done a thing for me. And thirty was next.

———

AS THE TRIVIA PROVES, I was trying to meet women, but I found—as many adults find every day—that it was really hard to meet people outside of work. For example, I once met a woman named Lorraine through a friend of a friend at a party, and she was not only strikingly attractive—with bright gray eyes that seemed to see right through you—but she was so sardonic and well-informed about pop culture that we were actually able to have a long conversation where I didn't once feel like an immature twit who needed to learn to like investing already. Plus I figured out she was single. Encouraged, I said, "You're really fun. We should get dinner some time."

She frowned. "Do you mean like on a date? I'm not sure that's such a good idea."

"Oh," I said, "Okay then. But I disagree with your judgment." It was supposed to come off as a joke, but I was serious, too. I thought, *I'll meet this woman again and again, and I'll wear her down with my charm until she can't help but fall for me.*

So far my plan had failed because I hadn't run into Lorraine again. If we had worked together, this never would have happened—and think how quickly, with daily exposure, I could have worn her down! Erosion was my only model for how good relationships actually worked. The only woman I'd ever dated was Jane, and it had taken me several months to notice her. I assumed things worked the same way in reverse; that I would have to insinuate myself gradually and grow on the women I liked. That whole "Ask someone out and go on a date" model was Hollywood; it led to unrealistic expectations and heartbreak. Better to

be friends, and friends don't ask each other out on dates. Friend-
ships emerge, just from hanging out with people.

Besides, every time I fought my instincts and actually asked a
woman out, she said no. So far all I'd gotten out of my adven-
tures was to discover that rum and Cokes weren't all that scary. I
kept to two drinks at a sitting, felt moderately adult in so doing,
and went home night after night, sober and alone.

"YOUR PROBLEM IS you want it too much," said Kenneth.
"You're trying too hard." Edgar agreed. That was, in fact, all any
of my friends ever told me. I just wanted to scream. Of *course*
it *seemed* like I wanted it too much. But I actually wanted it
exactly the right amount, considering. If you've been starving
for twenty-nine years, how do you pretend you're not hungry?
Who has that much deception in them? I seemed cursed by
my own honest need, like a beggar who can't get into the soup
kitchen until he buys a decent suit with the money he doesn't
have. And yet every TV show, every movie, every advice column was about temptation, adultery, people cheating. The world
seemed filled with people who actually had *two* choices about
who to have sex with. Two at once! Where was everyone else
getting their starting capital?

AS IF I DIDN'T ALREADY feel alien enough, we had another
creative renewal retreat out at the farmhouse. Since I still wasn't
writing, I really needed it. (Sometimes workshop poems became
cards.) This time the visiting poet was Mark Doty, who was well

known and so popular that we had to take two vans. With two vans leaving Hallmark, I found myself being picky. It was a forty-five-minute trip, and I didn't want to get stuck next to someone boring. So I loitered between the vans, and when I saw which van the cool people were getting into, I went there while it was still half full, convinced I was going to get some good conversation. (I noticed with disappointment that Josh Broward showed up late and went in the other van.)

On the way up I sat with Joy—the lovely little firecracker who'd gotten the "silence" message during her tenure on Nine—and although I expected a ride full of nonstop silly banter between us, to my shock, she spent at least fifteen minutes talking to the seatmate on the other side of her about, of all things, lawn mowers. Her seatmate wanted advice: should he buy a riding lawn mower or a push lawn mower? Was the riding one worth the extra expense? What about those old-fashioned muscle-powered ones? Joy had tried them all, and she had very specific opinions, which was a side of her I'd never thought existed. Since I still loathed the outdoors, I was hoping never to even need a lawn. (Back in Tucson, instead of lawns, people often use quartz rocks, which are very easy to maintain. And by the way, it's called xeriscaping, if you ever need a new Scrabble word.) My eyes glazed over, and I think I slept a little.

After that day's activities, I was determined not to get trapped near that conversation again, so I took the other van back, and I wound up beside two completely different people who broke into a ten-minute conversation about . . . lawn mowers. This time it was about whether or not to get the mulching attachment, and what other attachments were available, and if the special bags were any good for the price.

Wow, I thought. *What were the odds?* And then I looked out the window at these long stretches of passing prairie and I thought, *Pretty good odds. Grass is all they have out here.* Then a thought hit me—it actually felt like a drop of water on my forehead—*If I stay here, this is going to be me.* At that moment, being merely uncomfortable and bemusedly complain-y stopped being enough. I realized that, in all likelihood, I might have to shop for another life someday soon. I'd also need to find a place to have it. And of course, what the hell could I do for a living besides write cards, when writing cards was the only thing I'd ever enjoyed, and was still driving me crazy? Literary theory was fun to read, but it sure didn't feel like a respectable career.

ANOTHER TRY: HALLMARK EDITORIAL GOT a striking new hire named Jessica. She was not only a knockout, but stood out as being unusually funny and playful. Although she'd been hired as an editor, she was also capable of drawing very charming cartoons, and she was good with banter. I decided she must be mine.

As usual in these matters, I was hampered by my inability to read minds or parse social cues, and by my nice-guy, nerd-bred fear of being direct. We certainly seemed to hit it off as friends, and before long people were calling us "The Four Musketeers"— Kenneth, Angela, me, and (*fingers crossed; oh, let it be "and"!*) Jessica. When I eventually asked her out—shyly, with many an oblique side note before I got to the point—she said, "Oh, I'm sorry. We're friends. I don't date friends. I can't explain it, but it just doesn't work that way."

This made no sense to me, and like many a geek before me,

I still hoped she'd eventually realize what a great guy I was if I just hung around being interesting. Instead, maybe three months into her tenure at Hallmark, Jessica asked me for help. "There's this . . . unbelievably gorgeous guy in the Lettering Department, and I'm terrified to talk to him. Could you walk me over there and introduce us?"

This was technically beyond the call of duty. "You're outgoing," I told her. "Why don't you do it yourself? This isn't like you."

"You don't understand," she said. "I *dreamed* about him last week. I didn't know who he was then. But I just saw him today for the first time—the guy from my dream. It's freaking me out. I have to go talk to him, but I'm terrified. Please come!"

Say what you will, Jessica was never dull. I did in fact walk her over to say hi to Jun Lee, an extremely polite Chinese immigrant who was artistically gifted and intimidatingly handsome. They were dating by the end of the week.

I felt even more frustrated than ever. Here I was, an actual guy with a cool job and a great sense of humor, and I'd had my time beaten by a fucking *dream*. That's not bad technique; it felt more like a conspiracy by the universe to keep me frustrated for some powerful asshole's dark amusement.

MY LAST REAL HOPE FOR getting laid before I turned thirty looked like it would have to be the National Puzzlers League convention in July. It's the oldest puzzle organization in the United States, all the big names in the hobby are there, and it contains many of the sweetest human beings I've ever known. As you might expect, however, it also contains more than its fair complement of unsocialized geeks, and so having a good time involves an intricate process of steering for the cool people and avoiding the few annoying ones.

I did have one advantage, however: I was pretty well known—a regular contributor of funny puzzles to the League newsletter—and while I might not be competitive in the world at large, here in the puzzle world, with my reasonably good social skills and reliable hygiene, I was something of a catch. I might have any number of prospects if I played my cards right. Of course, the prospects might all be appalling—we geeks aren't usually pretty—and I hoped to have sex my first time with someone I actually found attractive, not just with someone available.

But this was still all theoretical. Since I'd never played my cards right before, it was hard to imagine how I'd start doing it now, just from scratch.

Still, I needed the hope, and this is how, in July 1997, I found myself in a hotel lounge in Atlanta on Saturday night, nursing a single nervous rum and Coke, sitting with Will Shortz (the *New York Times* crossword editor), a smattering of other puzzle folks, and a woman I'll call Nixie, who was one of my favorite members of the NPL—but, alas, married.

Will and Nixie were on big overstuffed chairs at the edge of the carpet, while I was sitting at a low table in the center of the room, which was ringed by four other guys, all of us geeky, all of us enjoying the geekery. One of the guys—a slovenly bespectacled college student nicknamed Inky*—set a large brown grocery bag on the table and said, "Hey, everybody. My mom sent me a care package for the Con. Snacks! Eat up." And he pulled

---

* In the National Puzzlers League, we all have nicknames. To protect everyone's identity, I'm calling my friends by the names of the ghosts in Pac-Man.

out some potato chips, a bag of grapes, a sleeve of Ritz crackers, and a can of spray cheese.

"Let me see that," said his neighbor, Blinky, grabbing the spray cheese. He read the label aloud. "*Easy Cheese.* Really? I mean, how difficult is cheese normally?"

Pinky grabbed the can from Blinky. "Oh, wow. It even has directions. *For best results, hold nozzle perpendicular to food . . .*"

"Really?" I said, and asked to see the can myself. I read the label and reported, "According to these instructions, it actually specifies you can only hold it perpendicular to *food*. So let's all be careful with our Easy Cheese. Don't get *too* easy . . ."

"No, that's not true," said Clyde, and grabbed the can from me. "See? You're reading it wrong. It says *For best results . . .*"

We all cracked up. Four jokes from a single container. It was hilarious and wonderful, and reminded me why I love puzzle people so much. For puzzlers, everything in the world is a potential game. Even my Humor comrades, funny as they were, often declined my offers to join in actual badinage. Here at the convention, though, the games just emerged as naturally as light.

Nixie, my favorite member, rose from her chair and tapped me sharply on the wrist. "We should catch up!" she said, and jerked her head conspiratorially to the corner. "Let's go over there."

Once resituated away from the crowd, she leaned forward in her kicky little dress and said in a quieter voice, "It's so good to see you! How are you doing?"

Oy. I sighed. "Well . . . I broke up with my fiancée."

She laid her hand on my arm. "Oh, honey. I'm so sorry. How are you doing?"

Nixie would have been number one on any list of people I'd want to sleep with, even outside the NPL. She was in her mid-thirties, with long black hair, and one of the smartest, funniest women I've ever met, a woman who seemed to be constantly living the role of the wacky gal Friday in whatever movie she was presently costarring in. I was very careful not to move my arm. Her hand felt great there. I explained the whole story, ending with, "I, uh, think it was for the best, you know. I mean I'm sure. I'm sure. And I'm ready now, for sure, because it's been—god, almost a year. But dating in Kansas City is really impossible."

"Oh, sure. I know. God. It's hard everywhere. You know, I'm divorcing my husband."

She didn't look crushed; I checked—carefully. Was there a trace of suggestiveness in her look? It seemed possible. My chest tensed. Opportunity! Oh, no! Because this was the part I was the worst at: sealing the deal. For one thing, I was terrible at reading women: at any given point, I couldn't tell if they were nice to me because they were being nice, or nice to me because they wanted to sleep with me. The difference is vast, and a clumsy overshot can cost you some serious likeability. And what if she *was* emotionally crushed, I was misreading her face, and I sounded like a guy who didn't care about her pain—a guy who just wanted to take advantage of her instead of be a friend in her hour of need?

But if this was an actual, happening-right-now opening, I'd need to come up with the right thing to say to move it to the bedroom. I had no models for how to do this. Kenneth and Edgar had apparently gotten lucky just by showing up and being normal, which I'd never been skilled at. My dad was no help at all. The one time back in high school when I asked him about dating, he'd looked uncomfortable and then cleared his throat, frowned at the ceiling, and said something that started with, "Well, David, when people begin . . . pairing off . . ." I stopped listening right there, since it was clear he was just theorizing. None of my friends in Tucson had ever dated conventionally. In fact, my college Christian group actively discouraged such behavior. Instead, the guys I knew had sort of found one woman to sit next to at Bible studies, and then wore her down, gaining ownership through squatter's rights. (My dad met my mom the same way: he was the elevator operator where she was a nursing student. They laughed together for weeks before he asked her out, by which time the question of dating was moot.) Where I was now, this was Lothario territory, and my only models were Cary Grant and Humphrey Bogart. And that didn't work, because they get their scripts ahead of time; they know the woman is interested because she's *always* interested. But in the real world, how the hell do you know?

Nixie leaned forward. "Are you still a virgin?"

"Yes," I said. "Though god knows I've been trying. I mean, Kansas City is so—"

"Come on," she said, with a nod and a wink. "Let's go take care of that." I can't tell you how lovely her smile was; it promised so much fun, without a trace of fear. She told me her room number. "I'm going up now. You wait ten minutes and then come up. Just knock and I'll let you in."

So *that's* how you can tell.

I waited ten minutes. I walked to her room, feeling like I was in a dream. I knocked on the door. She opened the door, and was already down to her lingerie. She was beautiful. The door closed on its own.

In my twenty-nine years of virginity, I'd read a lot about sex, and what people say over and over again is that the first time really isn't great—it's about getting it over with. You learn the good stuff later. I've also read, in article after article and interview upon interview, that a really common reaction after it's over is a bit of disappointment: all that buildup for something that isn't that much different from masturbation, physiologically.

Bullshit. For me, it was like the heavens themselves said, "You poor dumb son of a bitch, you've suffered enough. Here—take these keys to the ambrosia stash." As much as I have loved every woman I've dated since, I have to say that nothing has really equaled that first time. Even with the awkwardness you'd expect, it ranks first. As soon as the door chunked closed, she walked up to me, smiling, and slowly unbuttoned my shirt, while I eagerly took my pants off and stepped out of them. "Oh, god," she said. "Just one thing. You have to take your socks off. I just can't stand—"

"Got it," I said. And I made a mental note for the future: *In sex, always remove socks.*

When I was naked, she pointed to the bed and said, "I have to undress now. Just have fun while you watch me." This was a good plan; it distracted me so I forgot to get nervous. Then she lay down, invited me on top, and, with a little navigational help, we were off. I was initially amazed at how hard I was, even with a condom. That hadn't happened with Jane. I felt like I'd been cured of something.

Then, even more amazingly, she squealed with pleasure. It wasn't just the sex part. She liked having her breasts touched. She liked how I kissed her. I just seemed to have a delirious effect on her all over, and her screams got louder and louder and she dug her nails in my back and it was all so unlike anything I'd even imagined that I couldn't believe I was responsible for this amazing thing happening beneath me. I made another mental note: *If you're complimentary and enthusiastic, everyone has a happier time.*

I want to say it lasted for ten or fifteen minutes—which was also amazing, because I'd been warned that coming early was a real risk for someone starting late in life like me. And since then god knows I've had more than my share of confusion about and frustrations with my own unhelpful body. But for this night, and this first time, everything worked effortlessly. Then, and most amazingly of all, we actually came at the same time. I know this because in the middle of the screaming and the clawing and the bucking she stiffened and then she said, "Oh, god! I just came! How are you doing?"

"I just came, too," I said.

"Aw, that's a shame," she tutted, and kissed me. "You should have told me. That would have been even more amazing."

Mental note: Supply partner with updates on progress.

"Got it," I said. "Thanks so much."

We held each other, giddy and spent, and as I returned to reality I began to get a little more tense. This whole thing had just seemed so unprecedented. I couldn't wrap my mind around it. *I actually had sex. It all happened and it was all great. When does the letdown part appear?*

Nixie kissed me and said, "I hate to run, but I've got to get back downstairs. But you can use the shower if you want."

I didn't know how to express everything I was feeling, and all I could say was "Thank you" again, trying to push as much of my emotion into it as possible. "I think you've just improved my life forever."

She cupped my face with her hands and tilted her head, smiling. "You're welcome. I've always thought of myself as the Mother Teresa of fucking."

She went off and showered and dressed, we hugged once more, and then she left. But I didn't want to shower. I wanted her scent to linger on me; I wanted the feeling to stay. It takes emotions so long to seep into my consciousness, I was afraid that a shower would move me past this moment before I'd really had a chance to let it sink in. I stood in front of the mirror and looked at myself, waiting for the real emotion to come.

The real emotion I was expecting was guilt. It was inevitable. Everything I knew about sex—about responsible sex, like Dr. Ruth, not what you get from Benny Hill—suggested that sex was deeply meaningful. And every Christian speaker I'd ever heard taught us that recreational sex was unsatisfying and corrupting and empty. Even if I no longer believed in every tenet of the Christian creed, I expected that, like my nightmares of the Antichrist, I'd have some sort of leftover fear that would hit me and I'd have to deal with it. Better to do that up here, where no one could see me tremble or cry, than break down somehow in front of my friends downstairs.

But I stood there and stood there, and nothing happened. Eventually, I smiled, and I told the mirror, "I feel fine," as if testing the sentence out. It felt true. I went to the window and looked down over the nighttime city of Atlanta, thick with car lights oozing through various arteries. My reflection was cast on the window so you could sort of see the city inside me, and I thought of that line from Whitman: I contain multitudes. In a city full of people doing the normal activities of life, I had crossed a line tonight and I was now a man, and part of the human race. Being normal had never felt so deeply satisfying. "I feel fine," I said again, and this time I actually felt it—happiness tingling through me, every inch of skin feeling alive to the air in the room, and straining to hold in the joy of it all.

And Josh Broward had been right: happiness was easy. Then, with the emotional memory secure, I knew I was ready for that shower. If I cried actual tears then, I can't recall, but what's a few tears more or less when you've just had proof that you're lovable?

18

Milestone Birthday

THIRTY IS PROBABLY THE WORST MILESTONE BIRTHDAY, because it's the biggest transitional one. Hallmark does cards for sixteen and eighteen and twenty-one and twenty-five . . . but starting with thirty, you count them decades apart. It really is the first year of the rest of your life, which is apparently only going to be interesting at very long intervals.

Since I already wasn't crazy about my life's frustrating trajectory, starting at about twenty-nine and a half, I started changing things in my life. After taking the GRE, I figured I should save money, just in case I got into a Ph.D. program and had to move. So I moved to a different apartment away from the Plaza and got a roommate—a funny and brilliant Hallmark artist named Meg, who was a dream to live with despite a slight case of OCD and a predilection for exotic pets. ("While I'm on vacation, remember to spray the chameleon with mist four times a day or he'll die. Also, if the heat lamp burns out, replace the bulb or he'll die that way, too. The live crickets are in the top drawer. . . .")

As for the birthday itself, I planned the celebration with my new roommate. Key to our strategy was that Meg made sure I invited Edgar Allan (he was single, and she had a thing for him), and I would invite Lorraine, that smart, funny non-Hallmark girl I'd met a few weeks back and needed to wear down. The theme would be "Game Night," and there was going to be something to do every hour starting at seven P.M. Guests who arrived would be offered $100 in "Dave Money," which they were then permitted to wager on various events. Thanks to Kenneth, I had an old Atari 2600 in the corner where people could play Space Invaders. The top three scorers at evening's end would get $100, $50, and $25 in Dave money, redeemable for door prizes.

For the first two hours we also ran Wind-Up Monster Races. At a novelty store, I bought three wind-up King Kongs, three Godzillas, and three Creatures from the Black Lagoon. (Strangely, all three of them spit sparks. So much for verisimilitude . . .) After three runs—which took place along our coffee table, and which you could either compete in ($200, $100, $50) or wager on (up to $100), and after all three heats, the fastest Kong, the fastest Godzilla, and the fastest Creature all went head-to-head in a final racing showdown (more wagering).

The pièce de résistance, however, was a ballot that I'd handed out with the invitations: all evening, we'd take a vote, and if a majority of people wanted it, at midnight I would shave my head. You'd think this would be a no-brainer, but it turns out we're not in college anymore, and Hallmark people are very nice. The vote to shave my head passed by a whisker, thirteen to twelve. (About seven people showed up just at midnight to throw the vote and watch what happened.)

It was wall-to-wall geekery.

I got presents, I read some poems, I flirted with women and danced around, and everyone had a wonderful time. Except for one thing: Lorraine didn't warm to my charming attempt to wear down her resistance, and as the evening drew later, I noticed that she had spent most of the evening in the kitchen talking to Edgar Allan. They left together before the head-shaving. This should perhaps have been cause for some commiseration with my roommate, Meg, later, except that she'd met someone at the party, too. Loving was the one gift I didn't get.

Shaving my head, though, which was something I'd always been curious about, turned out to be a great move. Underneath that shaggy mane, it turned out, was a very nicely shaped skull. Everywhere I went the next day, I'd catch myself in the mirror and think, *This is a good look. I might keep this around for a while.*

Kenneth had recently purchased a video camera, and he'd filmed my whole birthday in bits and pieces. The next day, he gave me a copy of the tape, which I watched that night at home.

We didn't have a video camera growing up, so this was the first time I'd ever seen myself caught socially on video, and the experience was gob-smackingly awful. I was wearing the uniform I always wore—that seven-suits-from-the-Gap plan I'd made with my first paycheck—and it was, I could see now, a terrible mistake. My huge baggy pants not only didn't fit, but you could tell this from every angle. My shirt flopped all over me. I seemed to be constantly touching my nose or biting my fingernails. Even my dancing, which in theory is okay when I'm among other white people, looked bad when done in that outfit, and when surrounded by those geeky mannerisms. I swallowed hard. If I had seen myself at a party, I wouldn't have bothered to come over.

The worst, though, was my hair. I guess I'd always assumed it looked okay because I combed it from the front, straight back, and for as long as I stood before a mirror it was passable enough. But I'd always been a little curious about it, since I knew that, on my forehead, I had a sort of skinny strip of hair and I couldn't quite tell if it was connected all the way. Back in Tucson, I had trusted the stylist who told me I had "some marshy undergrowth." Now here, on the video, I could see that if this had ever been true, it was no longer. The hair that I was combing back actually formed an arc that, when you looked at it from the side, *you could see under,* like a bridge. Worse yet, my hair was wavy, and so the moment I stepped away from the mirror, that straight-back strip of hair tended to flop to one side or the other, and it looked like a comb-over.

Jesus! I felt betrayed. By myself, by my friends who hadn't stopped me from dressing like this, by life itself because its adulthood lessons were so unobvious that I'd missed them all this time. I'd been accidentally torpedoing myself for who even knew how long? (I'd even read *Dress for Success,* but I guess I didn't know what the author meant by "fit.") No wonder I wasn't attracting any women! If I didn't want to wait another thirty years for more sex, I was going to have to fix this.

My first step was obvious: I started shaving my head every day. It wasn't just a fashion statement or even self-defense. It actually felt like a kind of baptism or re-creation every morning; I literally scraped away my old look and, like a shiny new cue ball in hand, could set down anywhere on the table.

Then I started buying new clothes—shirts that had color in them and actual blue jeans. I had no sense of my style, really.

When I had eight new shirts and five new pairs of pants, I threw all of my old uniforms away. (I should have taken a picture of them first; no one believes me now that I ever had them.) When people said, "That looks good," I'd smile and say, "I know; that's why I'm doing it for once."

And another thing: I bought an exercise bike and started riding every morning for an hour. Two things happened as a result: I lost a surprising amount of weight very quickly, and I started getting hooked on country music. The latter was an accident. I was watching music videos to kill the time on the bike, and discovered that only the country stations—CMT and GAC—played any actual music for longer than six minutes at a stretch. Normally that wouldn't have been much inducement, but this was the era of early Shania Twain, and early Faith Hill, and Martina McBride and Mindy McCready and a whole string of women so gorgeous that initially I literally watched the videos with the sound off. But then I turned it up and next thing I knew I was in the music store hunting down Dwight Yoakam and Lucinda Williams. Next thing after that I was listening to "A Thousand Miles from Nowhere," growing an honest-to-god music collection, and dreaming of the wide spaces of Tucson for the first time in years. Maybe you can't really get escape velocity until you circle back one more time over where you've been. All I know is, within three months I felt practically unrecognizable, and more like my old college self than I'd been in years.

I HAD AN INTERESTING creative breakthrough around this same time. There'd been a call for writers to do quick writing for a new mysterious project. Since the only thing that had been breaking my writer's block was the demand for an instant sentiment, I volunteered.

The mysterious new project—which we were sworn not to reveal, but it's been over a decade, so what the hell—was a method of doing extremely intricate card cuts using computer-guided lasers. Back in the pre-laser days, the only way to cut a window or some other shape out of a card was to use a metal die, which had to be pretty simple—we could do big shapes, but nothing too fancy—and the dies themselves were expensive, because they tended to damage the printer rollers. Now, all of a sudden, anything you could draw, we could cut. We could create cards that had the shape of actual spiderwebs. We could have tree shapes and get as many individual leaves as we liked. We could make even a single, elegant, expressive hairline. It was truly impressive—and, as so often happened in the industry, they were planning to launch the cards as a new product based on what was the most eye-catching . . . but they hadn't actually figured out what any of the cards were going to say. We were invited to cast our eyes among the favored designs and see what called to us.

Ninety percent or more of the cards were nature scenes, and I'm not really a nature person. For me, a trip to the beach means moving outside where it's harder to read, and where my book might get messed up by sand or rain or bird shit. So I passed on most of them in favor of something more whimsical. Alas, the only thing that looked at all humorlike was my old nemesis, Mickey Mouse. *Fine*, I said, gripping the card grimly. *Maybe a deadline will make me come up with something for you, you miserable unfunny cartoon.*

The card was even halfway helpful, because, thank goodness, it wasn't just Mickey standing around. What it showed—in a series of really gorgeous silhouettes and a four-panel foldout—was Mickey Mouse playing the conductor for the Disney woodland band that often makes an appearance in his stupid cartoons. Goofy was on the fiddle, Donald had the trumpet, and there was some cow I'd never heard of playing the tuba. Surely, I thought, this would at least suggest a basic direction.

For hours—hours—it didn't. I paced. I fumed. I stared and stared at Mickey Mouse and his stupid friends, all enjoying themselves in their simple, moronic, not-funny-in-any-way way. Finally, I decided to just get the anger out of my system and write what I was feeling.

Fucking Mickey and his fucking idiotic orchestra are playing their goddamn instruments and pulling a lot of irritating, namby-pamby oompah shit. . . .

My brain suddenly stood up. Oompah! That's kind of a fun, silly word. There's *oompah*, and what other words? Flutes tootle. That'll work. Horns honk. Excellent! I can even make words up— the quonk of the clarinet, the sprash of the cymbals.

Suddenly, for the first time in months, I actually gave a shit about finishing a card. That it was a Mickey card made it all the more astounding. It eventually saw life as a Congratulations card with "Mickey and his woodland crew" celebrating "happy you!" With oompahs and tootles and crashes and plashes . . . et cetera. It was so amazing, so freeing, that ever since then I've used it as a last-ditch creative idea. If you find you hate working on something, embrace the hatred, and hate it so much that your hatred becomes the fun part.

I SHOULD HAVE EXPECTED THIS, but after taking the GRE,
even before I'd gotten any scores, I became deluged with college
brochures, most of which I dumped directly into the trash. But
now that I was getting letters from colleges, it suddenly seemed
important to have a more specific plan. A single afternoon of
poking around showed me that there were a number of Ph.D.
programs in English that allowed you to write a creative dissertation (i.e., a novel, instead of an analysis of the nipple references
in Jane Austen, of which I don't think there are any). The vague
wish I'd had for years turned out to be a real thing: after you'd
stopped caring about writing your novel, your committee would
care *for* you and threaten to take even more of your money if
you didn't get it done. Perfect!

In the end, I found three states to choose from: Colorado
(University of), Texas (Houston), and Florida (FSU). It wasn't
even close. Going back to school represented escape and a second chance to do it right this time—no to Bible studies, yes to
actual Spring Break shenanigans—and the last taste I'd had of
that had come when the woman in the van had flashed me.
Where was that most likely to happen again? Florida, surely.
Home of bikini tops. That, I decided, was where hope lived.
Before I sent off my application, I actually kissed the envelope
for luck. I hadn't even done that with my Hallmark portfolios.

It started affecting my everyday life the same way thoughts of
Kansas City had started to intrude on my life in Tucson. All
winter, I kept thinking, *If I lived in Florida, I would never have to
deal with snow again.* I would go to the UMKC university library
and think, *I bet FSU, with its forty thousand students and huge endow-*

ments, would actually have *frickin'* Simians, Cyborgs, and Women
by Donna frickin' Haraway in its frickin' stacks. And then one night
I found myself sitting in Kenneth Riley's apartment—the same
one where I'd collapsed after trying to rent *Casablanca*—and
since it was a quiet evening of mellow *South Park* watching, I
was able to look over the sofas and chairs at Kenneth and Angela,
Edgar and Lorraine, and Jessica and Jun Lee, and it hit me: *Every
woman here turned me down when I asked her out. Every woman here
met the guy they're with through me. I really hope grad school is where
people hook up, because here in Missouri I clearly have no goddamn mojo
at all. It's time for my catalyst phase to end already.*

Since my Hallmark friends were all coupled now, I went to a
party shortly afterward with the specific intention of meeting
non-Hallmark people. At this particular shindig, at a friend of a
friend's midtown house, which he actually owned, I found myself talking to three youngish architects (Kansas City is full of
architects for some reason) and a few of their non-Hallmark
friends.

One of the guys said, "Hey, did any of you see *Antz* or *A Bug's
Life*? I missed them in the theater. What did you all think?"

One woman said, "I liked *A Bug's Life* better." Another guy
said, "They were both good, but they're different."

And I felt that inform-against-their-will urge coming on, like
I'd had the time I told my colleagues about apes. It had been a
long time since I'd had it, and instead of worrying, I just gave in
without guilt. This wasn't Main Writing, after all.

"As it happens," I said, "I've just written a weird short story
about giant ants taking over the world, and I did a lot of ant
research. Then I saw those movies, and here's what's annoying.
Both of them do the exact same thing. In the movies, all the ants

are male, except for the traditional female roles—the queen, the love interest, and that's it. But in real life, *all ants are female*. Males only live long enough to impregnate the queen and create more females, then they die. So they just missed this amazing opportunity for satire, you know? What a great movie that could have been, using animation to explore what a completely matriarchal society would be like! Or maybe you could tell it from the point of view of these doomed males; I don't know. But it sure would have been more interesting than what we got."

And one of the guys listening said, calmly, "Dude. We're not in college anymore." In the silence that ensued, it was clear everyone agreed.

But this time I didn't feel bad about myself. I just remembered back to my MFA parties and thought, *No one ever said crap like that in grad school. Maybe I'm not a flawed person; I'm just in the wrong place, the wrong job, the wrong conversation at the wrong stupid party. I'll be a lot happier when I'm back among the overanalytical geeks who live in academia.* If I'd ever had doubts about going back to college, this sealed my determination. If nothing else, I hoped I would at least wind up in a smarter goddamn city.

Gee, I thought later, as I walked away feeling oddly centered, *I really have changed this year.*

AND THEN, just as I was getting the feel of this new me, at my end-of-year review, Constance looked at me a little wearily and said, "Well, we've talked about this among ourselves, and we're going to move you back to Humor."

Before it even sank in, just the idea of leaving Main Writing stopped my suffering for a heartbeat. It was dizzying. "Really? I mean . . . really?" Maybe I wouldn't have to move after all. God, that would be so much simpler. Maybe I could still turn my life into a Hallmark victory.

"Yes. I should warn you that Max isn't happy about this, and you'll have to take that up with him. But we think it might be better for your career at this stage to see if you can get along in that environment. We're all a little . . . Dave, we don't really know what to do with you. Let's hope this does something. It would be great if you could get back to how you were when you started here, because otherwise . . . you know. We just don't know."

That was it—the first time anyone had actually obliquely threatened me with firing. And yet it had no impact at all, because it came with a guaranteed prison release. *Do better? Of course I'd do better, you stubborn fucks! That's what I've been trying to tell everyone in Main Writing for the past year and a half!*

What was surprising was that, even as I packed my things with hands literally trembling, impatient to kick the dust of this boring-ass staff from my shoes, when I thought about the move back, I was only eighty-five percent thrilled to be returning to the staff and the job where I always felt I'd belonged. The other fifteen percent of my focus, which had been plotting my escape and thinking of a world of ideas where you could read good hard books and then talk about them, surrounded by a beautiful sunny Florida campus—perhaps one where women flash their boobies!—was a dream that wouldn't quite go back in the crate.

PART FIVE

Get Better Soon

My Months Back in Humor

19

Brinkspersonship

THE DAY I SHOWED UP BACK IN HUMOR, MAX HAD PRAC-
tically been lying in wait for me. "Look," he said, back in his
office. "I can't have you wandering around like you did before.
That's got to change. You have to stay in that cubicle."

"But you know I can't work there. If I could I'd have done it
by now. It's completely impossible."

He looked pained, as if humoring a lunatic as a matter of
duty. "I can't change the office around because of your disability
or whatever. You'll have to figure something out yourself. But
no walking around. I mean it."

After a few days of trying and failing, and looking longingly
at the conference room where Black Peter was ensconced every
day, I finally dared to demand something that would almost
certainly further piss off Black Peter, who scared me more than
anyone. Max agreed. So the compromise I finally wrung from
him was that I'd be able to come in at six A.M., before anyone
else (we had flextime, so six was a perfectly reasonable request
normally, but Max didn't like giving away the key codes for the

doors), and I could stay in the conference room for half the day—until ten—at which point Black Peter would take over and I'd have to go back to my cubicle. This worked perfectly at least in part because Max never scheduled any conferences before ten, so I was left entirely on my own except during midyear performance reviews.

But what to do while I was in there with the door locked? Even here, on the first day of this new plan, I started feeling the old frustration, the old writer's block. I wanted to break out and walk around! What I wound up doing was pacing inside the room—pacing furiously. I moved the chairs in really tight to give myself a decent oval runway, and I'd circle the table with my fists and jaws clenched, practically daring writer's block to hit me again. Somehow this didn't work, and I started jogging, feeling very silly . . . but it also felt good. What felt even better, I found, was jog-trotting around the table *and* staring fixedly at the floor. Not following any particular thread or stain, but literally blurring my vision a little and letting the floor's pattern pass before my eyes like so much static.

In three days, I had my new system. It was practically a religious ritual, and it went in this order:

1. Push all the chairs up against the table to provide floor space.
2. Close the blinds.
3. Turn off the lights, leaving the room almost completely dark. (At six A.M., a little ambient light streamed in from the streetlights outside, which was enough to prevent me from killing myself during what followed.)
4. Run around and around in circles, staring at the floor,

until overcome by a feeling of exhaustion, vertigo, and just a teeny bit of nausea.

5. Lie supine (i.e., on back) in a kind of fetal position, with the shins resting in the seat of a chair.

6. Pull notepad and pen out of pocket, and hold them, pen in one hand, pad in the other, with arms outstretched in a *Pietà* on the floor.

7. Drift in and out of sleep and write whatever comes to mind.

I'd get twenty ideas in four hours that way, which I would note roughly ("poem w/bug theme"; "snowman cartoon— where's my nose") and then work up into actual cards for the rest of the day.

It was terrible, because it worked like a charm and it was completely insane. There was literally no part of it that you could actually do while anyone was watching, and now that I knew that this was what I'd been trying to do all these years, I couldn't do anything less. Just walking around seemed absurd by comparison. Walking was such a small part of it; it was like trying to get high by licking an empty syringe. So with Max's further permission, I found another conference room that was never used—next door in Office Planning, right near the eternal soda machine, which Max thought of as our shared turf so it didn't count as walking around. I would wake up at four, exercise for an hour, then come in at six, run around in circles, lie on my back, drift in and out of consciousness, then leave at ten and go to a weirdly early lunch—the lunchroom didn't open until eleven, but you could grab sandwiches and salads at the commissary a floor above—and then spend from eleven to three in the Office Planning conference room, which was a square, sunny room that barely even had chairs, but it had a clean-enough floor and that's all I needed.

This worked beautifully in terms of productivity. I was getting twenty ideas a day again, and doing it so fast that if I made my personal quota by noon, I sometimes goofed off the rest of the day by reading more of my precious literary theory book, plus a few others I'd managed to find at the UMKC library. Professionally, I was, well, not in heaven, but at least I was out of purgatory, and that felt amazing all by itself. And with these books I was reading, intellectually, I was starting to be happy, too. But socially, everything about that workday—the aloneness of the conference room, the emptiness of the lunchroom in the off hours, the thinking thoughts I couldn't share with anyone— wound up making me feel like I was just circling through a series of the same four Edward Hopper paintings.

I got a call one day from Mia, the editor who had screamed when I startled her by emerging from under a table. She needed help. "We're doing these cards for kids," she said. "They're collectible, and the idea we've come up with is, each one has an animal on the front, and a series of fun facts about that animal on the reverse." Apparently she'd taken this project to the Idea Exchange for a quick brainstorm, and the hat had been left almost empty. No one could think of any animal facts, and one of the writers told Mia, "Why do a brainstorm for this? Just go ask Dave." Everyone agreed, and the brainstorm was adjourned.

I could come up with only half a dozen or so facts off the top of my head, and they needed at least thirty. So I asked Max if I could work on this project in my local library for a day or two.

And this is how I knew things had changed: Max agreed to let me out of his sight. "You've been doing good work lately," he said. "Your jokes for the Maxine calendar were really strong, and I'm not getting any calls anymore. So sure. Go ahead and do research if the editor needs you. But no more than two days."

I probably could have done it in one, but it was nice to get away from the office. So for two wonderful days I simply read every reference book I could find on animals of the world. I piled them around me as I sat on the floor between the stacks, taking note after note after note. It wasn't easy—the more scholarly books go a long time between anecdotes—but I did find the few following bits of information that I couldn't use, but which have stayed with me ever since.

- To keep cool in the desert heat, camels will pee on their own legs.
- Armadillos are one of the only animals that can contract leprosy.
- Male giraffes sexually mount other males more often than they do females.
- Sloths are so well adapted to climbing that when they die they often continue to hang in trees until they rot.

Use these freely at your next party.

It was a surprisingly important two days. First, because it was almost as if Hallmark itself was finally apologizing for complaining about my literary allusions. Here, at last, my tendency to inform people against their will was actually paying off. Second, and more surprisingly, it reminded me how much I loved research. I hadn't had a reason to do any in ages, and just being around those books, pursuing questions I was actually interested in, forced me to see another way I could be happy. *I bet this is what writing a dissertation is like*, I thought. *Sitting in a library, tracking a fun idea, planning a paper with piles and piles of information at your disposal.* I left it behind after two days, but for months afterward my brain remembered what it was like to be hungry, with a whole beautiful banquet right at arm's length.

ISOLATION IS NO FUN FOR ANYONE. But it's actually dangerous for me, because often a friend's outside suggestion is the only thing preventing me from following through on a terribly stupid idea. I'm not talking about greeting card ideas. I was having tons of those now—although because I spent all my time locked away from distraction, I didn't see my acceptances and didn't look at the results from meetings, and therefore had no real idea how I was doing. (I could have checked, but I felt like a superstitious batter on a hot streak. One piece of bad news might have thrown off a game that felt like it was maybe going okay.)

My problem in my sequestration was other non-card-related ideas, like, "Maybe I'd write better if I took off my shoes" (I didn't, but even when I left, the room still smelled like socks), or "Maybe this pain in my foot means I'm dying from cancer" (I wasn't, but I lost half a day stewing about it). I was now having a dozen of these crackpot notions every day, with only myself to edit them. In a way, I really was going mad, and thoughts of leaving for Florida didn't help. I may be exaggerating the cause a bit; even if I'd been going outside my lockup during the day, the fact was that all of my friends were in relationships now. Even if I'd wanted to call them up for lunch or to hang out after

work, they would have been less available anyway. Maybe I'd
have felt trapped and alone even if I hadn't actually spent all day
trapped and alone. All I know is, even while I was producing
cards again, some desperate part of me was, I think, angry about
my flattened life. In the isolation, the fear of failure, the lack of
any sense of how I was doing, the creative part of my brain came
up with at least two ways to get me fired.

KENNETH HAD MOVED all the way over to Shoebox as an artist,
and so I had begun to swing by every now and then when we
were planning to go to lunch. This is how I met Ryan Mueller,
the head manager of all the Shoebox writers. He was a funny
guy—bright, geeky, and lively. If we'd gone to school together,
I would totally have invited him to play Dungeons & Dragons.
Ryan seemed to feel the same way about me.

One day, as I was preparing to talk to Kenneth, Ryan called
me over to his office. "Do you play Diplomacy?"

"I've played it," I said. Diplomacy is a classic World War I
simulation game with an ingeniously simple premise. There are
no dice. You know who wins any conflict just by counting up
who's fighting. Everyone decides what they're going to do, writes
it down privately, and everyone reveals their moves all at once.

What this means is that the entire strategy of the game, literally, is just talking to people. "If you support me this turn against
Marseilles, I'll support you with my navy when you take Sevas-
topol." You can lie, cajole, or wheedle. People often pair off into
separate rooms to discuss plans. One friend of mine who played
it in college used to leave tape recorders hidden in popular planning rooms so he could hear what people were saying. It was

actual espionage. Depending on how many people you need to talk to and how involved the negotiations get, turns can take an hour each. A game lasts eight turns.

"Do you like the game?" said Ryan.

"In theory," I said. "It's a great set of rules. But you need six or seven players for a fair game and it takes forever, so I've only done it twice, back in college."

"Well, we've got six players and we really need a seventh, and I thought of you. We'll be running it for two weeks, talking to each other through e-mail and sending in orders Mondays, Wednesdays, and Fridays at noon. Can you commit?"

I don't know why I hesitated. I had just spent a year almost not writing at all, and it didn't seemed to have hurt me. But actively goofing off, instead of doing nothing and wishing things were different, seemed like going public with my sin. But then I realized that if the writing manager of Shoebox was doing this, then surely it must be okay. So I agreed, he handed me some photocopies of maps of Europe to keep track of things with, and by the time I got back to my home cubicle I got an e-mail saying I was England. Ryan was Germany, which made him a neighbor I had to negotiate with.

It turned out that playing the game was actually pretty easy and not at all time-consuming. One of the nice features of Hallmark's e-mail system was that all you had to do was type in a person's name and it would go straight to them. So I didn't even have to look up addresses. The only problem that nagged at me was that, precisely because I was forced to work by e-mail from the main building, and all the other players simply worked next to each other in cubicles at Shoebox, I was in a very vulnerable

position to be colluded against. What's more, since all my negotiations were written, there was absolutely no way to be sure the
other guys weren't over there printing out my e-mails and showing them to each other. I had no security at all.

Despite this, a surprising thing happened. I started to care
about the game. It started promisingly. All my immediate neighbors left me alone in the west, choosing instead to lunge to the
center, making lunch meat out of Austria-Hungary. While they
did that, Ryan and I were putting together a temporary truce
where he'd go north to Russia and I'd go south to Turkey, and
we'd see who was stronger when we met in the middle.

Another turn or two, and as far as I could tell no one even
knew England was a country. In fact, things looked really good
for me. For the first time in the history of my playing this game,
it seemed like I might actually have a chance to win. But just as
I was stretching myself really far south, with just two lone navy
pieces on a huge expanse of ocean, Austria collapsed, northern
Turkey trembled, and I knew, with the certainty of a Churchill,
that those other guys were looking around for a new and vulnerable target. I was isolated and easy pickings, and I had to defend
myself.

With no allies handy in my own office, I decided to protect
myself sort of like Nixon, by acting unpredictably. I poked ten-
tatively north and accidentally took over part of Greece. (Navies
can ferry armies around, so you can attack anywhere.) I savagely
charged through a French fleet that I'd left unbothered for four
turns. But in what I thought was my most brilliant act of skull-
duggery, I sent a fake e-mail. Ryan Mueller and I were allies, but
I knew you could see his computer screen through the glass of

his office. I suspected some of the other guys might be looking at his e-mail, trying to guess what was happening based on the subject lines and From Who.

So I came up with an idea—which I knew was risky, but in the thrill of the creative moment I didn't care. The idea was to fool any snoops who might be casually spying on Ryan's e-mail. I typed up a note to Ryan Mueller that had a fake opening paragraph, which went as follows:

If you don't move your jackbooted thugs off my border *tout suite*, I'll come down on you so hard that your heads will spin in your pointy little helmets and you'll fill your pants with last night's sauerkraut. Tell that to your schnitzel-munching kaiser. *Sprechen Sie* whoop-ass?

The next paragraph said, "Hi, Ryan! I know we're allies, but just in case someone was peeking at your mail, I wanted to give them the wrong idea. Our truce is still good. See you in the middle!" I gave it a provocative and misleadingly hostile subject line—"Die, You German Bastard!"—and sent it to Ryan.

This was my big gambit. I had to trust Ryan. Was he a thorough reader, or did he skim? Would I have accidentally planted an idea in his head, or would he appreciate its Machiavellian cunning? My game was riding on this. So although I looked at a few requisitions, tried to draw some cartoons, I was mostly pretty anxious to see how Ryan responded.

I got my answer ninety minutes later. "Hey, guys," he wrote in a mass e-mail. "Remember to have your moves in by noon tomorrow. I'll be calculating the results and should have them after lunch.—Ryan"

I waited, but no further note came. Not a "Ha ha," not a "You're so crazy," just nothing. I started to get really worried about what I had done to my game. I decided it might be smart to walk over there and actually talk to Ryan in person, just in case. So I hit "Reply" to send him an e-mail that I was about to come over, when I noticed something: he spelled his last name "Muehler," with *hl*.

I'd sent my e-mail to "Ryan Mueller," two *l*'s. It should have bounced back . . . but it didn't. Uh-oh! That meant that, according to the mail system, there must be an actual Ryan Mueller, with two *l*'s, *also* working at Hallmark. And even as I thought it, I felt a chill seize me. *Oh, god*, I thought. *What are the odds that he's German?* This wasn't a game anymore. I could probably get fired.

I immediately sent an abject and apologetic e-mail to "Ryan Mueller" (two *l*'s) and explained that that last message was a complicated inside joke between me and the writing manager of Shoebox and I was sorry for any misunderstanding. I got a pleasantly swift reply back from where he worked in the distribution plant, which said, "You aren't the first person who's made this mistake, and any time I get some crazy e-mail, I just assume it's for him instead, so don't worry." He wasn't a bastard at all. In fact, I never heard a single thing about this incident, so it seemed to have been nipped in the bud.

But even though nothing bad had happened, I had another of those sinking feelings that I'd been having more often lately. The way I was living now was almost animalistic—I was living eight hours a day in a set of rooms that I paced around in like a cage, and only came out for food, which I brought back to my lair—and my spirit was lashing out. This desperation had come out in my game, hadn't it? I hadn't been hurt yet, but what about next time? If this kept up, surely something horrible would happen and I really would get fired.

In the end, we kept playing, and I didn't even win. It turns out you need a strategy, and attacking randomly to throw people off guard isn't a shrewd use of resources. One good thing came out of it all, though. As a result of my erratic behavior in the middle of Diplomacy, when it was all over I discovered that those six guys, when they talked among themselves during the game, gave me the coolest nickname I've ever had: Mad Dog.

THE OTHER TERRIBLE IDEA CAME one evening when I was working late. I had a verse I was working on, and I wanted to be able to finish it before I left. It was so quiet, I found myself actually sitting at my cubicle without distraction. I looked around and realized I was the only person in the office. A quick peek showed that Office Planning was completely empty, too. It was seven o'clock. I thought back and realized that I hadn't talked to a single human being all day.

Jesus, I'm lonely. The thought came fully formed, unsurprising but definite, like the result of a bank book you merely have to get around to balancing. I thought about the woman in the van, about what the girls of Florida might be like. I thought about what shape hope might take.

And then, because I'm very good at self-deception, I thought of a fun prank I could do. I knew that Hallmark had a computer filter that would alert it if anyone went to a porn site. But here's the challenge: How close could you get to hitting a porn site while still plausibly doing card research?

I hasten to add that I truly thought this was a sudden, fun, and completely unrelated project, something to take my mind off my aloneness for a second. The idea that loneliness and porn are linked never occurred to me. I was just going to absurdly stick it to The Man by making the computer police gasp over something that would turn out to be nothing (whatever it was; I hadn't thought that far ahead). I would just do this experiment, set it in motion, and then leave, chuckling to myself, while I finished my poem. I figured I was a safe person to do this experiment because it was well known that I didn't actually look at porn. The closest thing I had to a porn collection was—and it pains me now to admit it—a series of nude-woman clips I had recorded late at night from Cinemax. It was a single tape, and it was rated a mild R. If I was accused of being some kind of pervert, all I'd have to do is enter that tape into evidence, and I'd be the subject of actual pity.

So . . . how to thumb my nose at the computer nanny with a legitimate search? The first obvious choice was "bunny." A search on "images—bunny" was apt to return *Playboy* images that an incautious person could theoretically click on accidentally. But as soon as I'd done it and seen the return—there was an obvious porn link right on the first page—I lost interest. That had been too easy. And also, it was too easy to tell the good links from the bad. What if there were a search you could do that *might* return naughty images, but wouldn't *necessarily* do so, and so it justified the putative card researcher to go and look? How could the nanny fail, and let an innocent card researcher go wrong?

After thinking through a number of unpromising options— *girl*, *honeymoon*, *consecration*—I finally hit on a great one: *Mardi*

Gras. A quick check of EDS confirmed that we did, in fact, do Mardi Gras cards. And of course, Mardi Gras has all the cool masks and costumes and such, so it would be important to look up "Mardi Gras images" to get the proper complement of domino masks.

But of course, why would I be working on a Mardi Gras card? We apparently didn't do Mardi Gras humor—a big mistake, by the way; the jokes write themselves—so I couldn't claim to have picked up a requisition. Fortunately I had another way to obtain plausible deniability: all the writers were encouraged every year to come up with at least one new product idea. I had already done that this year—instead of mugs, why not put funny labels on pencil holders? They'd said thanks for the idea and they'd get back to me, but it wouldn't hurt to work up another project.

So for verisimilitude, I actually went to the printing-area computer and started typing up an actual Mardi Gras Humor Cards proposal. I wrote an introduction that pointed out that we had only a few cards for Mardi Gras, and that none of them were funny, and that perhaps this celebratory event would be more popular if we had funnier cards. (My proposal was doomed, of course, but there's nothing illegal about having a bad idea. My pencil holders never went anywhere either.) With my back-story established, I now had the justification to check Yahoo for "photos—Mardi Gras." The next step—accidentally on purpose clicking a legitimate-looking link and finding nude images among the pictures of floats—took a little longer. There actually are a lot of Mardi Gras images on the Web that aren't rude in any way. It took me three screens to find the first page that actually showed the photos from someone's vacation that included domino masks, colorful floats, *and* young women flashing for beads. I clicked on it, noted the transgression, and the experiment was done. I clapped my hands together and actually said, "Perfect!"

It was very nicely done, if I say so myself. I think I might have even gotten away with it, except for one thing: the girls were really pretty. Once I got that one photo of these two young girls—so happy, so full of life, so defiant of both propriety and gravity—it was hard not to look for more. And the more I looked, the more I found. I found the photos quite . . . motivating. Why not gain a little release? It had been a difficult day. And did I mention I was lonely?

I looked around. I really was completely alone. I doubted there was another soul anywhere in the whole multistory building. And a quick scan of the ceiling didn't reveal any obvious cameras. Still, as I opened my zipper, a natural caution overtook me. If there *were* cameras, I'd be in real trouble, obviously. If only there were some way to hide myself a little . . .

That's when I noticed a stray umbrella. Like most weather-intensive cities, Kansas City tends to collect umbrellas the way rocks collect lichen. During any rainy spell like we were having, you just need to look in any office, or on any bus, and you're apt to find a cast-off umbrella somewhere. This one was on the floor beside the printer—black, retractable, tiny, and perfectly convenient.

I'd never done anything like this before, and it turns out that masturbating underneath an umbrella is actually somewhat complicated, if you're trying to hold the umbrella still and be completely hidden by it. I was obliged to hunch over beneath it—too high and some theoretically existent camera might see me from the side—and using my left hand alone didn't suffice to keep the umbrella steady. So I held the umbrella upright with my left hand, but also wedged the handle between my knees, letting the umbrella's edge rest on the back of the chair. Between this and the hunching over, I really didn't have a lot of room to maneuver. It was a bit like having sex in a pup tent while it's raining—you really can't afford to bump against any of the sides.

In for a penny, though. So I managed to meet my production goal (I closed my eyes and thought of Florida . . .), and then I carefully went over the scene to remove any incriminating evidence. As a final punctuation on the incident, I printed out the ersatz product proposal and left it in my cubicle for ready access in case of litigation.

I NEVER EVEN GOT TO my cubicle. Because I'd worked late that night, I came in later the next morning, and Max stopped me at the door and said, "Come here, Dave," and I was led into the conference room.

Max didn't even sit. "Dave, we know what you did."

Oh, shit. This is like the textbook reason people get fired. I felt the floor fall away beneath me.

"In light of this, I don't think you should have access to the building after hours, since it's just too tempting. I want you to come in at eight instead of six, and you can't be the last person in the office anymore."

Wait a minute—so I wasn't fired? I was safe? But now I was curious. I wanted to know how he'd found out. Was there a camera? Was it just a red letter on a database somewhere? How much did he know? But I was, naturally, so terrified and ashamed

that I simply nodded and said, "Uh, can I still have the conference room for four hours? You know—going until twelve?"

He mused. "You've got that other conference room over in
Planning. Just use that more often. That way you won't conflict
with Black Peter. Okay?"

I nodded, and while I stood there, waiting for the hammer to
fall, Max left the room. The meeting was over. I had survived. I
was still employed.

My first impulse, oddly, was irritation. Wait a minute! I wanted
to say. You want to limit my access *after* I've been nailed by surveillance? (I assumed I'd been caught by a camera, but having
just escaped firing, I had no desire to go back and find out for
sure.) Shouldn't I, of all people, be *least* likely to transgress in the
future, with this icky blot on my escutcheon? In fact, what the
hell—if you don't want people doing this, why not simply post
signs that say PREMISES UNDER SURVEILLANCE so people know
they really *are* being watched, instead of having it make the
rounds as a vaguely cautious rumor? You'll save management a
lot of embarrassing talking-tos.

The moment that thought hit me, though, I was struck by
the other odd element of our meeting: it had taken no time at
all, and Max had been calm throughout. Apparently I hadn't
committed a terrible unspeakable sin against all decency and
propriety and the proud name of Hallmark; I had been just a
notch on Max's managerial to-do list. So either Max was so
embarrassed that he exhibited no emotion at all . . . or my masturbating at work, for all its social unacceptability, wasn't that big
a deal. Just possibly this stuff happens all the time. Although I
felt horrible, maybe I wasn't a monster—just a statistic.

I've been dying to know the truth of this ever since. Not that

I ever bothered to ask even after I left, since I doubted I'd have gotten a straight answer anyway. But if my optimistic take on this is right, it suggests that sexual activity at work is a little-spoken-of commonplace in the world of nine-to-fiving. It suggests another truth as well: that caging people for eight hours a day is not the sort of thing that human beings take to very naturally. Sometimes the professional facade just can't compete with millions of years of evolution. There's something almost charming about the breakdown.

It also suggests, by the way, that security monitors are extremely ethical people. If they weren't, YouTube would be a lot more interesting. Not everyone is so considerate as to utilize the modesty of a trusty umbrella.

WITH THESE INCIDENTS on my record and no actual hand-slapping so far, I was pretty anxious in May, as I headed into my next performance review, to see exactly what sort of passive-aggressive backstabbing I was liable to suffer. I came expecting whiplash. Surely masturbating in the office was worse than using too many literary allusions, and look where that had gotten me. I felt the tom-toms in my bowels and a chill of possible dread when Max called my name. I fairly slunk in—quickly, to get it over with—and braced myself in the chair.

Max held up the report with a smile. A smile. Just like the old days. "I have to say, David, you've completely turned yourself around. I am very, very impressed. I get no calls, you're producing great work. And you did it all by yourself!" He shook my hand and pumped it joyously. He actually said that last point with pride, which I guess made sense to Max, since he tried never to be involved in any actual personal management if he could avoid it. I wanted to scream at him, "Of *course* I did it all by myself! What fucking choice did I *have*, you lazy prick?" But I stayed quiet and he ticked off a list of successes, and then he said, "Congratulations, David. You're now a Writer II." I'd been promoted at last.

I smiled, thanked him, and made my calls to Kenneth and Jessica, and I accepted their congratulations, too. But I honestly didn't feel happy or proud. I felt no emotion at all—just physical exhaustion so deep that even smiling felt like an imposition. And I was supposed to come back and do more tomorrow? That's when I knew it was over. For the next few days, people e-mailed and called and stopped me in the hallway to congratulate me on the promotion, and still I smiled and said "Thank you" the way people expected. But by day two, every time I said it, I started mentally adding *Good-bye; good-bye; good-bye.*

20

Heading South

A WEEK AFTER MY PROMOTION I DISCOVERED A MES-sage on my office phone left by a man named Breedlove who was calling on behalf of a head-hunting organization.

Head-hunting? I was flattered and curious. I called him back once I got home, and he answered right away.

"I represent a card company in the West that would like to hire you away from your current employment," he said.

"How have you heard of me?" I asked. "My name isn't even on any of the cards."

"I can't discuss that," he said. "The point is, would you be interested in the job? We obviously have a lot of details to work out, but they would definitely pay more than you're currently making, and they'd move you out to Colorado. I need an answer right away, and then we can get some sample cards to you so you can see what you'd be working with, and how your goals fit with theirs. So can I tell them yes?"

I said yes, I'd look into it, because what the hell, free cards. I was still basically committed to going back to college, but for a moment I also gave some thought to taking that other path: continuing forward as a greeting card writer. That's when I knew I had finally gotten back into my groove. If people had noticed— those same people who faxed *The Noon News* to our competition, maybe—and I was being headhunted, then by god, I must be good at my job again! The raise they were offering almost didn't matter; I was, by definition of being hunted, a recognized greeting card writer of skill, and I hadn't felt that way in a year and a half. A swagger filled my step. I took a long lunch. "I still got it," I said to the mirror at home.

The sample cards came the next week, and I could almost feel them burning my fingers with their suckiness—it was all cowboy art and ancillary hick jokes—and I knew there was no way on earth I'd want to even reread those "shee-it!" Slim Pickens-voice cards where every picture of a burro on the outside became an ass joke on the next page, much less go work to help pollute the world with more. In the keep-writing-cards-versus-go-back-to-college debate, college won easily.

I turned the headhunter down. But still, it was great to be asked. I felt even happier after that phone call than I had after the promotion.

I VISITED TUCSON THAT SPRING because I knew I was probably leaving Kansas City, and I had vacation days to use up. I also knew that going from being a Writer II to an English teaching assistant brought with it an eighty percent drop in salary. So who knew when I'd be able to visit Tucson again?

I expected for Tucson to feel more different than it did. Of course things had changed and moved around. But my friends from college were mostly gone, and this left me close to my family again—and as soon as I was around them, with their Bible studies and their "praise the Lords," I went into a familiar defensive crouch like I hadn't used in years. What was worse, this time I was an actual atheist, not just a Catholic, and I felt an urge to express it in person in a way that I hadn't been able to over the phone. So I argued with my brother-in-law until three in the morning about a throwaway verse in Joshua. I battled my brother into sullen silence over whether the Bible was even a sensible moral guide. I scorched the earth behind me. I sowed dragon's teeth.

Near the end of my visit, I got a chance to hang out with my dad late into the evening. This had always been my favorite time to talk to him, because he seems to come alive at night—we spent hours as kids listening to him posit amusing theories or put Bible stories in an interesting light or tell anecdotes about the characters he'd known in his life. I wanted to experience that again—that whole talk-all-night, slumber-party vibe I remembered so warmly. But I also had a brief window of opportunity, and I had a mission. I waited all night for Dad to slip, and when we walked into a twenty-four-hour diner on Grant and Swan, we sat at a cold little two-person booth, ordered a pair of omelets, and while we were waiting he took off his cowboy hat, frowned at the sparse tables around us, cleared his throat, and said, "You know, I've been thinking about doing a little missionary work now that I'm basically retired. There are opportunities in Spain—"

And I lunged. "Dad—why go to Spain? That's such an evangelical thing to do. 'Those poor benighted Catholics need to learn Christianity!' It's not only arrogant, it's unbiblical. Did you know that the sinner's-prayer model of salvation you sectarian

Christians are so obsessed with doesn't even emerge in Christian history until—"

"David," said Dad sharply, and when I stopped, he sighed. "David, I'm really proud of you. I'm really glad that you've got your master's degree and that you're so interested in this topic. But before you say another word, you should know why it's not going to work."

He paused and looked sad. He was remembering. "Before I became a Christian, I was miserable. I wanted to kill myself. I hated my life, I hated my marriage, I just wanted to end everything."

I remembered this. He hadn't talked about it very often, but once when I was in high school he'd told me about how he'd had a nervous breakdown, and how when he was driving on the highway, he'd actually been tempted to steer his car into oncoming traffic. He was so disturbed by this that he pulled over to the side of the road, found a phone book, and checked himself into a mental hospital. For a year after that, he couldn't read a single thing except the Bible, and even that in a sort of skeptical, clinical way. Every other form of reading reminded him of academia, and the department that had driven him mad.

I didn't know what he was about to say, but it was pretty clear that by choosing academia now, I had all but confessed to rejecting not just his religion, but his entire view of the world.

"So when I was looking around for some kind of hope," Dad continued, "I found Grace Chapel." Grace Chapel was *the* big charismatic church in Tucson, with the raising of hands, the speaking in tongues, the anointing with oil, and occasional miracle healings. "I remember walking in there and being so overwhelmed by the love I saw there, the way these people cared for one another. Then I found out what they believed and I said, 'Are you serious? Magic and spirits and all this stuff?' But I kept coming back. And finally one night I prayed and I said, 'God, if I have to take my own *head* off to be happy, that's what I'm willing to do.'

"So you can believe what you want," he said. "But I also know what I've felt. Jesus turned me into a better man. He gave me a life, he gave me a family, and I look forward to every new day. I never did that before, and all your arguments aren't going to convince me to go back."

Just like that, I lost my urge to deconvert anyone. I actually relaxed in my seat and swirled the lemon wedge in my Sprite. Maybe I *had* changed and had just needed a catalyst to see it.

"I'm sorry, Dad," I said. I didn't actually feel *deeply* sorry, but I felt like I needed to make a peace offering. "I'm sorry that, by going back to get my Ph.D., I'm basically ignoring all your advice since forever."

Dad nodded. "That's okay. I mean, I pray for you. I'm not going to lie. It makes me nervous. You don't just . . . forget that stuff when it happens. I hope you never find out." He thought a bit, then shrugged. "But for you, I think it makes sense. That's what it comes down to. It's really who you are, and I love you for it." He raised his Coke in a toast. "God bless you."

What was I supposed to say? I raised my Sprite. "Sure thing," I said, and we both laughed.

When I came back into town I made one more visit to a church in Kansas City, just to see if I still had some spirit in me somewhere. I had been to a talk given by Coretta Scott King and had noticed that it was being picketed by local crazy fuck Fred Phelps and his "God Hates Fags" contingent of inbred attention-seekers. (Coretta's sin was apparently that she had spoken in favor of tolerance for gays. In public!) And I noticed that one of the yahoo's placards read, GOD HATES BROADWAY BAPTIST CHURCH. Anything they hated had to be pretty good, so I made a note and checked it out online. The congregation was famous for being accepting of gays, for helping the poor in their community, for having a diverse congregation. This was exactly what I'd been hoping for. Still nagging at me, at the edge of my brain, I was wondering if I really was an atheist or if I just hadn't been satisfied by my options, churchwise. If there was a church somewhere that really exemplified the love of Jesus, the same Jesus I had loved as a child, maybe that love alone could win me over. I visited the next Sunday.

As soon as I walked in I saw people talking excitedly, shaking hands, hugging. Over in the corner a small cluster of women were spontaneously praying together, and the service hadn't even started. And damned if there really wasn't actual diversity. Black folks, white folks, Latino and Asian, gay and straight, old and young, hippies and squares—and they all seemed to be having a wonderful time.

The organ started up, something peppy and fun, and the people started clapping. As I had at the Unity Temple, I decided to sit in the back near the exit. From my safely distant perspective, the mood of celebration reminded me of Grace Chapel the way it must have for my dad—quite a far cry from the other churches I'd been trying since my apostasy. I scanned the crowd and there was joy and hope on every face; these people looked like they'd lived stories of redemption. They weren't just grateful in theory.

The pastor—who reminded me a bit of a taller Father Grady

from back in Tucson—opened the service by saying, "In the name of the Father, and the Son, and the Holy Spirit. Amen."

And I thought, *What a shame. The Trinity is completely nonsensical. It's a theology that rose relatively late in the formation of Christian thought and served more to unify two rival sects of the church than it ever served to make sense of actual felt religious experience.*

The pastor said, "Turn if you will to the Beatitudes, in Matthew chapter . . ."

And I thought, *Of course they're going to talk about Jesus blessing the poor. But they ignore the parts where Jesus says the ax is at the root of the tree, that doom is about to fall, or that even having a lustful thought is like committing adultery. Why do they hang on to Jesus when they only like parts of him?*

The sermon was lovely, I should add: a call to unity through compassion. He told the congregation that loving the least among us, loving those the world hates, is a way of being supremely radical and supremely peaceful. He told the story of his own life, of pastoring this church, and of standing up for gay rights when it led to acrimony in his congregation and in the local press. It made me want to enlist in the cause. And I saw the gratitude of the gay people in the audience—couples who squeezed hands as he talked, an old lesbian who dabbed at her eyes.

Then he said, "Jesus said, whatever you do unto the least of these, you do unto me," and I thought, *And then he says, Depart, evildoers, into the darkness prepared for you. Because this is Matthew, the Jesus who preaches an ugly hell of eternal torment.*

And then I knew, with a distinct sadness, that I could never join in the revelry. I stayed for the whole service, and smiled at the singing and dancing at the end just like I had at the beginning. But I'm not like my dad; I can't take my head off. While it would certainly be lovely to have a community like this to rely on, I found I couldn't imagine doing it in good conscience, not even as one of those unbelievers you occasionally hear about who join churches in the hope of learning to have faith. I not only don't believe this stuff, but I can't imagine ever believing it again.

On the way out, though, I blew them a kiss. The world needs more religious communities like this: humble, celebratory, loving. It's a part of Kansas City that I can honestly say I'm sorry to have missed.

ONCE I FORMALLY ANNOUNCED I was leaving Hallmark, no one was actually surprised. There was a party, but it was a Humor party, so we just went to a restaurant at lunchtime and came back. Aside from that, the only celebration at work was I got a lot of cards.

In the exit interview, a woman asked me if I had any suggestions, and I said, "For god's sake, tell people when they're in trouble before they endanger their careers. By the time anyone told me things were wrong, I had already done serious damage. Also, there's a lot of backbiting. Not from the good people, but from the assholes. I don't know what you can do about that."

She quietly noted something on her form. Then she also asked if I wanted to stay on contract. "We sometimes have assignments for writers who leave, and you might find you could use the extra money." That was definitely true. Plus, of course, where else would I be able to ply my skills? So I signed a contract with them for three more years, or possibly five. I don't remember. All I know is, they never called once, and all the contract did was prevent me from freelancing anywhere else. It seems fitting that the last thing I heard from anyone in management was just one more goddamned lie.

FSU HAD OFFERED ME a teaching assistantship, and I took student loans for the first time in my life, and that settled the money question. I found an apartment in Tallahassee online, crossed my fingers, and took it. I ordered a U-Haul. And this time, with no fancy corporate movers, I started boxing things myself, and deciding what to throw away.

I kept all my books, but I ditched my ties and sweaters. I also chose to leave behind boxes and boxes of vinyl Christian music, which my roommate, Meg, was curious about. I never listened to it anymore.

"But what should I do about the bed?" she asked, while I was gathering books.

That fucking king-sized bed. I walked around it, pressed down on its pillow-top mattress. Thousands of dollars invested. Four years of hoping and waiting. And I'd shared it with another human being only one time. We hadn't even managed to have sex.

"Sell it," I said. "You might want to call it lightly used. And warn them it's heavy as hell."

MY GOING-AWAY PARTY WAS SMALL, just my core group of friends: Josh and his wife, The Professor, Kenneth and Angela,

Edgar and Lorraine, and Jessica and Jun. Not even my roommate was there; she was out with the boyfriend she'd met at my birthday. They were planning to move in together once I left.

We all met in my apartment and, as had been the case at every party I'd been to for over a year, I was the only single guy in the room. I tried not to let it bug me. After all, that was one of my big hopes for Florida: college is where everyone meets their partner. There are lots of parties and lots of free time. This go-round, with no embarrassing virginity and no fundamentalist restrictions, I would definitely hook up with someone.

I was so excited I could barely stand still. All evening I was pacing in front of the couches where my friends sat, rattling on in answer to their questions. "I haven't decided what to major in yet, but I really like critical theory and cultural studies, and I'll probably center on some mixture of the two. I'm leaving for summer school because they've got an actual rhet-comp class they put you through, so I'm not even nervous about teaching. They train you. They've got a great program all around, and it's not even that far from New Orleans. I'm already planning to go to Mardi Gras." This sent me into raptures. "I'm going to actually do it right this time. No missionary trip bullshit! I'm going to Spring Break! I'm going to get drunk a time or two. I may even try marijuana. And there are girls there. That's where a lot of people meet their partners, you know. In college." No one in this room had done it that way, but they nodded politely.

When I'd calmed down a little and people had broken into subgroups, Josh took me outside on the porch and said, "Dave, there's just one thing I want you to think about. I think you need to go back to college, but I don't think you'll be happy if you go into theory. I think you need to teach creative writing."

My skull was burning with all these new names like Gramsci and Zizek and Derrida that I couldn't wait to deploy, and he was saying what now? I laughed. "I think you're wrong, Josh. I'm so excited about this stuff, I actually *want* to write an essay. I can't wait for a class assignment. I've never felt like this before."

"You're excited now, I know. But David—" He poised his hands awkwardly in midair, trying to capture exactly his own point. "You've read theory, okay. Then you know how ugly it is. I've tried to read it, too, and it's just impossibly . . . awful. I mean, I can scarcely express how . . . it does violence to the very *concept* of rhetoric. And *you*, Dave!" He pointed at me, almost laughing. "That first poem you gave me, how we met. That's one fucking great poem, and I can name only a handful of people who could have pulled it off. So I can't see you perpetrating that postmodern poststructuralist theory crap on other people as a career. You love the language too much, Dave. You'll want to be fun to read." He clapped me on the shoulder. "Do what you have to do to get through those classes, but my advice is, keep working on a novel."

I laughed and promised I would. Then I pointed inside, to where everyone else was. "This is what I'm going to miss. And right now, where my head is, it's the only thing."

I hugged everyone good-bye, got everyone's e-mail address, and we promised we'd stay in touch.

I PULLED OUT EARLY the next morning with Dwight Yoakam in my car's CD player, and when I hit the highway, I felt like I was flying. The Life of Dave, 2.0, was going to start today. I planned the whole thing in an invisible chart on my windscreen. I would become a cultural studies scholar, specializing in something cool. Figure that out later. I would learn how to teach, and maybe I'd even like it. I would live in warm weather again, and I'd have a lot of free time. No more nine-to-fiving! Who cares about an eighty percent pay cut if you're getting years of your life back?

I would go to parties. Maybe drink. I'd have a favorite alcohol, even, and feel cool ordering it. I'd smoke a little pot without any fear at all. And there would be girls. Beautiful girls. Don't they sometimes sleep with their TAs? College! Why does anyone ever leave?

I chose not to think that I might be disappointed. I noted briefly that I'd thought that Hallmark would be perfect, and that hadn't worked out, but I turned down that thought as well. This really wasn't the day for worry.

So then I just daydreamed for hours of the girlfriend I'd have in Tallahassee—the Girl Who Was Not Yet Here, but she was going to be there the same time I was. She would be smart *and* sexy, funny *and* affectionate, and she liked having her breasts touched, because honestly, who doesn't? I knew she'd be wonderful, and just imagining what she'd look like kept a smile on my face all the way to Tennessee. I hadn't smiled that hard in years.

The answer is d.

David Ellis Dickerson is a comic, storyteller, crossword constructor, and ex–greeting card writer, who is a regular contributor to *This American Life*. He holds an MFA in creative writing from the University of Arizona, and a Ph.D. in American literature from Florida State University. He has written for the *Atlantic Monthly* and the *Gettysburg Review*. His puzzles have appeared in the *New Yorker*, the *New York Times*, *Games* magazine, and *Time Out New York*. He lives and works in New York.